# Harry Hopkins

*Biographies*
IN AMERICAN FOREIGN POLICY

Joseph A. Fry, *University of Nevada, Las Vegas*
Series Editor

The Biographies in American Foreign Policy Series employs the enduring medium of biography to examine the major episodes and themes in the history of U.S. foreign relations. By viewing policy formation and implementation from the perspective of influential participants, the series humanizes and makes more accessible those decisions and events that sometimes appear abstract or distant. Particular attention is devoted to those aspects of the subject's background, personality, and intellect that most influenced his or her approach to U.S. foreign policy, and each individual's role is placed in a context that takes into account domestic affairs, national interests and policies, and international and strategic considerations.

## Volumes Published

Lawrence S. Kaplan, *Thomas Jefferson: Westward the Course of Empire*
Richard H. Immerman, *John Foster Dulles: Piety, Pragmatism, and Power in U.S. Foreign Policy*
Thomas W. Zeiler, *Dean Rusk: Defending the American Mission Abroad*
Edward P. Crapol, *James G. Blaine: Architect of Empire*
David F. Schmitz, *Henry L. Stimson: The First Wise Man*
Thomas M. Leonard, *James K. Polk: A Clear and Unquestionable Destiny*
James E. Lewis, Jr., *John Quincy Adams: Policymaker for the Union*
Catherine Forslund, *Anna Chennault: Informal Diplomacy and Asian Relations*
Lawrence S. Kaplan, *Alexander Hamilton: Ambivalent Anglophile*
Andrew J. DeRoche, *Andrew Young: Civil Rights Ambassador*
Jeffrey J. Matthews, *Alanson B. Houghton: Ambassador of the New Era*
Clarence E. Wunderlin, Jr., *Robert A. Taft: Ideas, Tradition, and Party in U.S. Foreign Policy*
Howard Jablon, *David M. Shoup: A Warrior against War*
Jeff Woods, *Richard B. Russell: Southern Nationalism and American Foreign Policy*
Russell D. Buhite, *Douglas MacArthur: Statecraft and Stagecraft in America's East Asian Policy*
Christopher D. O'Sullivan, *Colin Powell: American Power and Intervention from Vietnam to Iraq*
David F. Schmitz, *Brent Scowcroft: Internationalism and Post–Vietnam War American Foreign Policy*
Christopher D. O'Sullivan, *Harry Hopkins: FDR's Envoy to Churchill and Stalin*

# Harry Hopkins

*FDR's Envoy to Churchill and Stalin*

CHRISTOPHER D. O'SULLIVAN

ROWMAN & LITTLEFIELD
Lanham • Boulder • New York • London

Published by Rowman & Littlefield
A wholly owned subsidiary of The Rowman & Littlefield Publishing Group, Inc.
4501 Forbes Boulevard, Suite 200, Lanham, Maryland 20706
www.rowman.com

Unit A, Whitacre Mews, 26-34 Stannery Street, London SE11 4AB, United Kingdom

British Library Cataloguing in Publication Information Available

**Library of Congress Cataloging-in-Publication Data**
O'Sullivan, Christopher D.
  Harry Hopkins : FDR's envoy to Churchill and Stalin / Christopher D. O'Sullivan.
    pages cm. — (Biographies in American foreign policy series)
  Includes bibliographical references and index.
  ISBN 978-1-4422-2220-5 (cloth : alk. paper) — ISBN 978-1-4422-2222-9 (electronic :
alk. paper) 1. Hopkins, Harry L. (Harry Lloyd), 1890–1946. 2. Statesmen—United
States—Biography. 3. World War, 1939–1945—Diplomatic history. 4. United States—
Foreign relations—1933–1945. I. Title.
  E748.H67O88 2014
  327.730092—dc23
  [B]                                                                    2014027161

♾™  The paper used in this publication meets the minimum requirements of
American National Standard for Information Sciences—Permanence of Paper for
Printed Library Materials, ANSI/NISO Z39.48-1992.

Printed in the United States of America

~

# Contents

| | |
|---|---|
| Chronology | vii |
| Acknowledgments | xi |
| Introduction | 1 |
| Chapter One: The Social Gospel | 11 |
| Chapter Two: New Dealer | 27 |
| Chapter Three: "Lord Root of the Matter" | 45 |
| Chapter Four: Mission to Moscow, 1941 | 61 |
| Chapter Five: "Assistant President" | 75 |
| Chapter Six: Catalyst of the Grand Alliance | 93 |
| Chapter Seven: Defeating Fascism | 107 |
| Chapter Eight: The Final Mission to Moscow | 125 |
| Conclusion: The Lost Peace | 141 |
| Bibliographic Essay | 151 |
| Notes | 157 |
| Index | 187 |
| About the Author | 197 |

~

# Chronology

## 1890

August 17: Birth, Sioux City, Iowa

## 1912

Graduates Grinnell College

## 1913

Marries fellow social worker Ethel Gross

## 1931

June: Marries Barbara Duncan
Appointed head of Governor Franklin Roosevelt's Temporary Emergency Relief Administration (TERA)

## 1932

November 8: Roosevelt elected president

# 1933

March: Beginning of the Hundred Days
May 22: Appointed to head Federal Emergency Relief Administration (FERA)
November 8: Civil Works Administration (CWA)

# 1935

May 6: Works Progress Administration (WPA)

# 1936

Hopkins tours nation promoting New Deal and WPA

# 1937

October 7: Death of Barbara Duncan Hopkins
November–December: Harry Hopkins's first health crisis

# 1938

April: Hopkins arrives in Warm Springs to push for stimulus
Hopkins seeks 1940 Democratic presidential nomination
December 24: Appointed Secretary of Commerce

# 1939

Harry Hopkins health relapse
September 1: Germany invades Poland

# 1940

May 10: Hopkins begins residing in the White House
July 15–18: Democratic National Convention
July 18: Hopkins engineers Roosevelt's third term nomination
July: Hopkins engineers vice presidential nomination for Henry Wallace
August: Hopkins manages Henry Wallace's "Guru Letters" scandal
August 22: Resigns as Commerce Secretary
November 5: Roosevelt elected to third term

# 1941

January–February: Hopkins's mission to London
March 11: Lend-Lease passage
July: Hopkins returns to London
July 30–31: Mission to Moscow to meet with Stalin
August 9–12: Hopkins arrives at Atlantic Conference with Churchill
December 7: Japanese attack on Pearl Harbor

# 1942

April 7–17: Mission to London with General George Marshall
May 29 to June 1: Molotov Mission to Washington
July 18–27: Mission to London with Marshall and Admiral King
July 27: Hopkins marries Louise Macy
November 8: Operation Torch

# 1943

January 14–24: Casablanca Conference
October 23: Harriman appointment as ambassador to Moscow
November 23–26: Cairo I: Hopkins meets Chiang Kai-shek
November 28 to December 1: Teheran Conference
December 4–6: Cairo II: Eisenhower

# 1944

February 1: Stephen Hopkins killed in action
June 6: Operation Overlord landing in Normandy, France
October 9–19: Moscow "Tolstoy" Conference between Churchill and Stalin
November 7: Roosevelt reelected to a fourth term
November 8: Hopkins launches reorganization of State Department
December 1: Edward Stettinius appointed Secretary of State
December: British intervention in Greece

# 1945

January: Hopkins travels to London to meet with Churchill
January: Hopkins travels to Paris, confers with de Gaulle
February 4–11: Yalta Conference

April 12: Death of President Roosevelt
April 25: UN Conference opens in San Francisco
May 8: Victory in Europe Day
May 26 to June 7: Hopkins's last mission to Moscow
June 7: Hopkins visits the ruins of Berlin
July: Hopkins receives Distinguished Service Medal at White House ceremony
August 14: Japan accepts Allied terms of surrender
September 2: Victory in Japan Day

# 1946

January 29: Harry Hopkins dies in New York City

~

# Acknowledgments

I am grateful to the many scholars who have written about Harry Hopkins and FDR, far too numerous to mention here, but I am particularly indebted to the editor of the Biographies in American Foreign Policy series, Joseph "Andy" Fry, for his skilled and dedicated stewardship of every book in his series. I am also grateful for the assistance of the fine people at Rowman & Littlefield, particularly Elaine McGarraugh, Jon Sisk, Benjamin Verdi, and Desiree Reid. A number of research organizations assisted with the project, starting with the Franklin D. Roosevelt Presidential Library in Hyde Park, where I was supported by several people, starting with their dynamic new director, Lynn Bassanese, and their multitalented chief archivist, Bob Clark, and his helpful team, including Matt Hanson, Virginia Lewick, Kirsten Strigel Carter, and Sarah Malcolm. I was also aided by the archivists at the Special Collections Research Center at the Lauinger Library, Georgetown University, but particularly Scott Taylor. At the Virginia Military Institute, Paul Barron assisted with the George C. Marshall Papers, and Claryn Spies aided with access to the Henry L. Stimson Papers at Yale University Library. Also helpful were the many archivists, too numerous to name, at the Manuscript Division at the Library of Congress, the Houghton Library at Harvard, the Winston Churchill Collection at Cambridge University, the British National Archives at Kew, and the Mudd Library at Princeton. I would also like to thank Manaf Damluji, Ken Moody, Carol Grant Gould, Elizabeth Moorhatch, Kelly Hallisy, Elizabeth Klein, Sarah Reinheimer, Conor Reilly, Harrison B. Robbs, Natalie Kamajian, Steve Schulz, Charles Morone, Vince Dougherty, Halley Farrell, Kaylin Andres, Mirabai Collamore, Kendis Camacho, and, for his services as a muse, Alonzo O'Sullivan. And with respect to the august John Steinbeck, my deepest gratitude to my father, the redoubtable General Curtis H. O'Sullivan, who lived it, and my deepest love and admiration for my extraordinary wife, Maeve, who willed it.

# Introduction

When the history of these times comes to be written, you will stand out
as the greatest of American statesmen who served President Roosevelt,
and one of the best friends that Britain ever had.[1]

—*Winston Churchill to Harry Hopkins, July 1945*

Reflecting back on the Second World War, two years after its conclusion,
former U.S. Army Chief of Staff General George C. Marshall recognized
Harry Hopkins as a critical factor in the Allied triumph. As General Marshall frequently emphasized, the comparatively smooth functioning of the
Grand Alliance grew into an enormous advantage the Allies had over the
Axis. Marshall observed that Hopkins fully appreciated the global nature
of the war and the need to make the most of vital Soviet and Chinese
contributions.[2]

The *New York Times* Washington Bureau Chief Arthur Krock, one of
Hopkins's most determined critics, recalled: "Marshall once told me that if it
hadn't been for Harry Hopkins, the war would have lasted two years longer,
and we might have lost it."[3]

British prime minister Winston Churchill, who had dubbed Hopkins
"Lord Root of the Matter" for his talent at getting to the crux of an issue,
graciously hailed Hopkins after his negotiations with Soviet leader Joseph
Stalin in June 1945: "When the history of these times comes to be written,

you will stand out as the greatest of American statesmen who served President Roosevelt, and one of the best friends that Britain ever had."[4]

As these accolades attest, there certainly was no figure quite like Harry Hopkins among any of the other powers in World War II. No other official among the British, Russians, Chinese, or the French could compare, whereas coordination among the Axis powers was, by contrast, nonexistent. Chinese foreign minister T. V. Soong characterized Hopkins as the key to the smooth functioning of the Alliance, the de facto commander-in-chief of the entire wartime coalition. Hopkins played the role of conciliator and catalyst, but his efforts went beyond the story of harmonious Anglo-American relations and his maintenance of the Roosevelt-Churchill relationship. He became a catalyst for all facets of the Alliance and remained pragmatically focused on winning the war and playing to the strengths of Russian and Chinese contributions in defeating the Axis.

Hopkins and Roosevelt were the only members of the Grand Alliance who maintained a genuine interest in all aspects of the war. Churchill, Stalin, Generalissimo Chiang Kai-shek, and even Free French General Charles de Gaulle remained largely focused on their primary objectives and thus failed to fully appreciate the broader global view of Hopkins and FDR. Hopkins's assistant for Lend-Lease, General James H. Burns, reflected that, as the chief engineer of the Grand Alliance, Hopkins was one of the few wartime officials "who had a 360 degree view of the war." While others fought "local skirmishes," General Burns recalled, Hopkins "fought a World War."[5]

Because of the colossal size of the armies facing one another, and the enormous casualties both sides were enduring, Hopkins understood that the Russo-German front remained the war's most important strategic point. The defeat of the Red Army would have been a major disaster for all of the Allied powers, likely prolonging the fighting for many years.[6]

He grasped that the Soviet Union was crucial to the defeat of nazism, but he also understood that every member of the Grand Alliance, including the British, Nationalist China, and even the Free French had particular roles. He became key to the establishment and maintenance of the wartime alliance with Stalin and sought to make the Russians intelligible to the Americans and British. He worked, despite enormous obstacles, at keeping China supplied and in the war. He even strove, in the face of opposition from the president and the State Department, to smooth over misunderstandings with General Charles de Gaulle and the Free French.

Certain facets of the Hopkins story deserve further exploration or reexamination, such as the broader picture of his maintenance of the Alliance with regard to all its participants, but particularly the Soviet Union. Thus, this work provides an exploration of the precise nature of his views and objectives with regard to U.S.-Soviet relations, but also on China policy and relations with de Gaulle and the Free French.[7] There has been a massive amount of new source material since Robert Sherwood published his epic *Roosevelt and Hopkins* in 1948. Nearly fifty wartime volumes of the State Department's documentary series *Foreign Relations of the United States* (FRUS) series became available, and other materials related to Hopkins have been made available at the Franklin D. Roosevelt Presidential Library and the Hopkins Papers at the Special Collections Research Center at Georgetown University's Lauinger Library. A wide assortment of Hopkins-related documentary materials have opened at both the British National Archives and the Winston Churchill Collection at Cambridge. Even Robert Sherwood's papers themselves have not been thoroughly mined.

Most important, with the Cold War now ended, the goals Hopkins sought to achieve can be measured against his actual objectives, rather than projecting Cold War ideologies onto them. Operating in the context of World War II, Hopkins saw the enormous potential in the Red Army's contribution to defeating Hitler. His actions should be assessed against the actual objectives he sought to achieve, rather than in the context of Cold War ideological assumptions that did not factor into his goal of defeating fascism. Hopkins and Roosevelt sought to achieve the objective of winning the war expeditiously and with the fewest American casualties but also of creating a workable relationship with the Soviet Union that would survive into the postwar era.[8]

Hopkins shared with Roosevelt the goal of embracing the USSR and China. But his wartime efforts to pursue a balanced approach between Great Britain and Russia appeared vaguely sinister in the ideological climate of the Cold War. Postwar perspectives, often colored by Cold War ideologies, deliberately understated the wartime contributions of the USSR in defeating fascism.[9]

Hopkins's objective regarding the Soviet Union was to ensure military victory over fascism. Those critical of the wartime alliance with the Soviet Union are at pains to explain how the war might have been won without the Red Army's contributions. To think the war could have been won in the absence of Soviet and Chinese contributions, without hundreds of thousands more American casualties, is simply delusional. Second-guessers rarely explain how they would have done things differently and achieved the same, if not better, results.

Hopkins's views of the Soviet Union were based on an entirely different reality from his critics. His primary objective was the defeat of fascism. He did not see the Soviet Union as an immediate threat to American interests in 1941, whereas he certainly did see Hitler as posing such a threat. He thus saw the USSR, China, and Great Britain as various instruments in achieving the goal of defeating the Axis powers. He understood better than most, and certainly more than his later critics, the essentially anti-American objectives of nazism. While Stalin oversaw a brutal, loathsome regime, the USSR posed no immediate threat to U.S. interests. Hitler dominated an equally loathsome regime but, in Hopkins's view, he posed an immediate and perhaps increasingly existential threat to America. He thus pragmatically sought to guarantee that Hitler's search for victory in the vastness of Russia would prove elusive and ultimately result in the complete destruction of the Nazi regime.

This book is divided into eight thematic but chronological chapters. Exploring the origins of Hopkins's progressivism and value system, harking back to his origins in Grinnell, Iowa, chapter 1 examines the roots of his political views and values. He was never part of FDR's Brain Trust but rather saw himself as a man of action and demonstrated this talent in New York emergency relief under Governor Roosevelt, starting in 1931. Some critics accused Hopkins of having no core principles, but those who knew him felt he was in a constant state of ferment about how his ideas could be advanced into actual programs. The fact that he was a social worker has perhaps been overrated. By far his most important talent was bringing together people of different backgrounds, whether utilizing the previously unexplored speech-writing talents of the acclaimed playwright Robert Sherwood, pushing forward the career of General George C. Marshall for Army Chief of Staff, or recruiting Wall Street figures such as James Forrestal, Edward Stettinius, and Averell Harriman for top wartime appointments. FDR's daughter, Anna, felt that Hopkins had a unique talent for bringing people together, particularly people who might prove congenial to the president.[10]

Hopkins's role in the New Deal is surveyed in chapter 2. He achieved administrative miracles by creating the Federal Emergency Relief Administration (FERA), the Civil Works Administration (CWA), and the Works Progress Administration (WPA), and later overseeing the $50 billion Lend-Lease program (for comparison, the entire federal budget in fiscal 1940 was less than $10 billion). His innate pragmatism meant that if something failed, he would ruthlessly scrap the idea and try something else until he finally found a solution. He often spoke about William James and the philosophy of pragmatism. Perhaps it gave formal expression to what he was already doing instinctively. He possessed a rare talent for adaptability. Particular attention is also given to several episodes in the later years of the New Deal, such as his contributions reviving a weak economy in 1938 and his quest for the 1940 Democratic presidential nomination.

His role as catalyst for the Anglo-American wartime alliance is explored in chapter 3, with particular emphasis on his two missions to London in January and July 1941 and his efforts at managing Roosevelt's relations with Churchill and smoothing over the latter's rougher edges. Hopkins's assessments had enormous consequences for the outcome of the war. He pragmatically reported that Britain would likely survive despite its current predicament. Yet to achieve any lasting peace after the war, he believed the United States had to avoid narrowly organizing the world between itself and the British. Moreover, General Marshall recognized in Hopkins a shared determination to focus exclusively on winning the war and opposition to Churchill's "eccentric ideas" that threatened to prolong the war. The wonder is not that FDR and Churchill, or Hopkins and Churchill, for that matter, worked well together, but rather that they got on well for so long given their vastly different objectives.

Hopkins's mission to Moscow in late July 1941, where he met with Stalin and other senior Soviet officials and established the template for U.S.-Soviet wartime relations, is the subject of chapter 4. Based on this mission, Hopkins reported to the president that Russia would hold out and go on fighting. Hopkins's assessments justified the flow of Lend-Lease aid to Russia at a time when many officials in Washington were predicting that American supplies would fall into the hands of the Germans following a likely Russian collapse. Against the consensus, he asserted that Russia was a good bet to withstand the German onslaught, despite the Red Army having just been defeated on nearly every battlefield. He shrewdly grasped the significance of the USSR's natural advantages of manpower reserves, resources, geography, climate, and territorial depth. And his crucial assessment proved correct. A year after his Moscow mission, nearly five million German troops remained mired in the vastness of Russia, forces that could otherwise have been redeployed elsewhere, a point that Hopkins, along with the president and all of his senior officials such as generals Marshall and Dwight Eisenhower and Admiral Ernest J. King, all essentially understood in a way that postwar critics of Russian policy did not. "Every German killed by a Russian will kill no Americans or British," Hopkins said at the time.[11]

Hopkins's role as FDR's de facto "assistant president" is traced in chapter 5. An extraordinary evaluator of others' talents, his patronage contributed to the advancement of Marshall and Eisenhower. Some saw Hopkins as FDR's own personal Foreign Office, others as a prototype of future White House Chiefs of Staff.[12]

General Marshall perceived Hopkins, with his distinctive qualifications, his vast capacity for hard work, and, most important, the president's enormous confidence, as providing the necessary staffing level that an over-burdened White House so desperately needed during the war. In an effort to inject dynamism into his administration, the president used Hopkins as a troubleshooter and minister without portfolio. This chapter also assesses his evolving grasp of military strategy, as recognized by Marshall, Eisenhower, Admiral King, and Secretary of War Henry Stimson. Hopkins came closest to mirroring the president's knowledge of the war and thus became the chief figure in the effort to carry out what might be called FDR's "Grand Design" of supporting and engaging Russia and China and thus blocking Germany's and Japan's quest for victory.[13]

Chapter 6 evaluates Hopkins's oversight of the entire Grand Alliance, particularly his efforts to maintain wartime and postwar roles for China and the Free French. Roosevelt delegated to him several of the most difficult wartime portfolios such as managing the often unpredictable Churchill, cultivating the intractable Stalin, smoothing relations with the Chinese, and handling matters related to the fractious Free French. Unlike Churchill, Hopkins recognized that the day of the white European empires was drawing to a close and millions of people living in those empires would no longer tolerate ongoing exploitation.[14]

To avoid unnecessary postwar conflict, the Russians needed to be integrated into the world system, and the Chinese afforded an appropriate international role. In fact, he appreciated the contributions of China in a way few others did. China was often the forgotten ally, and the communist victory there in 1949 further obscured its critical wartime contributions. Hopkins became one of the principal advocates of assisting Generalissimo Chiang Kai-shek, realizing that China played a critical part in the war effort merely by tying down a majority of Imperial Japanese Army divisions throughout the war.

Chapter 7 examines how Hopkins struggled to uphold the Alliance until victory over fascism, often in the face of enormous challenges provoked by both British and Soviet actions in late 1944 and early 1945. As the war went on, Hopkins grasped that a "formula" had emerged among the Big Three, with each member conceding to the others on matters of their primary in-terests. This formula, which had served the Big Three effectively throughout the war, but particularly at Teheran and Yalta, might endure through postwar institutions such as the Council of Foreign Ministers and the UN Security Council. Yet Churchill's focus on the postwar status of the British Empire, Great Britain's primary interests in the Eastern Mediterranean, and in pre-serving its power and influence in the Middle East and Asia increasingly diverged from FDR's and Stalin's primary goals of opening a genuine Second Front in France, planning for the future of postwar Germany, and defeating

Japan as expeditiously as possible. Making matters more complicated, Churchill modified his primary objectives in unpredictable ways, such as altering his emphasis on British interests in Greece and the Eastern Mediterranean to increasingly pessimistic rhetoric about the future of Poland, or moving from the appeasement of Stalin's territorial aspirations between 1942 and 1944, to advancing a nascent containment strategy during the second half of 1945.[15]

Hopkins's final effort to revive the Yalta formula by traveling to Moscow in May 1945 is the subject of chapter 8. Although now in extraordinarily poor health, even by his own precariously low standards, he came out of retirement at the urging of President Harry S. Truman to pursue an understanding with Stalin during a critical moment in the war. Only a few weeks after FDR's death, he was given the task of negotiating with Stalin the outstanding issues that had emerged since Yalta. The fate of the future United Nations, the upcoming Berlin/Potsdam Conference, and the Red Army intervention against Japan hung in the balance, but he managed to wring significant concessions from Stalin on every issue, including modest ones over Poland.

Hopkins frequently served as a lightning rod for criticism that might otherwise have been directed at FDR. Roosevelt's genial demeanor often convinced people that he agreed with them, so when things went against them, they often looked for some nefarious influence to blame, and their wrath frequently settled upon Hopkins. Hopkins's lifelong indifference to his reputation and how he was perceived often hindered his effectiveness and played into the hands of his critics. In a similar vein, he was subjected to harsh criticism after his death in 1946, which left him open to attacks to which he could not respond. Because of his early death and failure to complete his memoirs, many thought Hopkins was easily and cruelly maligned after the war when *Yalta* became a code word for *treason*.[16]

Almost all of Hopkins's endeavors, dating back to his appointment to head the Federal Emergency Relief Administration (FERA) in 1933, were plagued by bitter and polarizing controversy continuing, and intensifying, after his death. Since his death, Hopkins has been sharply criticized as a dupe of the Kremlin, a Stalinist, or more grave, a spy for the Kremlin. This was perhaps inevitable given his role in Roosevelt's Russia policy and also the degree of deep suspicion and even paranoia that shrouds almost any matter related to the USSR. Yet upon closer examination, the accusations of Hopkins being a Soviet agent stem more from the ideological agendas of his accusers than from actual historical evidence. As has been pointed out by even conservative scholars, the lack of historical evidence undermines the most lurid of the accusations.[17]

In the absence of evidence, these accusations constitute political rather than historical opinion and are designed to reinforce accusations against Roosevelt's foreign policy.[18]

The documentary record that does exist is sharply at odds with the lurid caricature of a Soviet agent.[19]

Moreover, whatever his critics have later charged about his alleged naïveté about the Soviet system, he made it clear throughout the war that he had no illusions about the genuine nature of the Soviet regime. For example, after his July 1941 mission to Moscow, he observed that the differences between the American and Soviet systems "are clearer to me than any words of a philosopher, historian, or journalist could make it."[20]

During Soviet Foreign Minister Vyacheslav Molotov's mission to Washington in May 1942, Hopkins noted: "You don't have to know very much about Russia, or for that matter Germany, to know there isn't a snowball's chance in hell for either Russia or Germany to permit the International Red Cross really to inspect any prison camps."[21]

And shortly after his final mission to Moscow in May through June 1945, he observed that longtime relations with the Soviet Union would constantly be challenged by differences between Washington's and Moscow's "fundamental notions of human liberty—freedom of speech, freedom of the press and freedom of worship."[22]

His critics have also refused to look at the actual nature of the Grand Alliance, or at his relationships with the other members of the Allied coalition. Hopkins's relations with Churchill, the Chinese, Free French representatives, and Soviet officials are all of a piece. The consistent underlying thread was his promotion of cooperation among the Grand Alliance members designed to defeat the Axis powers as quickly as possible with the fewest American casualties. Many of his postwar critics, focusing exclusively on his relations with the Soviet Union, have contended that he favored Stalin at the expense of Churchill. Those who have focused narrowly on his relations with Stalin miss the larger point: Hopkins saw himself as the catalyst of the *entire* Grand Alliance, not solely the Anglo-American component, nor the Soviet-American component, but all of the Alliance's many facets. As the wartime record amply demonstrates, he not only sought to smooth over areas of potential misunderstanding with Stalin but also with Churchill, Chiang Kai-shek, and even General Charles de Gaulle. Many of his critics saw nothing constructive about wartime relations with the USSR and thus did not share Hopkins's appreciation of Alliance dynamics. Moreover, Cold War–influenced perspectives on scholarship often obscured the degree of wartime compatibility between the war aims and objectives of Washington and Moscow and the frequent incompatibility of Washington and London.[23]

Contrary to his postwar critics, those officials who served closely with Hopkins had an extraordinarily high opinion of him and valued his contributions to victory. He provided patronage and backing for such key wartime figures as General Marshall and Dwight Eisenhower and enjoyed strong working relationships with Admiral William Leahy, Admiral Ernest King, and Secretary of War Henry Stimson. Hopkins also served as a patron for figures such as Ambassador Averell Harriman, Ambassador Anthony Biddle, Navy Secretary James Forrestal, Edward Stettinius (who, with Harry's backing, would succeed Cordell Hull as Secretary of State in 1944), and State Department Russia hand Charles Bohlen. The press described some of these civilian appointments as "Hopkins's tame millionaires," and for all the criticism aimed at him as a wild-eyed radical he nonetheless pragmatically recruited such officials. He had no hesitation appointing Republicans or Wall Street figures, and they, in turn, appreciated his contributions. As during the New Deal, he considered the ability of any appointee more important than his political views.[24]

Perhaps anticipating his critics, Hopkins once observed that it was important for senior officials to have the "will to reach a decision and a will to act on what you decide." After-the-fact critics would forever find fault, he allowed, about the course he had pursued, but decisions had to be made with whatever information was available at the time, not an ex post facto knowledge of the future. With a paucity of information, leaders often have to act on intuition and draw upon their experiences and judgment and on the best advice available. "There is always some information that is not available to you," he reflected. "If you want to delay action until everything is known, you will never do a damned thing as long as you live. Your job as a public official is to make decisions. You can't just talk about what you might do. You've got to take a situation as you find it and do the best you can with it. Some people, of course, don't think so: this town divides itself into two parts—the talkers and the doers."[25]

Hopkins was one of the ultimate doers.

CHAPTER ONE

~

# The Social Gospel

Government seemed a pretty impersonal thing to me years ago, but now it lives with a vital human force.[1]

—*Harry Hopkins to Henry Morgenthau, 1940*

Progressive icon Frances Perkins, who served throughout the New Deal and the war as President Roosevelt's Secretary of Labor, once told Harry Hopkins that he had taken American liberalism to a new level, beyond its past crusades for antitrust and civil service reform. Perkins compared Hopkins's contribution to that of Jacob Riis's groundbreaking 1890 work, *How the Other Half Lives*. "I cannot but feel," Perkins wrote to Hopkins in 1940, "that what you did revealed on a scale of the whole United States the same kind of problem and brought the same kind of challenge, only this time on the whole National area. The work that you did in putting a decent, reasonable, human relief system into operation, and then revamping it into a constructive, as well as a human, program was, I think, brilliant and perhaps the most creative things that have been done in the whole New Deal. It was as though through your leadership the whole country, including the Government, discovered a new human area of need and did something about it."[2]

Hopkins was an important link between the Social Gospel progressivism of the late nineteenth century and the New Deal era of the 1930s and after. His life, spanning the time from the Social Gospel Movement to the

Hopkins proved himself a gifted administrator, both during the New Deal and the war. He built programs such as FERA, CWA, WPA, and Lend-Lease from nothing, distributed billions of dollars, and then broke them down when their tasks were completed. He developed a theory, deriving from his Social Gospel origins at Grinnell, that the federal government had a "responsibility" for the total welfare of its citizens and that only government was properly equipped to fight the Depression. He articulated a philosophy of government that defined the state as a guarantor of individual security.[3] All photographs courtesy of the Franklin Delano Roosevelt Library unless otherwise noted.

end of the Age of Reform in 1945, included stints as a social worker during the Progressive Era; leadership of major relief organizations such as the Red Cross and the Tuberculosis and Health Association; and leadership of several of the largest relief and public works agencies in American history, such as the Federal Emergency Relief Administration (FERA), the Civil Works Administration (CWA), and the Works Progress Administration (WPA).

Part of the secret to Hopkins's achievements was that he never saw public service as drudgery or a stepping-stone to future riches. "Government seemed a pretty impersonal thing to me years ago," he observed to Henry Morgenthau in 1940, "but now it lives with a vital human force."[4] Hopkins saw things differently from other people, discerning patterns and connections that eluded others. FDR respected this creative streak in Hopkins and, like him, did not like to think in terms of simplistic dichotomies.[5]

Many Americans felt that there was no place for government in the business of relief. Some believed that the Great Depression was merely a crisis of confidence and that doing nothing in the laissez-faire sense, or merely minor adjustments, would be sufficient. Even many of those in the social work field could only think in terms of private charity and remained staunchly opposed to the use of the government to provide relief. Most social workers understood very little about the challenge of mass unemployment. The stark reality of sixteen million able-bodied Americans, eager to work but without jobs, was totally incomprehensible to them. Hopkins understood that most of his critics had absolutely nothing to say about solutions for mass unemployment. Ideally, he would have preferred to get people back to work on private jobs, saying, "I'd damn well be in favor of hiring industry to give these people jobs if I thought it would work," but, in the meantime, public relief simply had to be provided.[6] He became a pivotal figure in the history of government welfare provision. He bucked the social worker establishment and embraced the idea of direct government aid. This decision enshrined the core of the New Deal philosophy that government had a responsibility for the total welfare of all citizens.[7]

Hopkins advocated that government relief should be administered directly to recipients and not only through traditional private charity organizations. He had originally favored the more traditional methods, and apparently FDR did, too. Hopkins announced his change of heart in June 1933 during a speech in Detroit when he came out strongly for the direct approach. He later convinced FDR that this was the right course. Although this received very little publicity or comment at the time, in retrospect this was one of the more far-reaching decisions of the New Deal. It signaled that relief was the citizen's right from his government.[8]

April 1935. FDR looking over his new car. In the rear seat are Hopkins, Missy LeHand. In the front seat is Franklin D. Roosevelt Jr., the president. Eleanor Roosevelt is looking into the car.

Hopkins served Roosevelt in so many different capacities that it remains a challenge to comprehend them fully. He wrote thousands of Roosevelt's wartime communications in his distinctive script, with the president merely affixing "OK, FDR" prior to their dispatch. A project of enormous importance might not receive official sanction until Hopkins signed off on it. One of his wartime assistants, Wayne Coy, recalled that when he once explained to Roosevelt, "You needn't bother with that, Mr. President, I can take that up with Harry Hopkins," the president sympathetically replied, "I don't want you to bother Harry with that. Harry has too much to worry about as it is."[9]

There is much about the Roosevelt-Hopkins partnership that outsiders will never know. Hopkins frequently acknowledged in his cables that he dare not say too much through official channels and that he preferred to brief the president privately upon his return. As General Marshall observed, those possessing even the most remote understanding of the depth of Hopkins's role formed a very small circle. Marshall recognized that Hopkins was much more than a mere executor of FDR's objectives, however. While his views as much reinforced Roosevelt's as influenced him, on the speculative question of influence, the fine line between Roosevelt and Hopkins remained a matter privy only to them. More might have been revealed in memoirs neither lived to write.

The relationship between Roosevelt and Hopkins grew upon a foundation of mutual trust and went beyond politics. It has been said that the enigmatic Roosevelt was a man with millions of admirers but few genuine friends. At the very least, Hopkins seems to have been one of the few people FDR fully trusted.[10] Roosevelt found Hopkins's company personally restful and enjoyed his companionship. Hopkins could talk very intelligently without being dull—in fact, with a mischievous frankness. "Harry did not bore FDR, ever," Hopkins's friend and New Deal official, Florence Kerr, observed, "because he was witty and quick and amusing, and I suppose a great relief to the President. Then, I think, too, Harry was available, night and day. A lot of people were available, but he was available *and* good company."[11]

At the end of the day's work the president would often sit down with Hopkins over cocktails. Hopkins intuitively understood when his chief wanted to relax and avoid weighty matters. The two men understood each other so well that it was rarely necessary to talk shop. Anna Roosevelt felt that her father could truly relax with Hopkins. Roosevelt's longtime adviser, Louis McHenry Howe, went into a slow physical decline in 1935 and died at the beginning of 1936. Many insiders observed that Hopkins grew far closer to the president than Howe ever was.[12]

As early as 1935 the newspapers began describing Hopkins as Roosevelt's alter ego, a trend in coverage continuing for a decade until the president died in 1945. He intuitively understood what kind of stories made Roosevelt laugh.[13] And yet, as General Marshall pointed out, Hopkins never shied away from challenging the president's views or finding clever ways to suggest alternatives.[14] Hopkins sensed the right moment to bring something to the president's attention. He understood that he had to be crafty because Roosevelt possessed a streak of stubbornness and did not like to feel that anyone was forcing his hand. The key to persuading the president was to do so without him realizing that he was being persuaded.[15]

Hopkins sought to bring FDR around to his position by preparing a paper for him to read and then wait until the right moment to give it to him. It was by this roundabout manner that Hopkins aligned the president's support behind his objectives.[16] But Hopkins would cease arguing as soon as the president had made up his mind, mostly because Hopkins deferred to Roosevelt's ability to gauge public opinion. "Harry will argue with the President," a friend said. "He knows when to stop arguing. Once the President has thoroughly made up his mind, you might as well butt your head up against a brick wall as try to change it."[17]

Hopkins possessed a talent for cutting through complicated problems. Navy Secretary and Hopkins protégé James Forrestal recalled that Hopkins possessed strengths that complemented FDR's. "Harry had a newspaperman's mind: direct, acquisitive," Forrestal recalled. "He was concerned with the immediate—not so much considering each problem in relation to the past or the future, as Roosevelt did."[18] Hopkins's friend, Supreme Court justice Felix Frankfurter, believed his chief strength was his "daring, intuitive, penetrating mind," his enormous energy and enthusiasm, and his ability as an administrator to change pace or direction instantly.[19] These were attributes he shared with Roosevelt.[20]

Hopkins had a thorough understanding of the way Roosevelt's mind worked. Hopkins once explained: "You must recognize that the most important thing in dealing with the President is to understand his signal system. With ordinary people you listen to what they say, watch their lips maybe. But with the President, you've got to pay attention to his eyebrows. They're his signals. They're more important than what he says with his mouth. The reason I've stayed with the President so long is that I understand his signals."[21]

Bernard Baruch, who considered himself a friend of both, recalled that Hopkins carried out his tasks with understated competence and discretion. The president understood that Hopkins would be 100 percent reliable in representing him and expressing his views without coloration or the injection of personal ideas, unlike most other officials.[22]

Hopkins's relationship with Roosevelt provoked jealousy and resentment. The extraordinary power and influence the president granted Hopkins placed the latter in the crosshairs of the hostile press and administration rivals. Critics poured resentment upon him when they dared not direct it at the president. Aside from the thankless job of providing cover for the president, Hopkins was uniquely Roosevelt's counselor, confidante, and friend. In Hopkins, the president found the kind of kinship he found in few other human beings. "He was truly another self for President Roosevelt," Perkins reflected. "The mutual trust between the two men sprang partly, of course, from personal sympathy and temperamental harmony, but more from a common devotion to the idea that their mission in life was to make things better for the people."[23]

Some critics described him as a latter-day Cardinal Richelieu, sinisterly moving behind the scenes, establishing his own court favorites or giving the knife to those in his way. Others charged that he was a man of no principles who simply acted through, and hid behind, the president. Lurid stories appeared with regularity about him being some kind of a Rasputin with control over the president and First Lady.

Yet for all the criticism directed at him, Hopkins's correspondence reveals an appealing man with a sharp wit, a profane sense of humor, a fabulous raconteur, but also a good listener.[24] Even his harshest critics acknowledged his good sense of humor and his amusement with the absurdities of life. "Harry could be a very agreeable cuss when he wanted to," administration rival Harold Ickes admitted after Hopkins's death. "He could be a VERY agreeable rascal."[25] A *New York Times Magazine* profile observed in 1942: "Let us start off by saying that—whether you are a Wall Street broker or a mechanic—you would be inclined to classify Harry as a 'good guy.' You certainly could not peg him as a man who had spent most of his life as a social service worker and he, for his part, would not attempt to impress you with his importance."[26]

Presidential speechwriter and the renowned playwright Robert Sherwood gave much thought to Hopkins's appealing qualities. Sherwood, who came to know Hopkins well, both during Harry's life and after while writing *Roosevelt and Hopkins*, observed that Harry was a delightful companion because of his sharp sense of humor and disarming fatalism. When thinking of Roosevelt and Hopkins's relationship, Sherwood thought Hopkins provided a distillation of information for Roosevelt to consume in one swallow.[27]

Hopkins's character and personality were inevitably rooted in his early life and college years in Iowa. He grew up at the intersection of Populism and Progressivism, and the history of the Social Gospel and nineteenth-century Progressivism is woven into Harry's family story. He came from the Midwest; lived in Grinnell, the epicenter of the Social Gospel movement; and eventually pursued a career in the Progressive mission of urban relief.

Hopkins had many unusual and contradictory characteristics. He once described himself as equal parts Baptist preacher and racetrack tout. His parents' marriage seemed to be an ill-fitting union of opposites, yet Harry was a striking hybrid of the characteristics of both parents. His mother, Ann, was born near Toronto in a well-educated, liberally religious family. Harry's brother, Lewis, described their mother as "a slight woman [who] did a great deal of work to keep her family clean, fed and clothed." She was a devout Methodist who gave her children a thorough Methodist upbringing, leading them in hymns around the family pump organ and demanding they attend church nearly every day. She saw her church activities as "the sum total of life" and dedicated herself to supporting Social Gospel missionary endeavors. While Ann Hopkins was a pillar of the church, friends recalled that Methodism never entirely "took" with young Harry.[28] Harry's siblings remembered him as extremely secretive. His mother would observe: "He never tells me anything about what he is really thinking or planning. I simply cannot make him out."[29]

Harry got his quick wit and intellect from his father, who was remembered as an engaging personality. Their garrulous, yarn-spinning father, David Aldona "Al" Hopkins, was frequently on the road as a harness maker, leaving their mother as the financial and managing head of the family. The Panic of 1893, the worst economic crisis in the nation until the Great Depression, hit the Hopkins family hard, destroying his father's business and leaving a lasting imprint on Hopkins's character. His easygoing father eked out a meager existence, a living made even smaller by his addiction to bowling.

Most of Harry's education occurred in Grinnell, Iowa, where his family moved when he was eleven. Settling in the town of Grinnell was Ann's idea. His father remained throughout his life scornful of the town's rigidly Methodist ethos. When Al Hopkins neared death from stomach cancer, Harry asked him where he wanted to be buried, and Al replied, "Any God-damned place except Grinnell!" When Harry learned that the other members of the family had decided upon Grinnell as his father's final resting place, he could only laugh.[30]

While more ambivalent about Methodism than his devout mother, Harry nonetheless became part of the "religious left" of Protestant Christian activism, attending Grinnell College, the crossroads of the Social Gospel reform movement. The college was one of the leading denominational institutions (Congregationalist) in the Midwest. A pious place, its charter stated that the town land and the college property would immediately revert to the Grinnell family if intoxicating liquors were ever sold within the town limits. In fact, Hopkins (class of 1912) nurtured within the New Deal a kind of Grinnell College circle consisting of former classmates, most notably influential New Deal administrators such as Paul Appleby (1913), Hallie Flanagan (1911), Florence Kerr (1911), and Chester Davis (1911).

Harry became the business manager of the Grinnell College newspaper, and he made arrangements to run a small-town paper in Montana after graduation. He also developed a strong sense of social justice. Already, in his late teens, he demonstrated character traits that would become well known during the New Deal. He placed special emphasis on what could be done immediately, rather than of what, hypothetically or theoretically, might be done in the future. Harry had his first experience with social work as chairman of the local YMCA employment committee. His interest in social work and the underprivileged came from the influence of a professor of Applied Christianity, Dr. Edward Steiner, who also sparked Harry's genuine interest in Tolstoy and the enigma that was Russia—an interest that resurfaced during World War II.

Professor Steiner arranged for Harry to work at Christodora House, the New York City settlement institution, which was looking for a young man to fill a counseling position at its summer camp for poor children. The opportunity presented small-town boy Hopkins with the chance to see the East. By contrast, his Montana plans seemed pretty remote. So after graduation in 1912, Hopkins moved to New York City, stopping off in Chicago to watch the exciting 1912 Bull Moose convention. Harry enjoyed the human drama of politics, also crashing both the Republican and Democratic conventions in 1912.[31]

Rejected for military service in World War I because of ill health, he joined the Red Cross. Close friends thought he was drawn to New York for reasons other than social work. When former Grinnell classmate Robert Kerr came to visit during the 1920s, Harry squired him around town, dropping in on the city's most expensive speakeasies. Kerr was astounded when, in one joint, Hopkins spent $20 on cocktails—a princely sum to small-town Midwestern boys like Kerr and Hopkins.[32]

Hopkins had artistic aspirations. He wanted to become a writer, which is evident in his wartime articles and some of his most personal letters. He once began work on a play promoting the establishment of labor unions for teachers and professors.[33] After his death in 1946, his first wife, Ethel Hopkins, recalled: "Harry was a great student of Byron, Keats and Shelley. His interest began while he was convalescing from an illness in 1920 and it never lagged. . . . He read and collected everything he could find in the way of biographical bookshops for any collections that he could find and we all knew that he would like nothing better as a gift. Of course he read a great deal of contemporary poetry besides. Carl Sandberg was a great favorite of his and he read and re-read everything he ever wrote."[34]

Harry actually saw the causes and consequences of poverty firsthand. As executive of the New York Tuberculosis and Health Association, he pointed out to specialists and doctors that the poor had little access to prescribed remedies such as fresh air, healthy food, clean water, and sunlight.[35]

Roosevelt recognized in Hopkins a compatibility of political and social views. In 1931, Governor Roosevelt appointed Hopkins as executive director of the New York State Temporary Emergency Relief Administration (TERA). After Roosevelt's election to the presidency in 1932, the new governor, Herbert Lehman, was eager to appoint Hopkins to the Industrial Commissioner post, which Frances Perkins had previously held. But Hopkins wanted to go to Washington. In March 1933, Perkins, Hopkins, and Bill Hodson, director of the Welfare Council of New York City, discussed the urgency of the relief situation and devised ways and means of bringing it to the president's attention.[36] According to the *New York Times* Washington Bureau Chief Arthur Krock, as FDR saw more of Hopkins, the latter "exercised that kind of magic personal spell on Roosevelt he did on so many people, especially women."[37]

Hopkins eventually married three times, the first in 1913 when, as a young Manhattan social worker just out of Grinnell, he met and married another young social worker named Ethel Gross. They had four children, one dying in infancy. When his first marriage began to falter in the 1920s, he underwent psychoanalysis under the supervision of Dr. Frank Wood Williams. People close to him observed that he became less secretive, but to the discomfort of many friends he began oversharing unflattering details about his most intimate life. Harry and Ethel divorced in 1930 after seventeen years of marriage. The divorce was wrenching for Hopkins. Some, such as his sister, Adah, severed communication with him.[38]

Hopkins had more than his share of turbulence and heartbreak, often agonizing over personal tragedies and his many self-acknowledged shortcomings. His papers reveal a man with an unsettled inner life, a complex personality, and a passion for the poetry of Keats. He grew fascinated with Freudian and Jungian psychiatry, and he endured anguish over leaving his first wife and children. Soon after, Hopkins married Barbara Duncan, a secretary at the New York Tuberculosis and Health Association, which Hopkins then headed. Harry was passionately in love with Barbara. They kept very much to themselves, and Harry preferred to stay at home with Barbara in the evening rather than going out carousing as he had previously. They had one child, Diana.[39]

No one rose from relative obscurity in the world of social work to the top ranks of the New Deal without a healthy measure of ambition. Hopkins's drive was aided by his elasticity and resilience. A man who had spent much of his life as a social-reforming administrator ultimately worked comfortably with Democratic political machines to secure the president's renomination in 1940, and then later worked harmoniously with the military chiefs and became the president's confidential liaison to Churchill and Stalin.[40] During both the New Deal and the war years, he proved adaptable and versatile, equally comfortable arguing about slums, sewers, storm drains, nursery schools, and later transitioning to military strategy. As Frances Perkins once observed, Hopkins's life revealed a strange quality of American life, in which a man trained and experienced in social work would emerge as the one official performing "the greatest job of organization, planning and releasing energy that the world has seen for a long, long time."[41]

Hopkins remained throughout his life a penetrating observer of human behavior and an excellent listener. This aided him in providing people with what they most wanted. "Harry's great virtue," New Dealer Jerome Frank recalled, "was that he intuitively went to the heart of a practical problem. He learned very quickly how to meet the practical problem of dealing with groups or personalities."[42] He was quick minded, keenly interested in things that could be done, shown, demonstrated, proven factually. He valued new ideas and was skilled at turning his attention from one complex problem to another. He possessed wide-ranging interests, which only broadened because of the nature of his jobs. He balanced the practical with the theoretical. He possessed a large measure of pragmatism, adhering to the Social Gospel creed of doing good for good's sake.[43]

Despite his display of a rough-hewn exterior, he remained one of the most empathetic of New Dealers, retaining a sense of spirituality, idealism, and social justice. Others took note that one of his outstanding character traits was an intense desire to serve, to aid, and to assist others. There were several paradoxes present throughout his life. He presented an outward impression of self-esteem, balanced with considerable private self-doubt. He possessed an enormous capacity for giving and receiving love and a talent for self-aware-ness. His sister observed in him an "unusual ability to grasp fundamental facts and needs, even if it admitted certain personal faults and weaknesses."[44]

While well organized as an administrator, his personal disarray was legendary. His clothes suggested an air of eccentricity. His appearance gave off an impression of sartorial indifference. One newspaper profile observed that "his clothes always reflected the angles of bony knees and elbows, and his general appearance was less that of the former farm boy he is than that of an actor made up to represent an old vaudeville conception of a farm boy."[45] Some colleagues suspected that he slept in his clothes, and it was an unending source of mystery how even his newest suits looked so threadbare only a few days after he began wearing them.

Hopkins rarely took a flattering picture, and photographs from the period failed to capture what his friends described as an unconventional charisma. Unhappy with how his appearance often came across in the press, he suspected that newspaper editors deliberately sought to capture him in "goofy situations." With his bony features and often loose-fitting suits, he inevitably became fodder for political cartoonists. His friends recollected with amusement when, kneeling before Pope Pius XI during his 1934 tour of Europe, the studs of Hopkins's tuxedo popped off and his starched dress shirt clumsily flopped open.[46] On another occasion, steaming to the Atlantic Conference with Churchill, Hopkins's cabin on the HMS *King George* was strewn with papers and clothing. Feeling sympathy for his defeated British valet, Hopkins gave him the expensive overcoat he had just purchased in London.[47]

Some friends thought Hopkins had a total disregard for money, the acquisition of which meant little to him, seeing it merely as something to spend. He was notorious for rarely carrying any cash and was frequently in debt, despite an above-average yearly salary of $6,000. Books became one of his extravagances, and he was known to impulsively purchase thirty to forty at a time. "If you should find Harry Hopkins with more than $50 in his pocket today, you could safely gamble that he just picked a good nag at Tropical Park," a friend observed. One unflattering news photo from the period showed Hopkins lining up at the betting window, standing below a sign for "Two-Dollar Bets." His friends joked that he could not afford higher stakes.[48]

His critical and analytical ability stood out above all. He loved to criticize and find flaws in plans and proposals, and he once described himself as the

Hopkins with Secretary of Labor Frances Perkins. "He was a natural executive," Perkins recollected, and "proved to have a natural talent, too, for those political adjustments which are so essential to a social worker carrying on a health and welfare program impinging on public policy. But he never forgot that the people were his clients and that it was in their interests that he directed the agencies he headed."[49] Credit: Library of Congress, Prints & Photographs Division, photograph by Harris & Ewing, Reproduction number LC-USZ62-123456.

Hopkins, as PWA Administrator, arriving at the White House for a conference with President Roosevelt on July 14, 1937. Source: Harris & Ewing Collection, Library of Congress.

Hopkins confering with his WPA Assistant Chief, Aubrey Williams, prior to testifying before the House Appropriations Committee on President Roosevelt's $4.5 billion stimulus package. April 20, 1938. Source: Library of Congress.

guy with a talent for taking proposals and translating them into administrative reality. He could be deliberative, but once he made up his mind he would vigorously work to implement his decision. He kept coworkers on the alert with his unexpected cross-examinations. He had little patience for long, drawn-out, digressive meetings. He could be curt and abrupt in halting discussions he felt did not bear directly on the issue at hand. Those who worked closely with him recognized the warning signs of his rising irritation. He would sink lower and lower into his chair, his shoulders hunched up, his arms folded across his abdomen as though he was hugging his unsettled insides, one of his eyes would half close, while the other would open wider and wider, or both eyes would suddenly look penetratingly, bug-eyed, at the speaker without blinking. His lips would shift to the side of his face and he would rasp: "I'm bored."[50]

Hopkins took several of the toughest assignments in the New Deal. He survived years of high-stress political crossfire and infighting while many other New Dealers fell by the wayside.[51] He picked excellent subordinates and worked them hard, expecting them to keep up with his killing pace. He considered the ability of potential appointees more important than their political views and made enemies in important states by appointing Republicans. By his own inclinations, and by directive of the president, Hopkins sought to keep political and patronage considerations out of relief as much as possible.[52] He came to be recognized by both friends and critics as an exceptionally able administrator. He developed a reputation for hard work, often laboring for long hours after his staff went home. Some observers, such as his WPA assistant Aubrey Williams, detected a streak of masochism. Williams recalled: "Harry always seemed to me to have an unlimited capacity for love and also an unlimited capacity for absorbing punishment."[53]

In his eulogy written for a memorial service a few months after Hopkins's death in January 1946, the author John Steinbeck noted that while there were thousands of physical monuments to Hopkins because of the public works of the CWA and WPA, the "still greater monuments are the saved lives and the purpose of the people who built them. The planted trees fed families; and wherever else these things may be disregarded they are known in the hearts of the people, and more than known, they are expected. The right to live in security has been acknowledged; government has undertaken the responsibility for that security."[54]

# CHAPTER TWO

~

# New Dealer

If you gave [Harry Hopkins] a piece of string, he would somehow manage to make a whole suit out of it.[1]

—*New Dealer Paul Appleby*

Harry Hopkins believed that the Great Depression created an extraordinary situation in which the American people looked to their government for relief from their economic problems with a comparatively open mind as to the form this relief should take. The economic crisis had shaken even the rich and powerful from their smug certainties about the American economy and political system. Even middle-class people gained a new, if temporary, perspective, as the stability of their jobs, homes, and savings evaporated. Hopkins observed in 1936: "New ideas and new solutions to old problems seemed less alarming under such circumstances." With the first flush of recovery, however, many of those who enjoyed the New Deal's benefits found themselves weary of government support, "bored with the poor, the unemployed and the insecure."[2]

Between 1933 and 1938, Hopkins became the spearhead of the New Deal and the world's largest employer, with more than fifteen million people (out of a population of 120 million) working in various programs he ran. He also became the world's biggest spender. More than $10 billion was distributed through New Deal programs he led, such as the Federal Emergency Relief

Administration (FERA), the Civil Works Administration (CWA), and the Works Progress Administration (WPA). To put this in perspective, Hopkins controlled an enormous portion of total federal spending at a time when annual federal budgets ranged from only $5 billion to $9 billion.

Hopkins's role in the New Deal, and the record of the New Deal itself, is rife with misperceptions. The actual record is at odds with popular myths about leaf raking, shovel leaning, and "boondoggling." By 1935, as head of the WPA, he had become the nation's biggest employer, with 3.5 million people on his payroll. Ultimately, the WPA created eight million jobs, built an estimated seventy-eight thousand bridges, six hundred and fifty miles of roads, hundreds of airports, seven hundred miles of runways, thirteen thousand playgrounds, 125,000 military and civilian buildings, 226 hospitals, six thousand schools, 325 firehouses, five hundred water treatment plants, twenty thousand miles of water mains, and repaired twenty-four thousand miles of storm drains and sewer lines. The New Deal also made enormous contributions to the subsequent war effort. Had it not been for the organization and experiences of the New Deal, the mobilization for war would have been delayed.[3]

To Hopkins, debates about the efficacy of New Deal spending missed a larger and much more important point. The crisis was not an abstract ideological debate about economics. Millions of *people* desperately needed help. He found abstract philosophical arguments about relief to be totally beside the urgent necessity of providing relief to millions of desperate people. Hopkins and FDR came to believe that only robust federal action could save the country. Yet the centralization and strong federal action that the New Deal came to represent was actually more of a Teddy Roosevelt Republican legacy. FDR, seeing himself as the legatee of Teddy Roosevelt, could easily reconcile himself to this.[4]

Hopkins understood the intensity of the hostility toward the New Deal. Many of the remedies he supported were seen as a staggering blow to the wealthy and their advocates in Washington. He believed that the wealthy controlled Washington through their outsized power over the priorities of government. As Hopkins saw it, many in both parties remained committed to austerity because they sought to defend the economic interests of the affluent, largely through opposing taxes on high incomes and fighting the regulation of banks and Wall Street.[5]

Roosevelt took office in 1933 in a nation characterized by enormous disparities in income and wealth. The shift during the New Deal toward the masses, the working class, and organized labor had a transformational impact, empowering workers and creating the beginnings of a middle-class society.

Any agenda that used the power of government to create jobs and old-age pensions, used spending power to stimulate demand, and put higher wages and buying power in the hands of workers was perceived by many critics as deeply "un-American" and "un-Constitutional." Hopkins expected a backlash. He would have been surprised had one not occurred.[6]

After Hopkins was sworn in as the head of the Federal Emergency Relief Administration (FERA) on May 22, 1933, he distributed more than $5 million in relief in his first five hours in office. The following day the *Washington Post* profiled him in a story titled "Money Flies!" Empowered to distribute $500 million, FERA represented an important step in getting the federal government over the fear of direct relief. In the early months of the New Deal, Hopkins concurred with the president that the federal government had a responsibility for unemployment relief, that the problems of the Depression would have to be attacked head on, and that a distinct federal program should be established to assist state and local governments in meeting their mounting relief crises. FERA, working through city and state governments, could still be reconciled with the idea of states and localities having the primary responsibility for providing relief.[7]

FERA would employ two million Americans. But relief, while vital in the short term, could do little to mitigate the long-term problems caused by widespread unemployment. Until the summer of 1933, the unemployed had been receiving only food aid. Hopkins and his staff often struggled with larger philosophical questions underpinning the challenges they faced. What was the chief problem of those on relief? Well, for the most part, they desperately needed paying jobs. Thus, if the primary challenge was jobs, why not give them jobs? Hopkins felt that a person out of work needed a job, not a series of endless handouts. He believed passionately in the principle that unemployment itself should be the measure of one's eligibility for work relief. Every unemployed American had the right to a job that should pay uniform monthly rates, and these wages should not be governed by whatever notions a social worker had about what the employee's monthly pay ought to be.[8]

Why not launch a public works program whose chief objective would be reemployment, one that would accomplish projects that could be launched immediately and inject demand into the stalled economy?[9] There had previously been modest public works programs under President Herbert Hoover, but these projects had unfolded slowly and had only a negligible impact on unemployment. Thus, after relief, a secondary objective was stimulating demand. These programs were designed not only to give jobs to the unemployed but also to bolster consumers' purchasing power and maintain it above a dangerous minimum level.[10]

To Hopkins, the crisis of the Depression was never about abstract philo-sophical or ideological arguments about economic theory. To the contrary, millions of *people* desperately needed help, and he sought to provide it. He found abstract arguments about relief to be totally beside the essential point of providing relief to *people*.[11]

Roosevelt and Hopkins subsequently created the Civil Works Adminis-tration in November 1933 to be run as a federal program to create immediate employment during the winter of 1933 to 1934 and to stop allocating money to people and instead allocate jobs. Meeting at the White House in No-vember 1933, the president said to Hopkins: "4 million people—that should require $400 million. We'll transfer the money from [Public Works Admin-istration head Harold] Ickes." Hopkins called up Ickes and told him what had just transpired—that the president had conceptualized the idea all on his own. Hopkins doubted Ickes was ever convinced that this was the case.[12]

Hopkins designed the CWA as a temporary emergency program to get the country through the coming winter. During its brief life, the CWA put four million unemployed to work constructing forty thousand schools, 469 airports, and thousands of miles of roads. Critics again began charging the CWA with "leaf-raking," "leaning on shovels," and "boondoggling."[13]

The CWA had a tremendous influence on Hopkins. It revealed to him the boldness with which things could be accomplished in the New Deal. His experience with the CWA was of inestimable value when, years later, he was confronted with the vast and urgent challenges of a world war.[14] Hopkins still opposed direct relief, such as the dole system in Great Britain. He preferred a system that would maintain and even upgrade workers' skills, sustain morale and their interest in the culture of work, and, simultaneously, provide them with relief and perhaps inject immediate demand in the economy.[15] He advo-cated providing jobs, medical care, clothing, and housing. Because of his in-terest in psychology and his experience in grassroots social work, he strongly believed that relief for paid work, however defined, as opposed to cash relief handouts would ultimately prove better for the psychology and self-esteem of recipients. This view coincided with FDR's and had a profound impact on the evolution of the New Deal.[16]

The CWA provided a precedent for the subsequent WPA. Established on May 6, 1935, with Hopkins at its helm, the WPA received an initial appropri-ation of $4.8 million, the single largest appropriation in history to that time, and it eventually allocated more than $8 million. Hopkins anticipated that launching a relief program on such an unprecedented scale would provoke fury from those who cared little for the plight of the desperate, but instead cared intensely about abstract arguments about "self-reliance" and "individualism."[17]

During his time at WPA, critics often derided him as a radical. But many of the things he fought for, such as old-age pensions, public relief, health care, and decent housing, became the centerpieces of the liberal agenda in the decades after the New Deal. Frances Perkins noted: "From what you led this country to know great reforms are bound to spring in the future, based on this foundation stone which you have laid so very ably and with such significance of purpose. You have done something very big for your country."[18]

Hopkins did not shy away from promoting the WPA's record, or making a broader case for liberalism through his speeches and his defiant testimonies before Congress. He frequently expressed his outrage that so many citizens remained improperly fed, clothed, housed, and otherwise denied the necessities and benefits of modern American life.[19] His achievement required administrative ability but, perhaps more important, it demanded the kind of personality that was impervious to criticism. Hopkins came to represent everything critics despised about the New Deal, provoking strong feelings in his many adversaries and even his close associates. Yet he reacted to it all with relative indifference. This only further infuriated his critics. Only rarely did he respond to personal attacks, philosophizing that criticism came with the territory, brushing off his critics with an indifferent "What the hell? I've got nothing to lose."[20]

Hopkins's enormous influence over policy provoked resentments and competitive relationships with other New Dealers. His most tortured rivalry was with Public Works chieftain Harold Ickes. The Interior Secretary could be bad tempered, irascible, and nasty. His voluminous diaries reveal a man with nary a kind word for anyone, even the president. His favorite target, however, was always Harry Hopkins.[21] The rivalry was perhaps inevitable given Ickes's enormous capacity for paranoia, but the roots of the conflict may have started in early 1934 when Ickes was insulted by the president's refusal to appoint Hopkins his undersecretary.[22]

The conspiratorial Ickes subsequently insisted that Hopkins deliberately created the acronym WPA in a deliberate effort to confuse the public with the achievements of his PWA. Ickes dictated lengthy rants against Hopkins and the WPA poaching on PWA turf. He suspected Hopkins's motives even when they were in agreement.[23] He accused Hopkins of manipulating the president and the people around him and fixated on Hopkins's closeness to the First Lady and his friendships with Jimmy Roosevelt and his wife, Betsey. Ickes had a peculiar fascination with Hopkins's relationships with women, once observing: "One of the principle cards played by Harry since the beginning has been the court that he has paid to the women who might be influential, either with the President or with someone who is strong with the President. He has assiduously and avowedly cultivated Mrs. Roosevelt, the President's mother, Missy LeHand and Betsey Roosevelt."[24]

Hopkins acknowledged the rift but nonetheless genuinely respected Ickes. He recognized that few battled as consistently for the New Deal and for the president, week in and week out, as did the Interior Secretary.[25] "Ickes is a doer," Hopkins admiringly observed of his rival.[26] Hopkins once baffled the conspiratorial Ickes when he explained that, while they had not always seen eye to eye on every matter, "I hope that you have never doubted my personal feeling toward you. Even when we have differed, you have added zest to my life."[27]

Too much focus on their personal disagreements overlooks the genuine philosophical differences between these two New Deal titans. They had fundamentally different perspectives on the purpose of public works and the means by which unemployment should have been addressed and the economy revived. Hopkins's WPA focused on creating jobs that might result in public works, whereas Ickes's PWA focused on public works that might, one day, result in employment. Ickes was terribly afraid of spending. Worried about even the slightest whiff of corruption, he applied the "green eyeshade" to every contract. The Interior Secretary was anxious to guarantee honest expenditures, but he failed to put a sufficient amount of money into circulation and his fear of spending became an obstacle to lowering unemployment by stimulating demand. His method, revitalizing the economy from the top down by allocating huge government contracts for heavy machinery, cement, and steel to be used in enormous public works, absorbed the unemployed far too slowly, if at all. Many businesses merely reduced their backlogs of inventory to meet Ickes's demands without tangible increases in their workforce.[28]

Hopkins's views were based on an entirely different reality. The human dimension was of greater importance to Hopkins than concerns about perceptions of profligacy or graft. He felt a sense of urgency about the unemployed and was thus much more audacious in his actions.[29]

Hopkins soon became distracted from the New Deal's second-term controversies by the failing health of his wife, Barbara, who had been diagnosed with cancer. Her subsequent death on October 7, 1937, was a devastating blow to Harry.[30] Added to the anxiety he felt over Barbara's death, more depressing news arrived in 1937 when specialists concluded that Harry had developed what doctors initially diagnosed as gastric ulcers. He had long been known throughout the New Deal for ignoring his health, and Barbara's illness and death made him more careless than ever. As he focused exclusively on her condition, he rarely slept, ate irregularly, consumed prodigious amounts of coffee and alcohol, and smoked more than ever before.[31]

FDR and the Roosevelt family leave the White House for Christmas Church Services, December 25, 1938. Left to Right: FDR's sister-in-law Mrs. James Roosevelt; Eleanor Roosevelt; FDR's mother Sara Roosevelt; FDR; the president's son Jimmy and his wife, Betsey Roosevelt; Franklin D. Roosevelt, Jr.; and Harry Hopkins. Front row: Sara Delano Roosevelt (daughter of Jimmy and Betsey); and Diana Hopkins.
Source: Library of Congress

Upon further examination, Hopkins's diagnosis grew much more serious: intestinal cancer, the disease that had taken the life of his father.[32] He faced a de facto death sentence, as Harry's physician brother, Lewis, examined him and surmised that he had only about four weeks to live.[33] When Harry departed Washington for the famed Mayo Clinic in Rochester, Minnesota, the president's personal physician, Admiral Ross McIntire, reviewed his medical records and doubted whether he would ever leave the hospital or whether he would live longer than a few weeks at most.[34] In fact, few people, except perhaps Roosevelt, ever expected to see Harry alive again. FDR refused to accept such a bleak diagnosis. The president, with his own experience with debilitating illness, called in specialists from all over the country. Hopkins miraculously survived.[35] It was said that he had undergone so many treatments at the hands of army, navy, White House, and Mayo Clinic physicians that neither he nor his doctors could remember who had administered which medication or treatment.[36]

Harry also worried about the future of the now-motherless Diana. Having lost her mother in 1937 and all indications that she might soon lose her father, her plight elicited the sympathy of the White House family, particularly FDR, FDR's longtime assistant, Marguerite "Missy" LeHand, and Eleanor, but also FDR's son Jimmy and his wife, Betsey, who considered adopting Diana if Harry should die. Eleanor became in effect guardian to six-year-old Diana.[37]

Harry agonized over Diana. He acknowledged that he was not father material and, after having three boys with Ethel (who did most of the parenting), he frequently felt perplexed about how best to raise Diana, particularly on his own. When, in the late 1930s, he shipped the seven-year-old Diana off to Grinnell to live with Florence and Robert Kerr, Robert observed to Harry that Diana was a shy and pensive girl who was difficult to get close to. Harry blurted out: "Well, now you know how *I* feel!"[38] "Diana, who outgrows her clothes every two months, has gone off to camp," Harry wrote to Missy LeHand in 1943. "I, never having been a very good parent, confess that I am not unhappy to have her in the mountains this summer."[39]

His brother, Lewis, suggested to the president that a genuine effort needed to be made to get Harry to reduce his consumption of cigarettes and coffee, the two staples that had sustained him throughout the New Deal years but had also helped to destroy his health. "Harry has been advised to this effect before, but I am asking if you would add the real weight of your request," Lewis asked the president, adding that Harry's doctors also recommended more rest, "which I feel sure Harry will not take without your orders."[40] The president conspired with Harry's doctors. One of Hopkins's physicians wrote to FDR: "I want to commend you for your kindly wisdom in asking Harry not to return to work until at least April 1, and secondly, to tell you that he has been not only completely cooperative, but brave in the suffering inseparable from a formidable operation."[41] Everyone conspired to assist Hopkins in cleaning up his act. Missy LeHand was particularly solicitous, gently admonishing him about his eating, smoking, and drinking habits.[42]

After Barbara's death in 1937, Harry threw himself into his work with a worrying zeal, yet he did not let his prodigious capacity for work get in the way of his private life. He distinguished himself for his love of life's pleasures, as one of the administration's better poker players, and a frequenter of the racetrack. Sociable, he liked to mix and mingle with people different from himself and enjoyed parties with the affluent in Manhattan, weekends at the track in Saratoga, poker with his New Deal cronies. He had many friends among the rich, moving comfortably in their circles.[43] "Everyone also knows of Harry's fondness for people with money," Harold Ickes once acidly observed, "especially the fast set, where the men gamble heavily and the women are little more than prostitutes."[44]

Hopkins became, improbably, one of Washington's most eligible bachelors. He was often seen in the company of well-known women such as the respected antifascist journalist Dorothy Thompson and the French-born actress Claudette Colbert, kindling rumors about his personal life. Friends and colleagues speculated, sometimes to the press, that he might remarry. Hopkins usually addressed these speculations by telling friends that his love life was nobody's goddamned business. One widely reported rumor had him marrying Dorothy Donovan Hale, thirty-three, a celebrated former chorus girl, actress, and widow of the muralist Gardner Hale. Hopkins weathered the sensation surrounding Dorothy's suicide in October 1938 (which some alleged occurred because of Hopkins's romantic indifference) as well as the haunting Frida Kahlo painting depicting her plunge from her Manhattan apartment building. Another rumor had him courting FDR's assistant Missy LeHand. Indeed, Hopkins had enormous admiration for Missy, and she grew protective of him, standing up for him to critics such as Ickes and Morgenthau. There was genuine affection between them, and he very well may have pursued a closer, perhaps even romantic, relationship. But Missy's devastating stroke in 1941 tragically removed her from FDR's coterie, severing an important link between the dynamic days of the New Deal and the increasingly weary and draining war years.[45]

The recession of 1937 to 1938 marked the return of Hopkins's influence from the low point of the death of Barbara and his own life-threatening illness at the end of 1937. After months of illness, the recession gave Hopkins an opening to reestablish his place as the most influential presidential adviser. After the 1936 election, President Roosevelt, under the influence of his fiscally conservative Treasury Secretary Henry Morgenthau, began calling for austerity and a balanced budget. The president informed Hopkins that the WPA would have to retrench.[46] These events occurred during the very months that Hopkins was preoccupied with Barbara's terminal illness, and then he faced his own dire prognosis. Hopkins's influence naturally went into eclipse, and Morgenthau's began to ascend.

Morgenthau's austerity measures, which included an 18 percent cut in federal spending, showed no positive economic results. Rather, the economy plunged into a deep recession as business declined and unemployment skyrocketed.[47] Morgenthau responded that things were not as bad as they looked, that more belt tightening was necessary, that big business required confidence, and only further austerity measures would prove adequate. "Stay the course," Morgenthau counseled. Fiscal conservatives around the president, sensing an opportunity to apply the austerity measures they had been advocating, demanded balanced budgets to restore "business confidence," but they left unexplained why business was suddenly less confident than it had been in the years prior to 1937.[48]

Hopkins argued that, on the contrary, spending was one of the most powerful weapons the president possessed for waging war on the 1937 recession.[49] He continued to urge spending in response to other influential officials who insisted stimulus was no longer necessary and would do genuine harm. He pointed to the plight of the cities, which felt the recession of 1937 to 1938 the hardest, as they were once again overrun with the needy and desperate unemployed. The big-city mayors and the urban political machines enthusiastically championed Hopkins's views and launched a massive lobbying effort to get the WPA taps flowing again. With the backing of the big-city mayors and machines, Hopkins urged massive spending increases to restart the stalled economy.[50]

Hopkins arrived at Warm Springs in the spring of 1938 and successfully pushed for larger appropriations. Hopkins ultimately won the battle with Morgenthau, and the spending taps flowed freely again in 1938. Hopkins demonstrated enormous influence with the president in convincing him to embrace spending as stimulus. Roosevelt authorized a massive spending bill. Of the $3.75 billion FDR requested, the enormous sum of $1.4 billion would be allocated to Hopkins, "appropriated directly to your Administration."[51] With the notable exception of Morgenthau, who was temporarily marginalized, Hopkins gained the support of other key members of the cabinet by sharing the stimulus.[52]

Hopkins threw himself into his new task with vigor. That summer of 1938, as most of the cabinet departed a sweltering Washington for cooler climates, he stayed behind, working eighteen-hour days translating the spending into action. His capacity for hard work and his innate fatalism sustained him. He became one of the chief advocates of what might be called "trickle up economics," or, more prosaically, spending to stimulate demand, focusing on restoring the purchasing power to the "submerged third" of the nation.[53] As he patiently explained to a dubious Senate committee in April 1938, spending to stimulate demand would lower unemployment, and lowering unemployment would further stimulate demand. "This program," Hopkins testified, "is not simply a security program. It would also provide a broad base of purchasing power . . . increasing the stability of the economic system."

Hopkins publicly lamented the millions of "idle men, money and machines, and all the resourcefulness, ingenuity and courage that reside in 12 or 13 million unemployed men, is helpless to take up this new frontier without tremendous organization of productive forces such as only Government can supply when business is in the doldrums."[54]

In the midst of the recession in 1938, Hopkins now had his $1.4 million appropriation, and the WPA soon had eight million Americans on its payroll. His supporters thought his push for stimulus, in the face of widespread demands for further austerity, was nothing short of heroic. But being back at the center of events and assuming the leadership of the push for the controversial stimulus bill meant that Hopkins would be subjected to fresh criticisms. Hopkins's concern for the dispossessed brought out the worst in some of his critics as a new sense of hysteria seized them, many of whom saw his actions as deeply threatening to their conception of America. Some characterized his advocacy of spending to reignite the economy as "socialism." The newspaper and political attacks became unrelenting as hostile columnists called him "socialistic," "un-American," or "redistributionist." Arthur Krock of the *New York Times* emerged as one of Hopkins's most determined critics, depicting him as the sinister Rasputin-like influence behind the New Deal. Krock accused him of "political bossism," "sycophancy," "machine politics," "class warfare," and balancing the budget through the "socialistic" "redistribution of income." He referred to Hopkins as "the taxer" and "the spender" and castigated the WPA as a "political agency" and nothing more than a "vote-getting" machine designed to keep the New Deal in power permanently.[55]

Other critics accused Hopkins of using the WPA for political purposes. Some feared that he was transforming the WPA into an enduring national political machine. He ran afoul of members of Congress who desired control over relief spending and patronage in their states and districts, but he refused to let the WPA become a pork-infested boondoggle, infuriating Congressmen who castigated him as little more than an unelected social worker.

In fact, Hopkins had evolved into a shrewd political observer, and he did indeed harbor grand ambitions. Evidence suggests that even before FDR faced his reelection campaign in 1936, Hopkins had his sights set on the Democratic presidential nomination in 1940, or perhaps the vice presidency as a stepping-stone to the presidency.[56] He traveled throughout the country during the 1936 campaign, exploring the nation, investigating the political situation in each state, getting to know thousands of Democratic officeholders and party leaders. His enemies suspected he was using his enlarged role in the campaign to create a network to serve his own possible bid for the nomination in 1940.[57]

Hopkins understood that the cabinet profile would confer upon him the kind of respectability required of a presidential candidate. But his goal of becoming the first cabinet-level Secretary of Welfare ended when Roosevelt's executive branch reorganization bill died in the spring of 1938. Opposition to the bill mounted when many on Capitol Hill grew concerned that Hopkins would transform a new Welfare Department into a vehicle for his own political aspirations, much as Herbert Hoover had used the Commerce Department in the 1920s as a launching pad for his election in 1928. As an alternative, friends and colleagues urged Hopkins to take over the War Department, which might prove to be a pivotal post in the years ahead. There was some plausibility to this idea. The WPA had engaged in thousands of defense-related projects, building, for example, 85 percent of the nation's airports between 1935 and 1941. Had it not been for such work, the war production effort would have been stymied. Moreover, FDR's use of Hopkins in late 1937 for top-secret inspection tours of defense installations suggests that the president might have been grooming him for just such a post.

Hopkins surprised many when he expressed his preference to become Commerce Secretary. One of only ten cabinet posts at that time, the Department of Commerce was housed in a magnificent $17 million monument commissioned by Herbert Hoover, who had ensconced himself in the opulent penthouse office. Many suspected Roosevelt had appointed Hopkins to Commerce to free him up to make a run for the presidency in 1940. One cartoon, appearing in the staid *New York Times*, portrayed Hopkins as a demented trapeze artist, visions swimming in his head of Herbert Hoover leaping from one swing labeled "Secretary of Commerce" to another labeled "The White House."

Hopkins might not have faced so much opposition had he not also been seen as the president's personal choice as his successor in 1940. His opponents in the Democratic Party, as well as the Republicans, understood that Hopkins, lagging in public opinion polls, had little chance at the 1940 Democratic nomination without the enthusiastic backing of the still-popular FDR. Columnist Walter Lippmann observed: "Appointing him to this lowly post, where there is nothing he has to do, is indisputably proof of how many as yet undefined things the president is ready to have Mr. Hopkins do." Lippmann also noted a number of similarities between Hoover and Hopkins. Both men had been born in Iowa and became known for their humanitarian endeavors. Hoover led enormous efforts to provide food relief for Belgium and Russia, whereas Hopkins led the largest government-led rescue of a nation during a depression.[58]

"Harry had been a rather well-known left-winger," speechwriter Sam Rosenman recalled. "His connection with the administration was in connection with the liberal policies of the WPA. Roosevelt thought, as a matter of politics, that he ought to have some identification with business, so over great opposition he made him Secretary of Commerce."[59] Hopkins also recognized that his biggest challenge in the months ahead was to get the economic recovery back on track and that this might require uniting the powers of business and government in a creative fashion. "If Harry Hopkins makes a success of it," a *Time* magazine profile observed, "and the businessmen feel he has accomplished something affirmative in the oft-talked-about but little-realized Government-and-business cooperation policy, it will be because the man now being suggested for the Department of Commerce portfolio will have brought left and right wings together in a practical way."[60]

The buildup began with Hopkins's dramatic swearing in on Christmas Eve at the White House.[61] "Don't kid me, boys," Hopkins joked to the cabinet upon accepting the appointment in late 1938. "This is the Christmas season and I'm accepting anything."[62] At the same time, many businessmen, formerly some of Hopkins's strongest critics, found him to be open-minded and discovered that his views were quite different from his critics' caricatures of a wild-eyed Rasputin. Several of the businessmen he recruited through his Business Advisory Council became Hopkins's "tame millionaires" who served the president during the war. Hopkins was amused by the prospect of transforming himself from the champion of the forgotten man to the champion of business. From the very moment of his acrimonious confirmation hearings, Hopkins exuded, "I am going to enjoy this."[63]

When Roosevelt's 1938 purge of the Democratic Party's conservatives failed, he instead sought to guarantee that the Democratic nominee in 1940 would be a liberal and New Dealer. Worried about a possible restoration of the conservative Democrats in 1940, Roosevelt kept his options open, but he also sought to cultivate a suitable successor, one who would uphold and expand the New Deal.[64] Early polls revealed the conservative vice president John Nance Garner as the strongest contender for the succession. One Gallup poll in 1939 revealed that if FDR did not seek the nomination in 1940, Garner would be the leading choice of 45 percent of Democrats. In the same poll, Hopkins had the support of only 1 percent.[65]

Roosevelt could not support Vice President Garner or Postmaster General Jim Farley because neither were New Dealers and FDR would only support a moderate conservative such as Secretary of State Cordell Hull if the ticket was balanced with a liberal running mate such as Hopkins or Agriculture Secretary Henry Wallace. Just as Teddy Roosevelt's departure from the presidency in 1909 marked the beginning of the Republican Party's return to its traditional laissez-faire ethos, FDR feared his exit might mean the restoration of the pre–New Deal Democratic Party—a southern-dominated party with a Jeffersonian small government philosophy. Roosevelt realized he had only temporarily changed the party and that the election of Hull, Garner, or Farley, or some other non–New Dealer, might restore the old, Jeffersonian Democratic Party. Roosevelt wanted to campaign vigorously for a liberal successor in 1940, but if the Democratic Party nominated a conservative, he threatened to make his displeasure known by taking a long presidential tour of the Philippine Islands for the duration of the campaign.[66]

Wallace and Hopkins represented to many the best possibility for the confirmation and extension of the New Deal's achievements. On the highest levels of politics, such as those related to progressive action and social justice, Hopkins's colleagues recognized that his intuitive skills in advancing the liberal agenda were equal to anyone else in Washington, including the president. "If you gave HLH a piece of string," Wallace's assistant, Paul Appleby, admiringly observed of Hopkins, "he would somehow manage to make a whole suit out of it."[67]

Despite anemic showings in the polls, Hopkins nonetheless possessed solid advantages in the jockeying for the 1940 nomination. First, he enjoyed the support of the president and First Lady, and as early as 1937 he was widely seen as FDR's personal choice and "logical successor."[68] The president regarded Hopkins as the very personification of the New Deal, a proven Progressive problem solver who had demonstrated his administrative skills with FERA, CWA, and the WPA. As Works Progress Administrator, Hopkins had little chance of vaulting into the presidential nomination in 1940. Now, brought into the cabinet as Secretary of Commerce—the same position Herbert Hoover had held in 1928 when he launched his successful bid for the presidency—Hopkins had a chance.[69] Ickes sourly observed in early 1939: "It is plain that Harry is a candidate—a very active one—and that it is pretty generally accepted that he is the heir apparent."[70]

As head of the WPA, Hopkins had established ties to a national network of powerful Democratic mayors and urban political machines, providing him with an enormously influential base of support. The president fully encouraged the mayors' efforts on Hopkins's behalf. Hopkins also enjoyed enthusiastic support from labor. As WPA chief he had worked closely with organized labor, and the WPA provided a means of livelihood for striking workers.[71] Many both inside and outside the New Deal saw these national networks as the potential base for an enduring New Deal–governing coalition, one bringing together New Dealers, liberals, organized labor, relief beneficiaries, and urban political machines. New Deal critic Arthur Krock later recalled: "Hopkins, by impressing upon Roosevelt the political allure of that combination which the New Deal philosophy made, won Roosevelt's favor and confidence. It looked to him as if Hopkins had the golden key to perpetuity of power, which proved to be true."[72]

The Washington political cognoscenti noted with increased interest Hopkins's emergence as the New Deal's political legatee.[73] "It is a fact that much of the best judgment in Washington thinks that Mr. Roosevelt wishes to make Mr. Hopkins the Democratic presidential nominee in 1940," observed the *Washington Post*'s conservative columnist Mark Sullivan at the beginning of 1939. "The same judgment thinks that Mr. Hopkins has the same idea in mind . . . the current judgment of Washington . . . is that Mr. Roosevelt, at this time, does not anticipate trying to nominate himself, that he does anticipate trying to nominate Mr. Hopkins."[74]

The president gave Hopkins encouragement and advice and persuaded him to establish residency in Iowa as a sturdier base for a national campaign.[75] His appointment to the cabinet as Secretary of Commerce, transfer of voting residence from New York to his native Grinnell, and application for membership in the Methodist Church at his boyhood home gave credence to the rumors that the president was directing Hopkins's embryonic candidacy. Harry even had little Diana dispatched to Grinnell to live with Bob and Florence Kerr.[76]

Hopkins leased an Iowa farm as an "official residence." The farm mostly grew corn. With his love of horse racing, he thought about starting a stud farm but worried about how the political humorists might react. He promoted himself as a Gentleman Farmer, but those who knew him understood that he would not have spent ten minutes in such a place. "I really get a great laugh out of Harry building himself up as a hard-working farmhand," a dubious Harold Ickes confided in his diary. "There is hardly anyone I know whom I would less spontaneously associate with farm life than Harry."[77]

He tentatively launched his candidacy with an address before the Des Moines Economic Club in February 1939.[78] Some speculated that the point of the visit was to line up potential delegates for Hopkins's campaign in 1940. *Time* magazine reported: "No political observer missed the point that the prize at stake in Harry Hopkins' performance was not just one State's convention delegates. The prize is presidential Prospect Hopkins'—and the New Deal's—standing with the entire US electorate in 1940."[79]

At the same time, Hopkins did not look the part of a candidate seeking the presidency. His critics played up his unprepossessing air with his thin, straggly hair, unsuccessfully combed over a growing bald spot; a face lined by years of long hours, constant smoking, and heavy coffee drinking; and his well-known penchant for profanity. As an "official" member of the cabinet, he worked hard to sharpen his public image. When King George VI and Queen Elizabeth came to Washington in 1939, the president arranged for his Commerce Secretary to attend a luncheon and garden party hosted by the British ambassador. Hopkins succumbed to the suggestions of Missy and Diana and was fitted for his first-ever morning coat. The press noted that the usually rumpled Commerce Secretary's sartorial sense looked perfect, but when he returned from a midday nap for the afternoon garden party his clothes appeared to be thoroughly covered with dog hair.[80]

Further health crises in 1939 derailed Hopkins's political aspirations. He suffered a severe relapse, and surgeons removed a large portion of his stomach and doubted his chances of recovery. Parts of his stomach revealed evidence of malignant cells, and he was again told his time was short and that the best he might hope for was a slow decline and a few remaining months living the life of an invalid. His case was seen as hopeless, that he would not live to see Christmas, and in September 1939 specialists at the Mayo Clinic discharged him, assuming he was going home to settle his affairs and die. This verdict was conveyed to FDR, who again refused to accept it. Roosevelt took control of Hopkins's care and ordered that all the medical resources of the nation be used to save his valued friend and ally.[81]

"As to Harry's long period of ill health," Lewis Hopkins recalled after the war, "his demanding work over many years comes first; his marital and financial worries can't be ignored; his operation in 1939 showed evidence of malignancy, word of which was carefully silenced and his operations deprived him of essential nutritional factors, which cannot be substituted for by medication."[82] Hopkins somehow suffered on, but he was never in denial about the severity of his condition and was not indifferent to his situation. Most of all, he wanted to get well, if only for Diana. "Stephen and I arrived around July first," Robert Hopkins recalled. "We were both amazed at how sick he was. His letters never indicated this."[83]

Hopkins's numerous attempts to resign in the months ahead were always rejected by Roosevelt, who understood the severity of his condition but felt it best that he soldier on, at least to maintain his own morale. The president, seeking to buoy Hopkins's flagging spirits, pulled rank and rejected his resignations, always pointing out that "his President needed him."[84] Hopkins remained Secretary of Commerce, and the president may have held onto a slim hope for Hopkins's future, harboring ambitions for him and mentioning him as a possible successor. However, Hopkins explained to friends that he was done with Washington and that he would probably edit a news magazine.

FDR throws out the first pitch on opening day, April 18, 1938. Hopkins, holding his hat, looks on from the president's right. Source: Harris & Ewing Collection, Library of Congress.

But on May 10, 1940, Roosevelt faced one of the greatest crises of his presidency, as the Germans finally invaded the Lowlands and a dizzying stream of dispatches flooded the president's desk. FDR looked up and ordered: "Send for Harry."

A call came from the White House inviting Hopkins to dinner that night, and within minutes a car was dispatched to Georgetown where Hopkins had been convalescing. He rose from his sickbed and arrived for dinner, and Roosevelt asked him to spend the night at the White House. Hopkins moved into the Lincoln Study of the White House that day, unaware that he would remain ensconced there for the next three-and-a-half years. Missy LeHand dubbed him "The Man Who Came to Dinner."[85] Now living in the Lincoln study, Hopkins became the president's principal strategist, overseeing FDR's unprecedented nomination for a third term, and his first task was organizing and then staging the president's renomination at the Democratic Convention in Chicago.

# CHAPTER THREE

~

# "Lord Root of the Matter"

Mr. Harry Hopkins has been with me these days. Last week he asked the President to let him go to Moscow. I must tell you that there is a flame in this man for democracy and to beat Hitler. He is the nearest personal representative of the President. A little while ago when I asked him for a quarter of a million rifles they came at once. The President has now sent him full instructions and he leaves my house tonight to go to you. You will be advised of his arrival through the proper channels. You can trust him absolutely. He is your friend and our friend. He will help you to plan for the future victory and for the long term supply of Russia.

—*Winston Churchill to Joseph Stalin, July 28, 1941*[1]

One morning in March 1941, the women of the Washington press corps gathered around the First Lady in her sitting room for an informal discussion when suddenly a shadowy figure in a bright silk dressing gown shambled past the open door. Harry Hopkins was only looking for his cigarettes, but when he grasped the nature of the gathering he quickly darted back into his bedroom and slammed the door before anyone could ask about his recent mission to London.[2]

When Hopkins moved into the White House on May 10, 1940, his influence grew even beyond what it had been during the New Deal. He remained the president's intimate adviser and boon companion, but now, living in what was then called the Lincoln Study, he had access to the president and First Lady day and night and needed only to cross the hall to discuss something with either of them. Presidential speechwriter Sam Rosenman perceptively observed: "Living with a man who is at the head of the government, when you can talk to him frequently and informally about things and he doesn't have to be on parade, when he's not hurried, when you can really argue with him, discuss things with him—you can really have more to do with helping him change policy than any other men, no matter how expert he is. In the first place, you wouldn't be living there unless he had some confidence that you were giving him your best judgment rather than some selfish interest; and you get him at his most relaxed moments."[3]

The intimacies between the Roosevelt and Hopkins families grew. Diana began calling the president "grandpa," and she and Eleanor collaborated on a small victory garden in one of the White House flowerbeds. The president served as a sort of kindly uncle to the Hopkins family. Illustrative of this, one night an embarrassed Harry admitted that he did not possess even the meager sum of five dollars to give to his son Robert who was visiting the White House on a twenty-four-hour pass from Fort Dix and needed the small amount to return to base before reveille. The amused president gave Robert the five dollars and genially offered to pen a note to his commanding officer explaining that the lowly private was needed at the White House to discuss important wartime matters. Robert courteously, and perhaps wisely, turned down the president's offer.[4]

Hopkins served as "the back-door to the White House," a vital conduit to the president. Those who had access to him also had an inside track to Roosevelt. To senior military officials such as Army Chief of Staff General George C. Marshall, Hopkins became an indispensible liaison, a shortcut to the resolution of problems overlooked by a busy commander-in-chief.[5] Some officials bemoaned the peculiarity of Hopkins's residence in the White House and his de facto membership in the Roosevelt family. To such critics, he was a pernicious influence, a breezy Rasputin whispering malignant rumors into the president's ear over cocktails. "Everything has to seep through Harry Hopkins into the White House," Ickes groused. "It is bad for the country to get the impression that any one person, no matter how strong and able he may be, is sharing in the President's councils to the exclusion of all others and perhaps influencing his judgment unduly."[6]

Hopkins never seemed too troubled about the negative impression his enemies had of him as a freeloading Svengali. Although, when a journalist casually mentioned that he kept a case of liquor in the Lincoln bedroom for his own purposes, he complained that it made him out to be a boozehound and that readers might suspect that he treated the White House like a fraternity house.[7]

Hopkins and Roosevelt were alike in many respects. Both had been severely racked by illness. Some saw in the Roosevelt-Hopkins relationship an element of mutual sympathy stemming from a shared experience of overcoming physical hardship. In a perceptive March 1941 profile for the *New York Times*, White House correspondent Turner Catledge observed: "Behind the President's reliance on Harry Hopkins is one of the most interesting, and at the same time most touching, stories connected with the New Deal. It is the story of the gradual development of mutual regard and admiration between two men as they worked together to translate into political action ideas which both doubtless will admit were a bit cloudy in the minds of each when they first met. The story has a personal flavor that is hard to convey in cold type because it involves, among other things, a warmth of sympathy each feels for the other out of his own experience of physical suffering."[8]

They no doubt developed a genuine friendship. Hopkins once revealed the anticipation he felt the night before reporting to the president about his missions to London and Moscow in July 1941. Only hours before arriving at the Atlantic Conference, he sat awake in his bunk on the HMS *King George*. "The man I was going to see that morning was President of the United States," Hopkins wrote in a revealing draft that was never published, "a great man in the world's reckons. It just happened that to me he was more than that. He was Franklin Roosevelt, my friend, incidentally president of the United States."[9]

The president had an enormous influence on Hopkins's views of the looming threat from abroad. As early as 1938, Roosevelt shared with Hopkins his growing pessimism that the United States would not be able to avoid another war. Influenced by Roosevelt's sobering appraisal, Hopkins, too, grew more resolute about the threats posed by Germany and Japan. The president dispatched Hopkins on a secret mission to the West Coast to inspect the aircraft industry and other war production facilities.[10]

Anticipating FDR's transformation from "Dr. New Deal" to "Dr. Win the War," Hopkins began redirecting his energies from domestic relief and toward the world crisis. The war, he told friends, was becoming his sole concern. Longtime Hopkins critic, *New York Times* Washington Bureau Chief Arthur Krock, later recalled: "Once the war began, Hopkins would say of any idea that came: 'Will it help win the war?' and, if they couldn't prove it, he'd say, 'The hell with it.'"[11]

This inevitably disappointed New Deal allies who suddenly found him indifferent to using his influence for liberal objectives. Some lamented what

Returning from Warm Springs on April 10, 1938. Harry Hopkins, Diana Hopkins, FDR, Cordell Hull, Henry Morgenthau. Source: Library of Congress.

they perceived as Hopkins's abandonment of the New Deal, further revealed by his patronage of Wall Street types such as Harriman, Stettinius, and Forrestal. As he threw himself fully into the war effort, others discerned a growing estrangement from Eleanor Roosevelt, who, it was alleged, thought Harry was not fighting to keep the president committed to the New Deal.[12]

Yet while he may have redirected his focus, his interest in social justice never wavered. His reformist Social Gospel ethos found expression in the effort to defeat German and Japanese imperialism. Even Churchill recognized this link between Hopkins's interest in social justice and his hatred of fascism. His deep detestation of fascism, deriving from his perception of it as antithetical to social justice and normal human aspirations, was revealed in the intensity of his comments about the Axis powers. The perceptive Frances Perkins later observed that Hopkins saw the issues of economic justice and peace as linked. Peace and individual liberty were only possible in a country with economic justice. The outrageous inhumanity of the Axis powers drove

Hopkins to the conviction that "he had to fight these evil forces in order to protect the opportunity of people to live in freedom from oppression and fear and want." Perkins detected links between the relief work and his later war work. "For his duties in statecraft," Perkins later related, "Harry Hopkins had no specialized training, but to them he brought the education and experience of the social worker's profession. These were combined with his great common sense, his rare insight into individual and social situations, his capacity for self-sacrifice, and a nobility of character, which would not be defeated by fear, misrepresentation, doubts, grief, or pain. This combination made him a unique man in his generation, and uniquely able to work with Franklin Roosevelt."[13]

In a revealing June 1940 letter congratulating his son, Robert, upon his graduation from high school, Harry shared his evolving thinking about the state of the world. He wrote of the many freedoms he believed were genuinely imperiled by the fascist threat. The Axis powers "represent the very antithesis of those things we hold dear. And you and I must decide whether these freedoms are worth fighting for—whether in war or in peace—this conflict is upon us."[14]

The war reinforced Hopkins's determination to secure the president's renomination in 1940, but he also believed that Roosevelt needed to secure a third term to protect the gains of the New Deal. "The big thing is the change that has occurred in the public thinking in the last eight years," Hopkins said in 1940. "Just look back and see that change. Remember the politicians who shuddered at the thought of voting for Federal old-age assistance. Who would think of opposing it now? . . . The Republicans don't oppose any of it publicly. It is not politically expedient to do so. They don't dare. They know the public won't stand for it. But what they will do, if they get a chance, is to start chipping off the corners, where they think it is safe, until after, say, eight years there will be nothing left of it."[15]

Hopkins began carefully laying the groundwork for the president's renomination, collaborating with Chicago mayor Ed Kelly weeks before the convention.[16] The president dispatched Hopkins to Chicago because Hopkins had replaced Jim Farley in Roosevelt's effort to realign the Democratic Party for the third-term campaign and after.[17] As the president's confidential emissary, Hopkins orchestrated FDR's third term nomination from his suite in the plush elegance of the venerable Blackstone Hotel, the very same "smoke-filled room," suite 308–309, where Warren G. Harding was selected in 1920. Hopkins's suite was the site of the real Democratic Convention. Hopkins had the only direct line to the president installed in the bathroom to guarantee privacy throughout the convention.[18]

Democratic Convention, July 1940, Harry Hopkins, Diana Hopkins, David Hopkins, John Hertz. Once in Chicago, Hopkins found himself in the crossfire, diverting resentment from the president to himself. He was blamed for everything that happened, and much that did not happen, during the convention. Officially, Roosevelt gave him very little instruction other than a brief statement the president had drafted turning down the nomination, but Hopkins was in complete harmony with Roosevelt's design for taking the nomination.

Hopkins sought to engineer something that at the very least looked like a genuine draft: nomination by actual acclamation. Failing that, he wanted Roosevelt's nomination by apparent acclamation. Taking no chances, Hopkins displayed a shrewd, cool ruthlessness that might have surprised those professional politicians who once thought him too inexperienced to be a national candidate.[19]

The most frequent callers to Hopkins's suite included powerbrokers such as Ed Kelly of Chicago, Frank Hague of Jersey City, and a long procession of politicians who had been vaguely promised the vice presidency. To keep everyone on board in the days leading up to FDR's controversial third-term nomination, an estimated seventeen candidates had been given hope that they might obtain the vice presidential nomination. Hopkins memorably paced around his Blackstone suite in his pajamas, cigarette in hand.

Hundreds of delegates visited his suite and, after a few days of conferring with Democratic powerbrokers, Hopkins grew certain of obtaining the support of 900 delegates for the president out of a total of 1,100. In fact, Roosevelt was renominated with 946½.

Hopkins had one more bridge to cross: FDR's running mate. Word went out from Hopkins's Blackstone suite: Roosevelt had blithely ignored everyone's wishes, including Hopkins's, and personally selected Henry Wallace. It was the president's decision, but the emissary charged with carrying it out was Hopkins. Despite reservations, Hopkins plunged into the thankless task of collaring delegates for Wallace. If FDR wanted Wallace on the ticket so badly, Hopkins was not going to fight it. In fact, Hopkins obediently rose to the task.[20]

Hopkins surmised that Wallace started with no more than a paltry fifty delegates, but, thanks to Hopkins's engineering, candidate after candidate mysteriously withdrew. The big machine leaders unhappily trooped into Hopkins's suite and grudgingly accepted what they had to do, but many of the delegates remained in a lather. Even Eleanor Roosevelt, who had flown into Chicago to address the convention, failed to calm them in an impromptu speech emphasizing the terrible burdens of the presidency in these times.[21]

The president employed maximum pressure by postponing his own acceptance speech until Wallace was safely nominated. Wallace had prepared an acceptance speech, but Hopkins told him the convention had already been contentious enough. Despite Hopkins's key role in the thankless task of securing Wallace's nomination, the new vice presidential nominee maintained a persistent grudge against Hopkins for his efforts. Perhaps Wallace remained stung by Hopkins's brusque treatment of him over the acceptance speech debacle. Seen from Hopkins's perspective, and surveying the tide of bile among the delegates, he was merely trying to shield Wallace from further humiliations.[22]

Hopkins later professed to be somewhat dubious of his tactics at Chicago. But he got the result he wanted—Franklin Roosevelt nominated for an unprecedented third term.[23] Hopkins may have also come to accept that he had become a liability to the president's reelection campaign, and he resigned as Commerce Secretary after the convention. In the public version of his resignation, Hopkins avoided personal matters and sought to use this, what might very well be his last big moment on the national stage, to address America's stake in the war.[24]

If he was indeed "retired" from the administration, it was a strange kind of retirement. He remained out of the spotlight but played a large behind-the-scenes role in the campaign. In a perceptive and sympathetic letter,

Labor Secretary Frances Perkins observed the toll that public life had taken on Hopkins: "I know that it has spent your energy, impaired your health and harassed your spirit. They don't give Congressional Medals, I suppose, for the kind of bravery and service which you have given to your country, but you have made just as great a sacrifice, and perhaps a harder one, as any soldier who draws a coveted decoration."[25]

At the end of the crisis-filled year of 1940, and with the tumultuous presidential campaign now over, he accompanied the president on a post-election cruise of the Caribbean. Freed from the pressures of the campaign, Roosevelt turned his attention to the plight of Great Britain. He had already aided Britain with the September 1940 bases-for-destroyers deal, in which he transferred fifty outdated American destroyers in exchange for basing rights on British possessions throughout the Western Hemisphere, but now he discussed with Hopkins the outlines of a bolder policy. Before they returned to Washington, they had created a rough blueprint for what would become Lend-Lease aid to Great Britain.[26]

Increasingly seeing Hopkins as his own private foreign office, the president decided to dispatch him to London at the beginning of 1941 as his "personal representative" to the British government, the first of his several wartime missions to London to confer with Churchill. His mission would clarify Great Britain's specific needs and offer a tangible demonstration of America's deter-mination to help.[27] Hopkins initially held no exalted opinion of Churchill, but he surmised that the success of the mission depended upon interpreting Roosevelt correctly to Churchill, and, conversely, Churchill to Roosevelt.

When he arrived in London in January 1941, Hopkins invited CBS radio correspondent Edward R. Murrow to his room at London's Claridge's Ho-tel to question the perceptive broadcaster about Churchill and the people around him. "You see," he confided to Murrow, "I have come here to try to find a way to be a catalytic between two prima donnas. I want to get a real understanding of Churchill and of the men who he sees after midnight."[28]

Churchill was nonetheless perplexed that the president was sending, of all people, his former relief administrator. The prime minister questioned why Roosevelt would dispatch a former social worker to discuss military matters. Yet appreciating the importance of the meeting, Churchill sought to put the American envoy at ease. The prime minister spoke with convincing enthusi-asm of his vision of the postwar world: "After the war," Churchill reassured Hopkins, "we must make a good life for the cottagers."[29] Hopkins replied with a firmness the prime minister had not anticipated: "I don't give a damn about your cottagers. I came here to see how we can defeat that fellow Hitler. . . . The President is determined that we shall win the war together. Make no mistake about that. He has sent me here to tell you that at all costs he will carry you through, no matter what happens to him—there is nothing that he will not do so far as he has human power." The two talked until four o'clock in the morning.[30]

The mission was no flying visit. He spent six weeks in Great Britain, two-thirds of that time as the prime minister's private guest. Hopkins, the student of the racetrack, liked the odds as he calculated them. The consistent tone of his cables: Britain remained a strong bet.[31] The prime minister and other British officials appreciated Hopkins's talent for sizing up things realistically.[32]

Not everyone was enthusiastic about Hopkins's mission. Harold Ickes acidly observed: "Apparently the first thing that Churchill asks for when he gets awake in the morning is Harry Hopkins, and Harry is the last one whom he sees at night. . . . Probably a good deal of this is true and the attachment of Churchill to Harry Hopkins may be entirely genuine. However, I suspect that if, as his personal representative, the President should send to London a man with the bubonic plague, Churchill would, nevertheless, see a good deal of him. This is not to imply that Harry does not have a good deal of charm. He has, although I have felt it much less than others."[33]

With the idea of Lend-Lease aid to Great Britain germinating, the mission to London had been an important moment for Anglo-American relations. The United States did not have an ambassador in London at the time of his first mission, and Hopkins thus became the Lend-Lease liaison between Churchill and Roosevelt.[34] "I shall never forget these days with you," Hopkins wrote to the prime minister, "your supreme confidence and will to victory."[35] He also sought to make Churchill's plight sympathetic to the American public and to explain America's point of view to the British. Hopkins briefed Churchill on his conception of Lend-Lease, and he shrewdly advised the prime minister to make public statements about Britain's sacrifices in the war and to always publicly emphasize deep appreciation for Lend-Lease.[36]

After returning from this first mission to London, the Lend-Lease Act was ready for passage, and the president made Hopkins its administrator with $7 billion to spend. He expropriated the palatial white marble Federal Reserve Building, surrounding himself with a staff of about thirty, all given the simple assignment of spending billions, miraculously conjuring more supplies for Great Britain (and later Russia), and guaranteeing that the bulk of those vital supplies arrived safely.[37]

While administering the Lend-Lease Act and allocating its appropriations, Hopkins also became the de facto executive secretary of Roosevelt's War Cabinet. The press described his duties as the second in importance to the president himself. Roosevelt told the press that Hopkins would suggest, plan, iron out, foresee, and confer. *Time* magazine observed that Hopkins "had become, in effect, Assistant President of the U.S."[38]

At the president's request, Hopkins returned to London in July 1941, the only passenger in a squadron of bombers bound for Great Britain, where he suddenly appeared before the British War Cabinet in an unprecedented session.[39] He briefed the War Cabinet that, since his previous visit in January, the production of munitions had greatly improved, particularly in the area of shipbuilding. Hopkins also explained that the political climate in America had perceptibly changed in the five months between his missions. He expressed optimism that the American people largely supported the president's recent decision to send troops to Iceland. "While it would not be true to say that the American people as a whole were anxious to enter the war," he told the cabinet, "if the President decided that the time had come to make war on Germany, the vast majority of the population, of all parties, would endorse his action and accord him their full support."[40]

While Hopkins accompanied the prime minister and his entourage during the subsequent sea journey aboard the HMS *King George* en route to the Atlantic Conference, Churchill peppered him with questions about the upcoming meeting. "What sort of man was Roosevelt?" the prime minister asked. What were the president's views on various subjects? Churchill expressed a genuine curiosity about the New Deal. "A New Deal was coming to the entire world," Churchill observed, still seeking to impress Hopkins with his liberal-mindedness. "What had happened in America, to Americans—that might guide the peoples of the world when Hitler had been crushed." Hopkins was discouraged that no one on board played poker. Instead, Churchill insisted that a reluctant Hopkins play backgammon every night, which the American dutifully, if unenthusiastically, endured. He observed that Churchill chatted so incessantly during the matches, and drove himself to distraction with his own rhetoric, that his game suffered greatly. Early mornings, when Hopkins finally dragged himself off to his cabin for a bit of sleep, Churchill would grumble that he was being "abandoned."[41]

Hopkins briefed Churchill and his entourage on how best to engage their American counterparts. He emphasized the magnitude of the gathering and recognized that it involved little, if any, sentimentality. "Neither Churchill nor Roosevelt had taken this dangerous voyage," he wrote, "taken these chances with German U-boats, merely to exchange felicitations, to reassure each other that their two hearts beat as one."

Through his binoculars, Hopkins spotted the president on the deck of the USS *Augusta*, positioned between Marshall, Chief of Naval Operations

Harold Stark, and Undersecretary of State Sumner Welles. Aware of how little rest Hopkins had obtained while entertaining Churchill, a sympathetic Roosevelt greeted him with a knowing look: "How are you Harry? Are you alright? You look a little tired." Hopkins laughed off the president's query and plunged into preparing the Americans for their meetings with the prime minister and his entourage.[42]

Hopkins continued to serve as the liaison between Roosevelt and Churchill throughout the conference. He not only handled much of the substance of the Anglo-American discussions that resulted in the Atlantic Charter but also the symbolic dimensions. For example, he helped engineer the legendary images of Roosevelt and Churchill singing hymns on the final Sunday morning.[43]

Historians and the public have come to see the Churchill-Roosevelt relationship as inevitable, but meetings between great personages do not always go so smoothly. Frances Perkins became convinced that Harry was responsible for the fortuitously "graceful rapprochement" between Churchill and Roosevelt. She observed that this dynamic carried enormous consequences for the war because, owing to Hopkins's missions to London and that first meeting between the prime minister and the president, Roosevelt gained greater confidence in the British ability to remain in the war. "I think probably Harry had caught onto the fact that Churchill was a very unconventional person, that he does very unconventional things," Perkins observed. "I think that Harry undoubtedly contributed a great deal of grace to this situation, both to Churchill and to Roosevelt. . . . Churchill is capable of letting himself go, being very gauche, very blunt, can make people dislike him." Hopkins achieved "a kind of conditioning of Roosevelt's attitude toward Churchill and toward the British . . . He did it so Roosevelt wouldn't take umbrage at some of the more awkward things that Churchill might do or say."[44]

Serving as FDR's special envoy to the prime minister entailed more than merely making several wartime missions to London. Churchill saw Hopkins as "the main prop and animator of Roosevelt himself."[45] That may have been because Roosevelt rarely possessed the stamina to constantly engage the prime minister himself. Churchill no doubt charmed Roosevelt at the Atlantic Conference, but the president grew fatigued by the prime minister's antics after he lodged at the White House for several weeks in December 1941 and January 1942. The prime minister's eccentricities and irregular hours took their toll on the president. Roosevelt increasingly delegated to Hopkins the challenge of managing the unpredictable Churchill, particularly on those matters that the president sought to avoid. Whenever it came to the prime minister, Roosevelt largely left matters to Hopkins.[46]

Having spent a total of nearly two months with Churchill in 1941, Hopkins understood that the prime minister could be temperamental, his soaring high spirits sometimes followed by black moods. Churchill suffered frequent bouts of melancholy and occasional despair, perhaps triggered by his prodigious consumption of alcohol. Hopkins thought the toxic cocktail of medications and alcohol Churchill was consuming in impressive amounts might explain his erratic behavior. Hopkins learned from the naval hospital that Churchill was consuming a variety of medications, including regular doses of hypnotics, pain killers, urinary antiseptics, fever reducers, treatments for urinary tract infections, antacids, and laxatives, all washed down with liberal amounts of brandy, whiskey, champagne, and red wine.[47]

In the weeks after the Atlantic Conference, Churchill began the practice of unburdening himself to Hopkins, who always sought to assure the anxious prime minister that his many fears and doubts were groundless.[48] He promised Churchill a sufficient supply of Lend-Lease to Great Britain, even if he had to wage war against the American secretaries of war and navy to make the diversions. He promised Churchill that once American production began to truly launch there would be an enormous amount of war matériel for everyone.[49] He gave the prime minister his word that every effort was being made to meet his requests, and he constantly reassured him that he appreciated the burdens under which he labored. "At times I get terribly discouraged about getting the matériel fast enough," Hopkins sympathetically cabled the prime minister in September 1941, "but then I think of your own overwhelming problems and I am tempted to try again."[50]

He understood that Churchill occasionally needed stroking. Writing to the prime minister during a particularly difficult period in the war, Hopkins added a touch of Churchillian purple prose: "What a gallant role you play in the greatest drama in the world's history no one knows better than I."[51]

Hopkins ran interference on any matters that might upset Churchill. For example, he took charge of the delicate Anglo-American collaboration over atomic research, known by the code name "Tube Alloys." Churchill, frustrated about the lack of genuine collaboration on the matter, looked for a sympathetic ear and directed his communications on the development and sharing of the atomic bomb to Hopkins rather than the president. Hopkins sought to appease the prime minister's concerns despite the reality that, as the development of the weapon advanced, the War Department became increasingly reluctant to share information about it with the British.[52]

Hopkins had plenty of experience with Churchill's eccentricities, yet an undeniable closeness developed between them.[53] For the sake of Alliance harmony, Hopkins shrewdly sought to look beyond the idiosyncrasies. The prime minister's old-fashioned imperialism and passions for unconventional military operations exasperated some American officials such as General Marshall and Admiral King, but Hopkins took a more practical approach. He recognized that Churchill, like Stalin, remained an important ally in the war against fascism. Germany had to be dealt with first, and problems related to empire and spheres of influence could be addressed later. "There are some of my countrymen who would destroy me by the assertion that I am your friend," Hopkins once wrote to the prime minister. "All I can say is that I am so proud that it is so."[54]

Hopkins's enormous capacity for punishment made him the ideal liaison to Churchill. The prime minister's self-absorption often knew no bounds. At wartime conferences he would launch into monologues, disrupting the agenda, and talking over and through even the most adept interpreters. Hopkins always stayed up late when he was with Churchill, listening to his stories, often in awe of his stamina.[55] "Do get some sleep," a genuinely concerned Roosevelt once cabled Hopkins during his stay with Churchill.[56]

Hopkins noted that Churchill's habit of indulging in numerous afternoon naps allowed him to stay up late, often well into the early hours of the morning. Those around the prime minister who did not have opportunities for afternoon siestas struggled to keep up. Hopkins marveled at Churchill's capacity for rejuvenation. The prime minister would go into the next room and a moment later he would be sound asleep. He would nap for an hour and awaken clear and ready as if he had had a full night's sleep. "Well up in his sixties he sets a killing pace," Hopkins observed in amazement, adding that Churchill, "an old man in the terms of today's world," was often "fresh, dynamic, clear-minded, certain in every move and word."[57]

Averell Harriman recalled that Hopkins could be completely frank with the British, even if Churchill did not like the result.[58] Churchill observed that Hopkins "had a gift of sardonic humor. I always enjoyed his company, especially when things went ill. He could also be very disagreeable and say hard and sour things."[59] Yet Hopkins was one of the few Americans who had genuine influence with Churchill. "Harry very quickly got onto jokey terms with Churchill," Frances Perkins observed, "which was a good way to handle him, and would say pretty sharp things to him, but in a way that struck Churchill as funny and would make him laugh. He would cap the joke with something else and get the best of Harry."[60]

"Churchill and the other Englishmen who enjoyed the President's company could never say they knew Roosevelt really well," recalled Churchill's intimate, Brendan Bracken. "At all the great war meetings work prevented much intimacy and when FDR was at Hyde Park he was as much surrounded by telegrams and official papers as he was in his office in Washington. But Harry lived with us and we got to know him almost as well as some of his closest American friends."[61]

After the war, Eisenhower paid high tribute to Hopkins's role as the catalyst of the Roosevelt-Churchill relationship. He characterized Hopkins's extraordinary relationship with both the president and the prime minister as "a Godsend" to military officials such as himself and General Marshall. Ike knew he could turn to the influential Hopkins to make headway with both leaders.[62]

Admiral King emphasized Hopkins's role in compelling those "two great but discursive gentlemen," Roosevelt and Churchill, to stick to the root of the matter and not drift offtrack. King remembered Hopkins forever reining in Churchill from his long-winded anecdotes about the battle of Blenheim, or Roosevelt from Delano family lore about the Clipper Ship Era, and getting both leaders to focus on the issues before them.[63]

"Harry Hopkins always went to the root of the matter," Churchill recalled after the war, adding, with a thorough lack of self-awareness: "I have been present at several great conferences, where twenty or more of the most important executive personages were gathered together. When the discussion flagged and all seemed baffled, it was on these occasions he would rap out the deadly question, 'Surely, Mr. President, here is the point we have got to settle. Are we going to face it or not?'"[64]

Illustrative of Hopkins's methods, when he arrived in Britain in July 1942 along with General Marshall and Admiral King to make the case for a cross-channel invasion, the three officials turned down an invitation to go directly to Churchill's country residence, Chequers, to spend the night with the prime minister. They were anxious to see Eisenhower, but Hopkins told Marshall and King he was having his head chewed off by the prime minister via telephone. Churchill complained that their bypassing of Chequers was a personal affront and a "flagrant breach of protocol and etiquette, good manners, and good taste." Marshall and King found this highly amusing and were delighted to let Harry face the prime minister's wrath. The American Chiefs cheerfully bade him goodbye and good luck and said, "We will see you tomorrow, Harry—we hope." Prior to the scheduled meeting on Monday, Churchill held an extraordinary session for the sole purpose of upbraiding the three Americans over his hurt feelings.[65]

Churchill frequently leaned on him for insights into what the president was thinking, and Hopkins carried out enormous favors on behalf of Churchill and Great Britain.[66] The prime minister and other senior British officials acknowledged that Great Britain required massive amounts of assistance from the United States to carry on and, without Hopkins, they might never have obtained it.[67] In one remarkable act of generosity, Hopkins came up with the novel idea of allowing Great Britain to rhetorically take a small measure of credit for supplies going to Russia from American Lend-Lease matériels. This was done for the sole purpose of lending Churchill a degree of stature with the Russians that might otherwise have been diminished had the Kremlin known of Britain's actual reluctance about sharing Lend-Lease with Russia or China. Credit went to the British for munitions because Hopkins thought it important that the Russians continue to see Great Britain as relevant to the war effort.[68]

Roosevelt often had his fill of Churchill's antics and assigned Hopkins to manage him. Churchill usually amused Hopkins more than he annoyed him, however. At the January 1943 Roosevelt-Churchill meeting in Casablanca, for example, Roosevelt, who reacted with annoyance when Churchill arrived with an enormous entourage after pledging not to do so, pushed Hopkins forward to handle Churchill. Hopkins had to calm the prime minister when the latter discovered that, as a gesture to the sultan of Morocco, there would be no alcohol served at an official dinner. Churchill noted: "Dinner. At the White House [Casablanca]. (Dry, alas!); with the Sultan. After dinner, recovery from the effects of the above."[69]

Hopkins faced further management challenges. For example, the following morning the president dispatched him to see Churchill in his villa. Hopkins noted: "I found Churchill in bed in his customary pink robe, and having, of all things, a bottle of wine for breakfast. I asked him what he meant by that and he told me that he had a profound distaste on the one hand for skimmed milk, and no deep-rooted prejudice about wine, and that he had reconciled the conflict in favor of the latter. He commended it to me and said he had lived to be 68 years old and was in the best of health, and had found that the advice of doctors, throughout his life, was usually wrong. At any rate, he had no intention of giving up alcoholic drink, mild or strong, now or later."[70]

He assumed that Churchill was storing up for further "dry" events. At the dinner with the sultan, Hopkins observed: "a good time was had by all, except the Prime Minister" whom he found "glum" and "real bored" because of the prohibition on alcohol consumption. He was amused by a stunt Churchill pulled to enliven the dinner, when an officious-looking British Marine marched into the dinner and dramatically handed the prime minister an "important dispatch." Hopkins had "a feeling Churchill cooked that up beforehand, because I saw the dispatch later and it certainly wasn't one that required the Prime Minister's attention at the dinner."

He also observed that Churchill seemed relieved when a press conference was cancelled. "It is perfectly clear that he has no confidence in his own ability to meet newspapermen, which is due to the fact that he never does see the newspapermen in England. . . . Churchill asked his man Sawyer for his false teeth and said he wished the pictures were going to be taken later in the day, because he didn't look his best at twelve o'clock, but that he liked the idea of pictures because he loved publicity. He told me he could put on a very warlike look whenever he wanted to."

And yet Hopkins was never Churchill's pliant tool. While maintaining warm relations with the British, he believed the United States should resist subordinating its own strategic objectives to Churchill's. Hopkins grasped the critical distinctions between Churchill's strategic goals and those of the British military chiefs, as Marshall and King confirmed for him. He became convinced that the British Chiefs, like the American Chiefs, remained interested in the military objective of defeating the Axis as soon as possible while Churchill had more narrowly eccentric objectives involving preserving Britain's tottering empire and shoring up its faltering status as a world power.[71]

Marshall frequently heard accusations that the British, particularly Churchill, unduly influenced Hopkins. The general believed, however, that anybody who had actually been present at the wartime meetings with Churchill understood the baselessness of this accusation. To the contrary, Marshall said that he often thought Hopkins was going too far in pushing the British to do things they had no desire to do. When Hopkins felt Churchill was wrong, he opposed him as resolutely as he supported the prime minister when he thought his objectives coincided with American interests.[72]

Hopkins would only take the Anglo-American alliance so far, and probably not nearly as far as Churchill desired. As the war continued, Churchill occasionally felt snubbed by him. The prime minister complained bitterly when Hopkins refused to stop in London for meetings. But Hopkins was operating from a different set of objectives. Earlier in the war, he understood the importance of demonstrating intimate ties to Churchill. Great Britain's continuance in the war was absolutely essential to America's hopes to eventually defeat the Axis powers. As the war continued, Churchill's desire to demonstrate a complete commonality of interests between himself and Roosevelt ran counter to Hopkins's efforts to prevent the United States from becoming too closely wedded to British objectives, particularly in the imperial sphere. Hopkins appreciated that the American people did not want an alliance with Great Britain to the exclusion of Russia and China. And despite his obvious affection for Churchill, Hopkins, like the president, persisted in seeing the United States as an honest broker between Churchill and Stalin rather than part of an Anglo-American partnership against the Soviets.[73]

# CHAPTER FOUR

~

# Mission to Moscow, 1941

> This was no time to hold back because Russia's ways were not ours. If by helping Russia with arms Hitler could be broken, the President wanted to give that help. He cherished no other dream. Russia wanted nothing but arms from us. We wanted nothing but victory from Russia.
>
> —*Harry Hopkins*[1]

As the German Wehrmacht moved toward Moscow in late July 1941, foreign military experts in the city predicted it would fall in a matter of weeks. These assessments claimed the Red Army had few supplies, suffered from low morale, was poorly trained, and that the beleaguered Russian people would never withstand the invincibility of Hitler's armies. Many officials in Washington gave the Red Army only a few weeks against the irresistible surge of the German war machine.

Shuttling through the streets on his way to the Kremlin in late July 1941, Harry Hopkins observed that, despite all of the activity, a strange calm hung over Moscow. He had arrived during some of the darkest days in the history of Russia; only weeks after Hitler had launched his Barbarossa offensive. The entire population of the city seemed to be methodically preparing for the inevitable, anticipating the coming onslaught as even old men, women, and children focused on the grim task of preparing for the siege of the city.

Hopkins was encouraged by the endless procession of trucks moving through the city and the thousands of soldiers manning antiaircraft guns. Soviet fighter planes from the airfields east of the metropolis flew low over buildings on their way to engage the Luftwaffe.[2] Hopkins discovered that only the foreigners believed that Moscow would collapse. He was instead impressed by the grim determination of the Muscovites as they anticipated the murderous ferocity of Nazi Germany. What choice did they have but to resist?[3]

A month earlier, when news of Hitler's attack reached Hopkins on the morning of June 22, 1941, he immediately realized that the German invasion of Russia had the potential to transform the war. He believed that the USSR possessed innate advantages in its struggle with Nazi Germany. The USSR's manpower reserves were enormous, and nature had bestowed upon Russia huge advantages in a land war against Germany. He believed that everything possible should be done to make certain the Russians held a permanent front even though they had been swept from the battlefield in many of the early engagements.

He appreciated that the USSR's vast resources and industrial capacity had to be prevented from falling into Hitler's hands. He never deviated from his conviction that everything possible should be done to make certain that the Red Army kept fighting.[4] He pragmatically recognized that if the Germans ultimately triumphed in Russia, it would free up Hitler's war machine for a new offensive against Great Britain, in the Atlantic, the Middle East, or elsewhere. If Hitler subdued the Soviet Union, or if the Russians left the war, Hopkins feared the war might drag on for many more years, perhaps with millions of American casualties.[5]

Several months prior to his mission to Moscow, Hopkins began emerging as a player in the nascent origins of an American alliance with Russia. The German invasion of the USSR came as no surprise to him. Beginning in 1940, he began seeking insights into the USSR by sounding out officials with knowledge of Russia.[6] In the months prior to the German attack, he began reading communications from Moscow, particularly those of the military attaches. He calculated that a German attack was likely when he read that the wives of senior German and Italian officials had been ordered to leave Moscow.[7]

Five weeks later, while in Great Britain arranging the Atlantic Conference, Hopkins conceived the idea to go to a besieged Moscow and meet with Stalin. "I am wondering whether you would think it important and useful for me to go to Moscow?" he cabled Roosevelt on July 23. He added that the air routes into Moscow remained open.[8] Hopkins believed it vitally important that the president obtain an unbiased assessment of Russia's likelihood of survival.[9]

"Now Russia had been invaded and this was something to ponder," Hopkins recalled. Vital decisions had to be made immediately, and Washington needed to make clear to Moscow that it was serious about aiding it against Hitler. If Stalin could in any way be influenced at this critical time, Hopkins believed it worth doing by a direct communication from the president through a personal envoy. He and Roosevelt agreed that it was important that someone directly representing the president see Stalin.[10]

"And clearly too," Hopkins later reflected, it was "better all around that that someone have the significance of a special agent, commissioned solely to consult with the government of the USSR in the particular crisis of the moment. Moreover, it was important that he be an American closely identified with the President." In Britain, the invasion of Russia might have posed a serious political problem if not for Churchill's forceful declaration of support on June 22. The prime minister regaled Hopkins with the story of his decision to offer unconditional support for the USSR. Hopkins recalled: "There was only one man to defeat, one philosophy of government to destroy. Russia was now fighting that man and that philosophy. England was already doing so. Any enemy of Hitler was to be England's ally."[11]

Hopkins set out to reassure Stalin that American assistance would be forthcoming and that the United States would assist in turning back the German offensive. He sought to strengthen Stalin's faith that the United States shared the goal of defeating Hitler but also to determine if Stalin would remain in the war against Hitler to the very end and not opt for a separate peace as the Bolsheviks had done in 1918. "I think the stakes are so great that it should be done," Hopkins cabled the president. "Stalin would then know in an unmistakable way that we mean business on a long-term supply job."[12]

Roosevelt wanted Hopkins to go to the Kremlin, talk to Stalin, and report back to him, face to face. "Welles and I highly approve Moscow trip and assume you would go in a few days," the president cabled. "Possibly you could get back to North America by August eighth. I will send you tonight a message for Stalin."[13] Hopkins and Churchill stayed up late discussing this very subject at Chequers when a reply cable came from the president. "The first message was short enough," Hopkins recalled, "go to Moscow. See Stalin."[14]

"See Stalin?" he reflected afterward. "Of course one would have to see Stalin if one wanted to know what Russia was going to do, what she had to do it with, how she proposed to go about it. Stalin is Russia. In this or any other crisis, his would be the only word of authority, his ruling would be the only law."

In sending Hopkins, Roosevelt sought to demonstrate to Stalin the importance he placed on the mission. Hopkins would get to the root of the matter with Stalin in a way no other emissary could. Moreover, a Hopkins mission would bypass the State Department with its anti-Soviet officials whom Hopkins deemed too consumed with their ideological hostility to the USSR to focus on the larger goal of defeating Hitler.[15]

Exhausted after his days and nights with Churchill, Hopkins suddenly felt reinvigorated by the president's cable. Early the next morning he received a second confidential cable from Washington elaborating in greater detail what the president expected of him. FDR explained that he wanted to know "the strength, the size, the equipment, the morale, the will of the Russian air corps, army, navy," Hopkins recalled. "He wanted to know whether Russia was prepared to halt the hitherto victorious march of Germany up and down the mainland. He wanted to be sure—he hoped to be sure, that Stalin could hold Hitler off while America and Britain were reaching their peak of defensive and offensive arming."[16]

Roosevelt began his message to Stalin: "At my request, Mr. Hopkins is going to Moscow to discuss with you personally, and with each other officials as you may designate, a question of vital importance—how to make available most expeditiously and effectively the assistance that the United States of America is able to render your country in the magnificent resistance which it is making against the treacherous aggression of Hitlerite Germany."[17]

Hopkins told Churchill that they had to figure out how to get him expeditiously to Moscow. Hopkins had already arranged the president and prime minister's upcoming meeting in the Atlantic in early August. The date of that meeting was near enough that Hopkins had no time to waste getting to Moscow and back to London. "Mr. Harry Hopkins has been with me these days," Churchill cabled Stalin on July 28. "Last week he asked the president to let him go to Moscow. I must tell you that there is a flame in this man for democracy and to beat Hitler. He is the nearest personal representative of the president. A little while ago when I asked him for a quarter of a million rifles they came at once. The president has now sent him full instructions and he leaves my house tonight to go to you. You will be advised of his arrival through the proper channels. You can trust him absolutely. He is your friend and our friend. He will help you to plan for the future victory and for the long term supply of Russia."[18]

"No one except Churchill discussed my mission with me," Hopkins later recollected. "Actually no one but Churchill, Ambassador Winant and perhaps one or two others had the remotest idea what I was about to do."[19] The Russian ambassador in London, Ivan Maisky, took the extraordinary risk of writing a visa in his own hand, and the American ambassador rushed to London's Euston station and handed the passport to Hopkins through the window of the departing train.[20]

A visibly exhausted Hopkins arriving in Moscow, July 1941. Upon initially landing in Archangel, he had been promptly introduced to Russian vodka. "Vodka has authority," he observed. "It is nothing for the amateur to trifle with. Drink it as an American or an Englishman takes whiskey neat and it will tear you apart. The thing to do is to spread a chunk of bread (and good bread it was) with caviar and while you're swallowing that, bolt your vodka. Don't play with the stuff. Not while you're drinking it—something that will set as a shock absorber for it."[23]

"I wasn't tired any more," Hopkins recalled. "I had never been to Russia. I don't remember that I thought much about what I was going to do or hear or see when I got there. If I had any immediate concern it was to get to Moscow as fast as possible and let the gods who had been so good to me thus far take care of the rest. After all I was going to see a man whose word was the law of a hundred and seventy million, who to millions inside and outside of Russia was an almost legendary figure. And heaven knows what would come of it—particularly if I fumbled. . . . I had executed a number of assignments for the President. None had impressed me more."[21] He made a circuitous and harrowing journey to Moscow—a twenty-one hour flight just to Archangel.[22]

As the most influential administration figure charged with dealing with Soviet officials, Hopkins's views of the USSR were relevant to the policy that was ultimately pursued. He did not share the visceral and ideological hatred of the Soviet Union of many of his colleagues. As suggested by evidence from his papers, he believed communism had some admirable objectives in theory but had failed almost entirely in its execution. On the other hand, he believed that fascism began with the wrong objectives, and thus its execution was entirely beside the point.[24]

To Hopkins, many of the American Soviet specialists were so ideologically fixated on the evils of the Soviet regime that they were unable to see the bigger picture of the Red Army's centrality to destroying nazism. Hopkins's views and actions derived from an entirely different reality. "What I thought of the government of the USSR, what I thought of Stalin, what I had heard from his friends, his critics, from diplomats and newspapermen—all these things had to be set aside."[25]

To obtain a clearer picture of events, Hopkins concluded, such American officials needed to be bypassed. By July 1941, even after Hitler's attack on the USSR, official American assessments remained plagued by misperceptions and rigid ideas about the Soviet Union's prospects for survival. At the time of the German invasion of Russia, Colonel Ivan Yeaton, the military attaché in Moscow, drew heavily upon his own anti-Soviet feelings and also on Nazi propaganda broadcasts. He underestimated the capacity of the Red Army and the Russian people to withstand the German onslaught, and his reports to the War Department grew increasingly pessimistic.[26]

Hopkins was dubious of the motives of the State Department's Russia specialists and the War Department's military attachés. He was often dismayed by the way officials personalized their reporting, contributing to his suspicion that they allowed personal piques to cloud their assessments.[27] Hopkins had been reading Yeaton's reports from Moscow, and what he read troubled him. Only a week after the Germans launched operation Barbarossa, the panicked attaché warned Washington that the Wehrmacht would reach Moscow within five days and provoke a complete collapse of the Stalinist regime.[28]

Yeaton's predictions of an imminent Germany victory influenced the highest officials in Washington and gave his pessimistic telegrams a cumulative and exaggerated effect. Hopkins became increasingly concerned with Yeaton's pessimism, as he had under consideration substantial Lend-Lease shipments to Russia. The mission to Moscow would allow him to see for himself whether the situation was as disastrous as Yeaton depicted and whether Lend-Lease material shipped to Russia would likely fall into the hands of the Germans.[29]

Hopkins challenged Yeaton's reporting. Blitzkrieg had overwhelmed Poland, Norway, France, the Low Countries, Yugoslavia, and Greece, but Russian geography presented an entirely different challenge for Hitler. Hopkins expressed his conviction that there was a strong possibility that Moscow would not fall and that the Red Army would continue fighting. Prior to returning to London, he engaged in a heated argument with the attaché. At Hopkins's request, Colonel Philip R. Faymonville, who had been military attaché at the Moscow embassy in the 1930s, returned to Moscow as his Lend-Lease representative.[30] Faymonville kept Hopkins briefed on the situation in Moscow and reinforced the assessment that Moscow in all likelihood would not fall. Indeed, the Red Army's resistance in the autumn of 1941 damaged the myth of Wehrmacht invincibility.[31]

"Facts were what the President had asked for," Hopkins later recalled of his first mission to Stalin. "This was no time to hold back because Russia's ways were not ours. If by helping Russia with arms Hitler could be broken, the President wanted to give that help. He cherished no other dream. Russia wanted nothing but arms from us. We wanted nothing but victory from Russia."[32]

Upon arriving in Moscow, U.S. ambassador Laurence Steinhardt briefed Hopkins about the obstacles to any effort to assist the USSR, such as the Kremlin's excessive secrecy and unwillingness to grant foreigners freedom of movement. Hopkins learned that Stalin disdained ambassadors and envoys and only valued negotiations with the highest-ranking officials.[33] During his initial Kremlin meetings, he observed that no one, not even Foreign Minister V. M. Molotov or senior Red Army generals, felt free to share information with foreigners or make substantive decisions. He thus concluded that high-level personal meetings, either between himself and Stalin or, eventually, the president and Stalin, would be necessary.[34]

Hopkins maintained that he could never be entirely candid about his discussions in the Kremlin. "All I can do is tell you that I went to Moscow to ask some questions of Stalin," he later wrote, "to observe the Soviet Union, so to speak, under fierce attack, and to report back to the President when he met with Winston Churchill in the Atlantic."[35] The substance of his discussions with Stalin can be pieced together, however, by a close reading of the unexpurgated versions of his Moscow communiqués to the president and his own notes of conversations with Stalin, his early drafts of a magazine article he was preparing on the meetings, and various accounts of U.S. officials closely involved with the meeting.[36]

Hopkins later penned a colorful, if melodramatic, impression of the Soviet warlord: "Not once did he repeat himself. . . . He welcomed me with a few, swift Russian words. . . . It was like talking to a perfectly coordinated machine. . . . Joseph Stalin knew what he wanted, knew what Russia wanted, and he assumed that you knew. We talked for almost four hours. The questions he asked were clear, concise, direct. Tired as I was I found myself replying as tersely."[37]

Hopkins acknowledged that no one would describe Stalin as possessing a "pleasant" personality. He observed that his true nature remained difficult to fully gauge, and he detected an undertone of menace in Stalin's voice and opinions. He recollected the image of the Soviet leader, "an austere, rugged, determined figure in boots that shone like mirrors, stout baggy trousers and snug fitting blouse. He wore no ornament, military or civilian. He's built close to the ground. . . . He's about five feet six, about a hundred and ninety pounds. His hands are huge, as hard as his mind. His voice is harsh but ever under control. What he says is all the accent and inflection his words need."[38]

He told Stalin that his stay in Moscow must be brief and that he wished to accomplish as much as possible during his short visit.[39] Stalin replied: "You are our guest; you have but to command." Hopkins explained that Roosevelt considered Hitler "the enemy of mankind and that he therefore wished to aid the Soviet Union in its fight against Germany." He made clear that his mission was not a diplomatic one. He proposed no formal alliance of any kind and, in fact, not a diplomatic phrase or word passed between them. He instead emphasized Roosevelt's determination to extend all possible aid to the USSR in the shortest possible time. He informed Stalin that the American government, and the British government (Churchill having authorized him to say this) were eager to do everything they could to dispatch matériel to Russia. He emphasized that plans should be made for a long war.[40]

Hopkins inquired about the USSR's immediate versus long-term needs. "Give us anti-aircraft guns and aluminum," Stalin declared, "and we can fight for three or four years."[41] Hopkins asked for Stalin's candid analysis of the struggle between Germany and Russia. Hopkins observed that the Soviet leader did not rely upon his advisers and possessed detailed information about his war machine. "The man told me his story," Hopkins later recalled. "It was a frank, forthright story taken from his personal knowledge and from his extraordinary memory and written records." Hopkins and Stalin both appreciated that they spoke candidly to each other. He observed of Stalin: "Except when he spoke of Hitler or when the name of Hitler was mentioned, he was at ease, relaxed."

"When he spoke of Hitler his manner was more eloquent than his words. It was only when he mentioned Hitler that he discarded his suave assurance. Then his body grew tense. He didn't raise his voice; rather it went as cold as his eyes and the mellow harshness of it became grating. Of Hitler he spoke slowly, not measuring his words nor considering his phrasing but as if he wanted the interpreter they had assigned to me to convey to me every syllable in its implication and direct meaning. For Hitler he had more than the anger he would necessarily have for a man who had double-crossed him;

it was a personal hatred that I have seldom heard expressed by anyone in authority. I don't want to over-dramatize the scene; I'm not at all sure that I can. But the cold, implacable hatred he has for the German Fuehrer was clearly evident. Stalin's huge hands half clenched. I think that Joseph Stalin would have liked nothing better at that moment than to have had Hitler sitting where I sat. Germany would have needed a new Chancellor." Hopkins sensed in Stalin "a hatred of Hitler that nothing but the death of the German Chancellor could lessen."

Hopkins was tremendously relieved by the grim certitude that Stalin exuded about the USSR's chances of survival. "He seems to have no doubts. He assures you that Russia will stand against the onslaughts of the German army. He takes it for granted that you have no doubts either."[42] Stalin predicted that he could mobilize at least 350 divisions in time for an anticipated spring offensive in May 1942. Hopkins found it encouraging that the Kremlin was already making plans for a 1942 counteroffensive rather than planning to abandon Moscow.

Stalin confirmed the USSR's innate advantages in its struggle with Germany and asserted that Hitler had underestimated Russia's underlying strengths. The recent Wehrmacht penetration so deep into western Russia, over extended lines of communication, would prove catastrophic for the Germans. The Red Army possessed much more familiarity with the terrain. Hitler had failed to appreciate Soviet geographical depth and industrial potential. The laws of geography and manpower would ultimately prevail.[43]

This portion of their discussion had an enormous influence on Hopkins's views of the role the USSR would play in the war. He not only highlighted Russia's geographical advantages in his reports but also he emphasized these factors in conversations with American and British officials. The USSR's "manpower reserves are huge," he observed. "The protection that nature has given Moscow is all but impenetrable from land and water."[44]

Stalin observed that Germany's might was so great that even though Russia might defend itself against the German offensive, it would prove difficult for Britain and Russia to crush the Nazi war machine without the United States formally joining in the military struggle. He predicted that America and Russia would eventually come to grips with Hitler on some battlefield, and he bluntly said that an immediate U.S. declaration of war against Hitler would guarantee the defeat of Germany. He concluded their initial meetings by telling Hopkins that he wanted him to convey to the president that Hitler's gravest weakness was the vast millions of oppressed who hated nazism.[45]

"We Russians shall win this war," Stalin said, leaning toward Hopkins, his hands flat upon his table in front of him. "The battle front will remain west of Moscow. Russia will not fail. Russia is huge. She is inexorable. Russia is fighting—for Russia. She will not again be enslaved. Once we trusted this man . . ." Stalin concluded, not finishing his sentence. "Hitler again," Hopkins observed. "I hope never to be hated as Stalin hates Hitler."[46]

He had conducted two lengthy audiences with Stalin and was given a glimpse of Russia's huge military arsenal. He developed an appreciation of Soviet armor, particularly tanks. After his four-hour meeting with Stalin on July 31, Hopkins met briefly with Molotov and later with Red Army officials to discuss technical aspects of Lend-Lease.[47]

Kremlin watchers concluded that the reception accorded Hopkins revealed the tremendous importance that had been attached to his visit. To almost everyone's astonishment, Stalin had promptly received Hopkins and granted him extended, multihour interviews and discussed sensitive war matters with an unprecedented frankness. Illustrative of the special treatment afforded Hopkins, during one of the Luftwaffe air raids, he reacted with astonishment that the shelter provided for him was stocked with "basic necessities" such as fine Russian champagne, caviar, gourmet chocolates, cigarettes—this in a country often on the verge of starvation and economic collapse. Hopkins laughed heartily when the morose Ambassador Steinhardt complained to him that no such shelter, nor such provisions, had been placed at *his* disposal.[48]

Hopkins told the press that his meetings with the Kremlin had convinced him that Hitler would not prevail. He never wavered from the public declaration he made in Moscow that "anybody who fights Hitler, anywhere, is on the right side."[49] He departed Moscow on August 1 bullish on the prospects for Russia's survival and concluded that Russia, like Great Britain, would hold out, an assessment doubted by virtually all U.S. military officials. He concluded that the prospects of Moscow's survival "are better than some pessimists would have us believe."[50]

Ever the gambler, he reassured Roosevelt that the Russians were, if not a sure thing, at the very least a good bet. "I have had two long and satisfactory talks with Stalin," he cabled the president on August 1, "and will communicate personally to you the messages he is sending. I would like to tell you now, however, that I feel ever so confident about this front. The morale of the population is exceptionally good. There is unbounded determination to win."[51]

Hopkins was glad he made the effort to go to Moscow. He felt he had obtained what he needed from his mission, but he was never entirely sure. Writing to Brendan Bracken, Hopkins observed: "I would have liked so much to tell you about my visit to Uncle Joe which I think went off fairly well, but only events can tell."[52]

He grew fascinated with Russia, asking State Department Russia specialist Charles Bohlen numerous questions about its history and culture, explaining that such knowledge might aid him in making better-informed decisions.[53] Yet he also recognized that maintaining good relations with the Kremlin would prove a challenge. Problems provoked by the alliance with Stalin plagued Hopkins throughout the war. While a vital ally in the war against Hitler, Stalin remained a murderous tyrant, his worldview warped by paranoia and a ruthless realpolitik.[54]

Hopkins shared with Roosevelt the hope that the Russians would furnish the land armies and that the Americans could focus their participation in the war to production, supplies, logistics, the air, and the navy.[55] Yet, Hopkins retained few illusions about the Soviet-American relationship. He anticipated that relations with the Russians always had the potential to "blow up at the last minute."[56]

Nor did he harbor illusions about the nature of the Stalinist regime. Yet he did not allow the loathsome nature of the regime to obscure the fact that the Red Army provided an enormous weapon to thwart Hitler's objectives. He noted the genuine unpleasantness of Stalin and his blunt cynicism about human behavior. "I would hardly call Uncle Joe a pleasant man," he wrote privately upon his return, "although he was interesting enough, and I think I got what I wanted, but you can never be sure about that."[57]

Whatever his personal feelings, they had to be set aside if he were to take maximum advantage of the opportunity presented by Hitler's invasion of Russia.[58] "Before my three days in Moscow ended, the difference between Democracy and Dictatorship were clearer to me than any words of philosopher, historian or journalist could make it. I'm making that observation and letting the subject rest."[59] He kept such misgivings mostly private. In public, he faced the challenge of widespread skepticism about aiding the USSR. He sought to focus publicly on the difference between the immediate dangers posed by nazism as opposed to the less threatening loathsomeness of the Stalinist dictatorship. Hopkins concluded that the Soviet system, while odious, in no way posed the kind of immediate threat to vital American interests as did Hitler.

For Stalin, Hopkins's mission represented a tangible sign that six weeks of stubborn Red Army resistance had inspired the Americans to support Russia. Hopkins remained enormously popular with Stalin and the Soviet leadership. The Russians made no secret of the gratitude they felt toward him as the first official to come to them from the West bearing the promise of aid and, most important, fulfilling that promise. "Hopkins was the first foreigner that came in to help," Averell Harriman later recalled, "and made a very deep impression on Stalin, incidentally—this frail sick man arriving . . . Stalin was at a pretty low point at that time."[60] This proved to be an important asset for Roosevelt, and later Truman, in their relations with Stalin. The credibility Hopkins had earned from his no-nonsense negotiations with the Russians in 1941 earned him a standing with the Kremlin that no other American possessed.[61]

When he returned from Moscow to London in early August he carried with him ninety pages of handwritten notes of his meetings with Stalin. Despite Churchill's persistence, he refused to share anything of substance about his meetings in the Kremlin. Hopkins maintained his determination to report to the president and shrewdly refused Churchill's transparent offer of a "stenographer" to help dictate the disorganized notes into a coherent manuscript. "I never lost sight of the fact," Hopkins recalled, "that I had but one chief—the President. All that I knew was for him alone."[62]

At the Atlantic Conference, Roosevelt and Churchill devoted a portion of their first luncheon speculating about the war in Russia. Both leaders turned to Hopkins and asked his assessment of Stalin's views of the prospects for Russian survival. Hopkins said that Stalin believed that Hitler would need to secure his enormous Russian front before contemplating his next moves against either Great Britain or the United States.[63]

Upon returning to Washington in mid-August, Hopkins predicted that the next several months of the German-Soviet war would be critical. If the Red Army could hold off the German offensive, it might prove to be the turning point of the entire war. He surmised that the USSR would recover from its initial setbacks and gradually increase in strength and manpower while Hitler's power could only gradually decline. With the United States remaining formally out of the war, Hopkins believed that getting supplies to Russia quickly was the most important contribution Washington could make.[64]

Harriman observed that Roosevelt agreed with Hopkins that supplying the Russians was entirely about keeping them in the war against Germany and that Washington should not be stingy "in answering the requests, if they asked for something we should try to give it to them—was in order to do two things: One, to help them in the war, Two: to create a friendly atmosphere and try to live down the years of ill will that had existed between us."[65]

Hopkins worried about the challenges the president would face in convincing the American people that Russia's struggle was also America's, and that Russia "was our ally in arms though not in our separate philosophies of government."[66] As he had done with Great Britain following his first mission there in January 1941, Hopkins now sought to make the Red Army's plight sympathetic to the American public. "There is still an amazing number of people here," he lamented to a sympathetic Churchill in September 1941, "who do not want to help Russia and who don't seem to be able to pound into their thick heads the strategic importance of that front."[67]

Hopkins shrewdly developed the idea of using Churchill as an example of the sort of pragmatism the United States might adopt toward Stalin and the USSR. He sought to pose the challenge as a question: If the prime minister were prepared to put everything aside to join with the Soviet Union to destroy Hitlerism, why not the United States? "With the courage that is Churchill's, obeying his mind as well as his heart, he pledged Britain to Russia's cause," Hopkins noted. "And he did it boldly, without consulting anybody." He took inspiration that the prime minister did not hesitate to consider any possible political consequences. "There was only one man to defeat, one philosophy of government to destroy. Russia was now fighting that man and that philosophy. England was already doing so. Any enemy of Hitler was to be England's ally." Hopkins respected Churchill's "undying determination" to destroy the Nazi menace, "a menace compared to which all other political and economic threats were puny."[68]

In the weeks and months after his return from Moscow, Hopkins sought to make the case for aiding Russia before the court of public opinion. He published a public version of his meeting with Stalin in an effort to reorient American views toward the Soviet Union and its leader. "Before I left Stalin's office many such questions were answered for me," Hopkins wrote for publication. "Put your prejudices aside. Ask yourself whom you want on the west shore of the fifty miles of sea that separates Asiatic Russia from Alaska. Whom do you want—Stalin or Hitler? Whom would you choose, the Axis powers or Russia?"[69]

Throughout the remainder of 1941, Hopkins sought to use Lend-Lease to exploit Hitler's blunder in invading the vast Soviet Union. He also contemplated the consequences of Barbarossa for the United States. But matters in the Pacific would soon take precedence. Shortly before Hopkins's departure for London and Moscow in July 1941, Undersecretary of State Sumner Welles had warned Hopkins in a prescient letter: "the German invasion of Russia may very possibly serve to cause Japan to take some further aggressive action"—one which might entangle the United States in a Far Eastern war.[70]

# CHAPTER FIVE

∾

# "Assistant President"

Your presence in the White House and with me in England has always
been a great reassurance and I pray for the continued improvement of
your health, and damn your indiscretions.[1]

—*General George Marshall to Harry Hopkins, December 1942*

On Saturday evening, December 6, 1941, President Roosevelt sat in his
leather chair in the oval study on the second floor of the White House
while Harry Hopkins paced about nervously. At 9:30 p.m. a navy lieutenant
entered the room carrying a locked pouch. The president looked over the
just-decoded papers—the first thirteen parts of the final Japanese reply to
Secretary of State Cordell Hull. Roosevelt read them and then waited for
Hopkins to read them. The president observed: "This means war."[2]

Hopkins replied: "It's too bad we can't strike first and prevent a surprise."
The president nodded—but said, "No, we can't do that. We are a democracy
of peaceful people. We have a good record. We must stand on it." Hopkins
speculated about where the likely point of attack might be directed. Neither
man mentioned Pearl Harbor; neither knew the time or place the war might
begin. Roosevelt then tried to contact Chief of Naval Operations, Admiral
Harold R. Stark, who was at the theater. The president decided not to disturb
him lest it cause "public alarm."

The following afternoon, on December 7, 1941, Hopkins lunched with
the president at his desk when the phone rang at 1:40 p.m. Navy Secretary

Frank Knox told the president that the navy had picked up an urgent message from Honolulu advising all stations that an air attack was underway and that it was "no drill."[3] A disbelieving Hopkins said there must be some mistake and that surely Japan would not attack Honolulu. The president thought the report was likely true and said it was just the sort of unexpected thing the Japanese would do—at the very time they were discussing peace in the Pacific. Roosevelt told him that if this action of Japan's were true it would take the matter entirely out of his own hands because the Japanese had now made the decision for war.

Admiral Stark called the president at 2:28 p.m. and confirmed the attack, stating that very severe damage had already been done to the fleet and that there were casualties. The president called a conference of Secretary of War Henry Stimson, Secretary of State Cordell Hull, Secretary of the Navy Frank Knox, Admiral Stark, and Army Chief of Staff General George C. Marshall at three o'clock. The conference met in a tense atmosphere. Hopkins reflected that "all of us believed that in the last analysis the enemy was Hitler and that he could never be defeated without force of arms; that sooner or later we were bound to be in the war and that Japan had given us an opportunity. Everybody, however, agreed on the seriousness of the war and that it would be a long, hard struggle. During the conference the news kept coming in, indicating more and more damage to the fleet."

Churchill called from London, and the president told him that they were all in the same boat now and that he was going to Congress the next day. Churchill informed him that the Malay Straits had also been attacked and that he, too, was going to the House of Commons in the morning and would ask for a declaration of war. Churchill cabled to Hopkins that night: "Thinking of you much at this historic moment."[4] The United States was now, officially, at war.

At the end of that day, shortly before turning in, Hopkins had a conversation in his Lincoln Study bedroom with CBS reporter Edward R. Murrow. He suggested to Murrow that, upon further consideration, the Japanese attack would prove to be a "Godsend" for the United States because by no other means could the country have entered the war without serious internal dissention. Just before getting into bed, he sat on the edge for a moment, looking frail and exhausted, barely filling out his loose-fitting pajamas. He spoke, more to himself than to Murrow: "Oh, God—if I only had the strength."[5]

From somewhere deep within him, Hopkins found the strength. Officially, Hopkins was the president's special assistant, a member of the War Production Board, chairman of the Munitions Assignments Board—the top

Anglo-American body that, with the combined Chiefs of Staff, allocated all Allied war equipment. "Unofficially," a *Time* magazine profile observed, "Harry Hopkins often serves as the president's eyes, ears, hands, feet, brains. His bony shoulders are piled high with the war's weightiest military secrets. . . . . By nature outspoken and gregarious, he frankly tells reporters why he avoids them: he knows too much and he loves to talk."[6] As he worked eighteen-hour days, one of his colleagues counseled: "Cut it out, Harry, you'll kill yourself." He fatalistically replied: "Do you know a better way to die?"[7] "All of us get older," he laconically wrote to Missy LeHand, "some of us falter, drink more or less and occasionally do a little work."[8]

The president had to fight a twentieth-century total war with a White House staff system based upon nineteenth-century notions of limited government. Hopkins transferred his skills as a New Deal administrator into assisting the Allied war effort. The talents compelling Roosevelt to place more and more power and responsibility with Hopkins during the New Deal prompted the president to lean increasingly on him during the war. Unlike secretaries Stimson and Knox, both of whom had enormous departments to manage, Hopkins was free from such institutional restraints. His supervision of Lend-Lease and his chairmanship of the important Munitions Assignments Board gave him power over the distribution of vital war materials.[9]

Hopkins believed that a handful of senior officials were indispensable to the success of the war effort. Although his own influence was extensive, he was usually inclined to follow the advice of the president's senior military advisers. Convinced that Hopkins had been primarily responsible for his appointment to Army Chief of Staff in 1939, General Marshall naturally grew impressed with his personnel acumen. He respected his skill in selecting talented subordinates during the New Deal and assumed this was but one of many talents that recommended Hopkins to the president during the war. Marshall paid high tribute to his physical and moral courage and fearlessness. Shared trials forged strong bonds with Marshall, with the general observing in December 1942: "Your presence in the White House and with me in England has always been a great reassurance and I pray for the continued improvement of your health, and damn your indiscretions."[10] Hopkins also shielded General Dwight D. Eisenhower during several wartime controversies. With Hopkins in his corner, Ike recollected, he never doubted that he was fully supported by his commander-in-chief and did not fear making mistakes.[11]

He frequently deferred to the venerable Secretary of War, Henry Stimson, and appreciated the important roles that Secretary of State Cordell Hull and Secretary of the Navy Frank Knox played in public perceptions of the administration as being above politics in wartime. He worked hard to maintain good relations with the president's Chief of Staff and Chairman of the Chiefs, Admiral William Leahy, forming a mostly harmonious alliance that all too easily could have been plagued by jealousy and rivalry.

Inside the war cabinet, Hopkins was often seen as the logistical maestro, but his strategic sense also evolved. A close reading of his papers, and the postwar recollections of senior military figures such as General Marshall, Admiral King, and General Eisenhower, reveals his evolving instinctive strategic sensibility and a set of consistent military objectives governing his actions throughout the war.[12] He became a quick study of strategic questions. From observation, senior military figures grew impressed with his rapid and pragmatic grasp of military matters and came to respect Hopkins's views, recognizing his remarkable aptitude for grasping the basic principles of grand strategy.[13]

Hopkins revealed his emerging strategic acumen in the days after Pearl Harbor, raising a series of penetrating questions the armed forces needed immediately addressed. How best could they get desperately needed planes and reinforcements to Hawaii? How could they best hold the Philippines? What about reinforcing China? Could they now get bombers to China and under whose command? What did they have in mind should the Philippines or Singapore fall? The president checked off these menu items, leaving question marks on those without immediate answers.[14]

Several fundamental objectives influenced Hopkins's strategic sense of the war. These included the necessity of expediting aid to Great Britain and maintaining the British Isles as the forward base for the eventual liberation of Europe. He also placed enormous importance on keeping the Red Army in the war against Hitler. Confronting indifferent and often hostile anti-Soviet officials in both Washington and London, he reminded them that the war might be lost if Hitler defeated the USSR and redeployed hundreds of German divisions elsewhere. He also never wavered in his commitment to maintaining China as a vital ally in the war against Japan. He became one of the staunchest supporters of aid to China, partly for the strategic objective of tying down hundreds of Japanese divisions on the mainland of Asia, divisions that could not be deployed against American forces.[15]

Because of the genuinely global nature of this war, Hopkins concluded that questions of supply and logistics would prove vital, particularly to a nation like the United States with its enormous capacity to outproduce its adversaries and supply its allies. He always sought a compromise between the demands of the Alliance and the requirements of the American services. He pursued, as George Marshall recognized, a shrewd form of realpolitik. He fought to aid the Allies, but he always, very subtly, placed American interests ahead of those of Russia, Britain, and China. He further won the enduring loyalty of the reticent Marshall during a December 1941 controversy over the Hopkins-led Munitions Assignment Board. Marshall bluntly told the president that he could not continue as Chief of Staff unless the board was under his direct authority. To the general's astonishment, Hopkins pondered the arguments and reversed himself, vigorously supporting the general before an audience made up of the president, the prime minister, and Lord Beaverbrook. The two British statesmen reacted to this *volte-face* with ill-concealed dismay, but the Chief of Staff thought it rare indeed that any official would ever argue on the merits of an issue, at significant loss to his own power, rather than merely seeking self-aggrandizement.[16]

All such problems between the Allies and the American services required endless and exhaustive explanation, but General Marshall felt that Hopkins was the one person capable of this liaison duty. Whatever his duties, Hopkins always attained a mastery of his brief and possessed an enormous capacity for details, which Roosevelt respected and relied upon. Marshall felt that Hopkins understood logistics better than FDR who, the general lamented, understood logistics from the perspective of the navy, whereas Hopkins came to grasp logistics from the army perspective, as well. Undoubtedly his FERA, CWA, and WPA experiences in meeting the needs of millions of people proved critical to his achieving this broader understanding. He believed the United States could best contribute in the areas of war production and providing supplies to its British, Soviet, and Chinese allies, and he thought that American forces might eventually open up fronts in both Europe and the Pacific or Asia to relieve pressure on their Chinese and Soviet allies.[17]

Hopkins perceptively observed that experience in the previous world war might not prove entirely applicable to this one. He recognized the current conflict as "an entirely different kind of war" featuring a dominant role for technologies such as airpower, aircraft carriers, tanks, and new lethal "super weapons."[18] The prospect of Axis "super-weapons" deeply troubled him because he knew the Americans were racing to develop them ahead of the Germans. American scientists began holding regular discussions about this frightening subject and understood the threat that Germany was seeking to develop superweapons and that Hitler would not hesitate to use them. Top scientists presented a plan for a National Defense Research Committee (NDRC) to Hopkins, who immediately sensed its enormity, discussed the scientific community's concerns with FDR, and arranged meetings between scientists and the president.[19]

The president grew more dependent on Hopkins, not merely for his labor, but also his counsel. "Harry L. Hopkins is referred to in Washington today as 'the Assistant President,'" observed a *New York Times Magazine* profile in

"Certainly Harry Hopkins never expected life to bring him to the central point of military and political strategy," Frances Perkins observed. "It often seemed ridiculous to this modest, simple man that he should be there. But the quality of dedication in doing what came to him to do, made him unselfconscious as he used his whole personality, his whole strength, for his task."[22]

July 1942. "Almost everyone, from Cabinet members and ranking diplomats to humble government clerks, uses the title. Not only his unique position as a White House guest and the man closest to the president, but the increasing authority he wields and the mantle of mystery flung about him, have made this New Deal old-timer the liveliest topic of capital conversation."[20] When Chiang Kai-shek cabled Roosevelt in July 1942, requesting the president send Hopkins on a mission to Chungking to meet face-to-face as he had with Churchill and Stalin, the president replied: "He is playing a most vital role in the war effort here, and I did not feel that I could spare him for an extended period."[21]

Hopkins, like Roosevelt, also had an enormous personal stake in the war. Roosevelt's four sons served in uniform, and Hopkins's three sons entered the army, navy, and marines. Private First Class Stephen Hopkins served as an infantryman with the marines, deployed to the Pacific, as was Lieutenant David Hopkins, U.S. Navy, while Sergeant Robert Hopkins served as a signal corps photographer in Europe.

Hopkins's public service took a toll on both his physical health and his family life. He acknowledged being a negligent father and often admitted that he was not entirely suited to fatherhood. It pained him when he learned of important news of his family from secondhand sources. He was often a faithless correspondent, including with immediate family members who resorted to seeking news about their famous father from other people. His sons often went many months without any communication from their father, and close friends admonished him that he should do more to maintain contact with them.[23]

For several months in early 1942, Washington buzzed with rumors that Hopkins was about to be married again. Many presumed that the bride-to-be was actress Paulette Goddard. Instead, he had met Louise "Lou" Macy, a Manhattan divorcee and onetime Paris fashion editor for *Harper's Bazaar*. Louise was well known in Manhattan café society, a bon vivant and elegant dresser who sometimes matched her outfits with a ginger-brown French Poodle on a pink patent-leather leash. She had served as the model for a recruiting poster prepared by the Office of Civilian Defense. Hopkins grew enamored of Louise's high spirits and witty conversation.[24]

Harry's background could hardly have been more different from Louise's, and many speculated about the relationship. Some called it the union of the social worker and the socialite. In an effort to quell the gossip, he and "Louie" held an awkward White House press conference, presided over by Eleanor Roosevelt with a firm hand. An embarrassed Hopkins grinned self-consciously and fidgeted throughout the ordeal. Under the prompting of the First Lady, the couple announced they would be married on July 30 at the White House, the first marriage there since 1914, when first daughter Eleanor Wilson married William Gibbs McAdoo. They would embark upon a honeymoon trip whose route was a well-guarded "military secret" and would then move into the White House. Unable to think of anything memorable for the occasion, he inelegantly blurted: "I like the whole business. It suits me. That's an unqualified endorsement!"[25]

"To be very frank," George Marshall wrote to Louise in a revealing note, "I am intensely interested in Harry's health and happiness, and therefore, in your approaching marriage. He has been gallant and self-sacrificing to an extreme, little of which is realized by any but his most intimate friends. He is of great importance to our national interests at present time, and he is one of the most imprudent people regarding his health that I have ever known. Therefore, and possibly inexcusable as it may seem to you, I express the hope that you will find it possible to curb his indiscretions and see that he takes the necessary rest."[26]

They were married in a White House ceremony and lived there for a year before moving to Harry's house in Georgetown. Friends of the couple credited Louie with slowing down Harry's tempo, putting him on a healthier regimen, and keeping him from overwork.[27]

Throughout 1942, American officials worried about developments in the Russo-German war but also about the state of public morale in Great Britain and the United States. What if Hitler knocked the USSR out of the war? One proposal pushed by the Americans, Operation Sledgehammer, was a contingency landing in France in the event of the threatened collapse of Russia or actual collapse of the Germans.[28] Central to Roosevelt and Hopkins's vision of the war was the establishment of a second front in France. Stalin had been urging this as far back as Hopkins's mission to Moscow in July 1941—four months prior to America's formal entry into the war.

Thus, an important moment in Grand Alliance relations occurred during V. M. Molotov's mission to Washington in late May and early June 1941. The Soviet commissar had a reputation as a tenacious negotiator, and Hopkins noted that it had been "pretty difficult to break the ice." In carrying out the president's Russia policy, Hopkins encountered numerous obstacles, particularly from the State Department. Roosevelt and Hopkins felt that dealings with the Russians required a particular kind of temperament and a genuine effort to remember that, for all of the problems an alliance with Stalin provoked, the Red Army's enormous manpower and sacrifices nonetheless remained essential to the defeat of Hitlerism. Molotov's visit exposed such fundamental differences with the State Department over Russia policy. Hopkins felt that the State Department was missing the larger point of the Second Front. Secretary Hull thrust upon him a list of items the State Department wanted raised with Molotov during his visit. Hopkins lamented: "None of these things has anything to do with the war on the Russian front." One of Hull's issues was a well-intentioned desire to obtain Soviet adherence to the Geneva Convention for the treatment of German prisoners of war. "You don't have to know very much about Russia," Hopkins observed, "or for that matter Germany, to know there isn't a snowball's chance in hell for either Russia or Germany to permit the International Red Cross really to inspect any prison camps."[29]

During a May 29, 1942, White House dinner that ran for more than four hours and did not conclude until midnight, Roosevelt had an opportunity to outline some of his views on American wartime and postwar aims.[30] Tensions developed the following day, however, when it became obvious that the Americans were reluctant to commit to a specific date for a second front in France. "If you postpone your decision," Molotov warned during their May

30 meeting, "you will have eventually to bear the brunt of the war, and if Hitler becomes the undisputed master of the continent, next year will un-questionably be tougher than this one."[31]

Conferring with Hopkins, Marshall, and King prior to the final meeting with Molotov, the president expressed concern that the perilous situation on the Russian front necessitated a more specific answer to Molotov regarding a Second Front in France.[32] Hopkins observed: "The President told General Marshall and Admiral King that he thought the matter was a little vague and the dangerous situation on the Russian front required that he, the president, make a more specific answer to Molotov in regard to the Second Front."[33] The president desired to send a clear message to Stalin that he was serious about a meaningful Second Front in France because he did not think the Russians could hold out indefinitely, and he sensed the danger that the war would be disadvantageously transformed if the Red Army was defeated or if the USSR left the war.[34] "Molotov's visit went extremely well," Hopkins cabled Ambassador John Winant in London. "He and the President got along famously and I am sure that we at least bridged one more gap between ourselves and Russia. There is a long way to go but it must be done if there is ever to be any real peace in the world."[35]

After Molotov's departure, Hopkins struggled to make America's commit-ment to a Second Front more convincing to the Russians. He sought to apply subtle pressure by making public the case for a Second Front. He took advan-tage of a joint appearance with Soviet ambassador Maxim Litvinov in New York City commemorating the one-year anniversary of the German invasion of the USSR. With Litvinov at his side on the podium at Madison Square Garden, Hopkins declared: "And what of our 3 million trained ground troops with their modern mechanized equipment? I want to assure this audience tonight that General Marshall, the great leader of our Army, is not training these men to play tiddlywinks. A second front? Yes. And, if necessary, a third and fourth front, to pen the German Army in a ring of our offensive steel. . . . Make no mistake about it. Russia and the Russian Army are in danger—just as they have been in danger for the last 365 days. We know they are fighting against great odds. We know that the Russian front is the most important strategic front in the world. A defect of the Russian Army would be a major disaster and prolong the war for months."[36]

The president had also assigned to Hopkins the difficult task of persuad-ing the British to accept what the Americans regarded as a genuine Second Front, preferably a cross-channel landing in France. Hopkins made two trips to London in 1942 in an effort to obtain Churchill's agreement. He faced the challenge of seeking to reconcile widely divergent American and

British objectives.[37] He sought to capitalize on his ties of friendship with Churchill in the hope of persuading the prime minister to make concessions on a cross-channel invasion.[38] This initially seemed to pay off when, during an April 1942 mission to London, Churchill welcomed both Hopkins and Marshall to sit in on a session of the War Cabinet, but the prime minister remained largely unmoved by their arguments.[39]

In July, Admiral King joined Hopkins and Marshall on yet another trip to London to push for a substantive Second Front. They had explicit orders from the president to acquiesce to Torch, a landing in North Africa in 1942, only if Round Up, the cross-channel invasion, was out of the question for 1943.[40] While in London, Hopkins, Marshall, and King confronted the ferocity of British opposition to an early cross-channel operation. Hopkins served as a buffer between Churchill and the less indulgent Marshall and King, both of whom found the prime minister's digressions and monologues exasperating. The American chiefs feared that Churchill's desire for a Balkan misadventure was due primarily to his love of what Marshall and King characterized as "eccentric operations." Hopkins understood that Marshall and King held no high opinion of Churchill. King was dismayed that Churchill, fancying himself a great military strategist, overruled his Chiefs of Staff, forcing them into compliance with policies preferred by the prime minister. The admiral suspected that, given the chance, Churchill would indefinitely delay the cross-channel landing until the war ended through other events. General Marshall fretted that Churchill's enthusiasm for diversions implied that the Allied forces could afford to take many years conquering Germany. All three Americans shared the objective of defeating Germany in the quickest possible time by the shortest possible route because the Americans could not indefinitely endure hardships in the Pacific.[41]

General Marshall appreciated Hopkins's determination not to deviate from planning for a cross-channel operation, but the Americans nonetheless considered alternatives. One, a landing in French North Africa, worried the Americans because it would be a diversion from the main object, which was the buildup to the liberation of France.[42] Hopkins felt that the staffs should not consider other alternatives until the American Chiefs received instruction from the president. He warned that Roosevelt had been emphatic about laying the groundwork for a cross-channel invasion and would be unhappy to learn that no agreement on it had been reached. "It was imperative," Hopkins continued, "that no breath of this disagreement should get noised abroad; neither America alone, nor Great Britain alone, could win this war. It had to be a joint effort."[43]

After five days of argument in London, he and the chiefs reluctantly concluded that the British would not agree to Round Up—the cross-channel invasion of France. He reported this to the president, who instructed them to begin discussions for a landing in North Africa, or Torch.[44] When Roosevelt gave the final okay for Torch, Hopkins and Marshall accepted it as a fait accompli, but both were deeply depressed.[45]

Hopkins accepted the fact that the calendar days favorable for a cross-channel operation were extremely limited. May or early June were the only really favorable times, not only for the landings themselves but also to provide a period of reasonably good weather for the buildup on the beaches before one or more ports could be transformed into supply bases.[46]

In the months prior to the December 1943 Teheran Conference, Hopkins grasped that the appointment of the Supreme Commander for what was now called Overlord, the cross-channel operation, had tremendous bearing on Grand Alliance relations. He understood that the Soviets remained dubious of Anglo-American seriousness about a Second Front without the appointment of a Supreme Commander for the invasion of France. More-over, choosing a commander would further pressure Churchill to accept the inescapability of Overlord.[47]

This would be no easy matter for Hopkins. Throughout much of 1943 he assumed General Marshall would be appointed to lead Overlord. Through shared trials, he and the Chief of Staff had developed an enormous respect for each other. The general attributed the president's extraordinary confi-dence in him and the enormous degree of independence he enjoyed to Hop-kins's influence. Several months prior to Teheran, Hopkins began preparing the way for Marshall's appointment. "I feel very strongly," Hopkins wrote to the president in October 1943, "from the point of view of organization, Mar-shall should have command of all the Allied forces, other than the Russians, attacking the Fortress of Germany."[48]

Hopkins also knew, however, that Admiral King was adamantly opposed to the appointment of Marshall, whose presence in Washington was deemed too valuable to relinquish. He emphasized that he did not want the "winning team" of the JCS dismantled in wartime. In fact, King, Admiral Leahy, and General Hap Arnold all lobbied Hopkins and the president "in the strongest of terms not to separate General Marshall from his post as Chief of Staff in Washington."[49]

While Hopkins remained Marshall's staunchest backer, he gradually came around to the logic of General Dwight D. Eisenhower's appointment as Supreme Commander.[50] Eisenhower had first met Hopkins in late 1941 and learned from Marshall that he was one of the few civilian officials the army could genuinely depend upon. Ike was immediately impressed with his instinctive understanding of military matters. As for Hopkins, he sensed in

Eisenhower an ability to read people and situations and a shared recognition that, at this level of leadership, a shrewd combination of diplomacy and political savvy was absolutely necessary. Ike soon came to see him not only as his ally but also as a genuine friend, a person he could turn to for sympathy, understanding, and support.[51]

When Roosevelt and Hopkins were on their way to Teheran in November 1943, they met with Eisenhower. The president told Ike that Marshall very much wanted to command Overlord and made clear that he was prepared to grant Marshall's wish. "Ike," the president said, "you and I know who was the Chief of Staff during the Civil War. But practically no one else knows, although the names of the field generals are household words. I think that George Marshall is entitled to establish himself in history as a field general."[52]

Returning from Teheran, at the Second Cairo Conference, which ran from December 4–6, Roosevelt gave Hopkins one of his toughest assignments of the war. At the president's request, Hopkins discussed with Marshall that the president was "in some concern of mind" over the general's appointment as Supreme Commander. Instinctively recognizing Hopkins's tone and other cues, Marshall understood "what the president's point of view was and in my reply I merely endeavored to make it clear that I would go along wholeheartedly with whatever decision the president made. He need have no fears regarding my personal reactions. I declined to state any opinion." The very next day, Roosevelt summoned Marshall to his villa and revisited the topic that Hopkins had already broached with the general the night before. Marshall repeated that, whatever the decision, he would go along with it wholeheartedly and that the issue was too important for any personal feelings to be considered. Roosevelt ended their conversation by telling Marshall: "I feel I could not sleep at night with you out of the country."[53]

Anticipating that the matter had been settled in Marshall's favor, Eisenhower presumed that he would be dispatched back to Washington as Acting Chief of Staff. When FDR came back through Cairo, he and Eisenhower met alone. "Well, Ike, you'd better start packing," Roosevelt bluntly stated. "You are going to move." Eisenhower assumed the president meant that he should pack for Washington to take up his new task. Roosevelt then clarified that he was being dispatched to London to serve as Supreme Commander of Overlord.[54]

Another enormous challenge Hopkins faced was how to best manage U.S.-Soviet relations. The public and press perceived Hopkins's views on the U.S.-Soviet alliance as most closely expressing the president's. While many continued to see aid to Russia as a political expedient, it was, Hopkins stubbornly insisted, a question of vital military necessity. He made every effort to provide more supplies to the Soviet Union through Lend-Lease. He understood that assistance to Russia was vital and that only the Americans were in a position to render it.[55] He continued to be the nagging conscience of the Grand Alliance, pushing for support of the convoys to Russia.[56]

His public emphasis on the contribution of the USSR was interpreted as dispelling rumors of a growing rift between Moscow and Washington. In October 1943 he publicly described the USSR as "the keystone of the war" and declared: "If we lose her, I do not believe for a moment that we will lose the war, but I would change my prediction about the time of victory. Then, indeed, we would have a long war ahead of us."[57]

Hopkins anticipated opposition to his views on Russia. He related a story in 1943, illustrative of his view of U.S.-Russian relations, that a colleague had confronted him, questioning how he could even imagine cooperating with Russia: "She's out to Bolshevize the world," this official told him. "You fellows in Washington are blind. You haven't been around. Russia will bleed us dry and then double-cross us. We'd better start protecting ourselves from Russia, not helping her." Hopkins claims he replied: "Russia is a mighty nation with a political philosophy different from our own. But, like us, she is motivated by a desire to better her people, express her genius, and make her contribution to life on this planet."[58]

In his effort to manage relations among the Big Three, Hopkins sought to restrain Churchill and Anthony Eden from making commitments to Stalin that the president did not support. Hopkins had reacted with concern to the negotiations over the Anglo-Soviet Treaty of 1942, where Churchill and Eden sought to acknowledge Stalin's aspirations in the Baltic by hinting at de facto recognition of Soviet territorial objectives. Hopkins considered this naïve. He felt that any promise of territorial concessions to Stalin early in the war would be subject to changes as the Red Army advanced across Europe. And the longer Churchill blocked a Second Front in France, the greater would be the advances of the Red Army across Europe. The president, representing a nation increasing in strength every day, sought to delay decisions until the United States was in a better position in Europe and had built up its strength in France.[59]

Relations with Moscow grew more complicated during the early spring of 1943. The contentious issue of the Second Front had intensified, and the Lend-Lease supply losses on the Murmansk route to Russia had risen to unsustainable levels.[60] Equally troubling, relations between the London-based noncommunist Polish government-in-exile and Moscow had reached a breaking point in early 1943 when German occupying forces uncovered enormous mass graves containing thousands of Polish victims in the Katyn Forest near Smolensk. Rightly suspecting that the Soviets had committed the massacre, and aiming to drive a wedge into the Grand Alliance, Hitler proposed an international investigation of the mass gravesite, a call immediately seconded by the London Poles. The Kremlin castigated the London Poles and broke off diplomatic relations. The shocking revelations from Katyn poisoned Polish-Soviet relations. The Kremlin exploited the crisis to its advantage by moving immediately to promote its "Union of Polish Patriots," a group of communist Poles in Moscow (later based in Lublin, Poland) seeking to organize postwar Poland along Stalin's desired lines.

Hopkins grew increasingly concerned about the Kremlin's threatening attitude toward Poland. He understood that revelations from Katyn underscored legitimate concerns about an anticipated Red Army reoccupation of territories to the USSR's west. Given the Soviet threat to its neighbors, serious problems would arise if the United States were unwilling to defend the interests of small countries.[61] Hopkins harbored few illusions about Soviet-American relations and understood that the fragile relationship with the Russians had the potential to "blow up at the last minute." This, he feared, might be that moment.[62]

For all the difficulties provoked by Soviet behavior, Hopkins understood that it nonetheless remained absolutely necessary to continue nurturing the alliance, not only for the enormous manpower the Red Army was providing in the struggle against nazism, but also for any hope of a postwar world that would not be overwhelmed by great power antagonisms. With matters growing increasingly complicated between Washington and Moscow, Roosevelt and Hopkins considered suggestions by two former U.S. ambassadors to Moscow, Joseph E. Davies and Laurence Steinhardt, that Hopkins might best be suited to make yet another mission to Moscow and stay on as the new U.S. ambassador. After discussing the matter with Hopkins, the president concluded that he could best serve by remaining close at hand in Washington.[63] At Hopkins's urging, Roosevelt instead appointed one of Hopkins's protégés, W. Averell Harriman, who would serve as Harry's eyes and ears in Moscow.[64]

The growing challenges of U.S.-Soviet relations reinforced Hopkins's desire for a Roosevelt-Stalin meeting. Churchill had grown anxious to take the lead in negotiations between the Western allies and Moscow, seeking to establish himself as Roosevelt and Stalin's go-between. The president sought to avoid the prime minister playing the role of intermediary and instead sought to meet one-on-one with Stalin, without the interference of Churchill.[65]

Roosevelt wanted to get away from the difficulties of large staff conferences and ideological agendas, but he also wanted to get away from the prime minister. Hopkins, too, felt that the meeting should be a bilateral Roosevelt-Stalin tête-à-tête without the distractions of Churchill's presence.

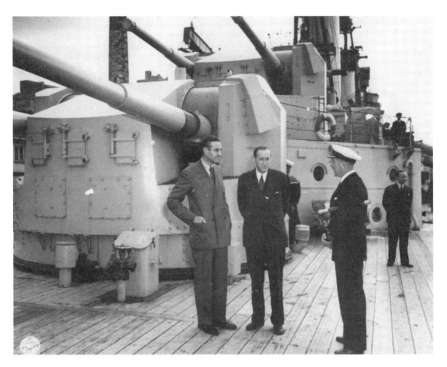

Hopkins and W. Averell Harriman.

He recalled with dismay the often unfocused and rambling meetings between Churchill and Roosevelt throughout 1941 and 1942.[66]

Roosevelt also sought to avoid the perception of a common Anglo-American front against Moscow. This was, in part, because the president had fundamental disagreements with Churchill with regard to such matters as the Second Front and the colonial question. He also sought to avoid the impression of ganging up on Stalin. It was not so much that Roosevelt thought that he and he alone could persuade Stalin, but rather that only Stalin could make the big decisions for the USSR, an idea Hopkins brought home from Moscow in August 1941.

Roosevelt wrote to Stalin in May 1943 proposing "an informal and completely simple visit for a few days between you and me." The proposed geography seemed designed to exclude Churchill: "I suggest that we could meet either on your side or my side of Bering Straits," Roosevelt added. "It is my thought that neither of us would want to bring any staff. I would be accompanied by Harry Hopkins, an interpreter and a stenographer—and that you and I would talk very informally and get what we call 'a meeting

Teheran, Iran, December 1943. Standing outside the Russian Embassy, left to right: British Field Marshall Sir John Dill; General George C. Marshall, Chief of Staff of the United States, shaking hands with Sir Archibald Clark Kerr, British ambassador to the USSR; Harry Hopkins; Marshal Stalin's interpreter; Marshal Joseph Stalin; Foreign Minister Molotov; General Voroshilov. Library of Congress Prints and Photographs Division.

of the minds."[67] Roosevelt later explained that he had desired to establish a genuine communication with Stalin, despite the challenge of "interchanging thoughts through the medium of two widely divergent languages" to get through to the "Russian mentality." He desired that both his words and intent be thoroughly understood by Stalin.[68] Ultimately, Churchill would not be denied, however, and, rather than a bilateral meeting in Alaska or Siberia desired by Roosevelt and Hopkins, a tripartite meeting including Churchill took place in Teheran in November to December 1943.

For all of the attention and notoriety the February 1945 Yalta Conference has received, Teheran was more significant. Hopkins was probably never more influential than at Teheran. He sat at the president's right elbow, passing him notes throughout the conference and providing Roosevelt with another brain and another set of eyes.[69]

Hopkins met Stalin for the first time since their dramatic Kremlin encounter back in July 1941. Stalin, upon entering the conference hall and spotting Hopkins, walked across the room and greeted him warmly. Harriman noted that it was never Stalin's habit to take the initiative this way: "Stalin showed Hopkins a degree of personal consideration which I had never seen him show anyone except Roosevelt and Churchill."[70]

Hopkins sat in for the absent Cordell Hull and, meeting with the British and Soviet Foreign Ministers, found himself wedged between Molotov, who dogmatically adhered to a Kremlin-focused agenda, and Eden, who, perhaps influenced by his undisciplined chief, did not seem to be following any agenda whatsoever. Hopkins sought to get to the root of the matter, but Eden, and even Molotov, made matters enormously difficult.[71]

Hopkins anticipated that Churchill might seek to pursue new diversions from Overlord. He also worried that Churchill's strategy of indefinitely delaying a Second Front in France entailed enormous risks. Eden, sensing that Teheran offered an opportunity for more Churchill-inspired sideshows in the Eastern Mediterranean, and sharing Churchill's penchant for empire-salvaging misadventures, spoke enthusiastically about the possibility of compelling Turkey, perhaps by force, to enter the war on the Allied side.[72]

Hopkins stood firm and voiced his concern that any diversion in Turkey might unnecessarily expand the war and result in delaying Overlord indefinitely. Upon hearing this, Molotov, who initially seemed to relish the prospect of Anglo-Soviet meddling in the Turkish Republic, abruptly interjected that he opposed this if it meant even the slightest delay of the cross-channel invasion. The following day, during a plenary session, Hopkins again sought to thwart the prime minister's incurable enthusiasm for eccentric Eastern Mediterranean operations by repeatedly pointing out that any such endeavor would divert vital matériels from an eventual landing in France.[73]

For Hopkins, the crowning achievement of Teheran was the Big Three agreement to establish a Second Front in France in May 1944 (it would occur in early June), despite Churchill's best efforts to push for a Balkan operation. Stalin also pledged to launch a simultaneous Red Army offensive on Germany's Eastern Front. Hopkins was well aware that, at the time of the Teheran Conference, Anglo-British forces in Italy were facing an estimated fourteen German divisions, while the Red Army was in the process of annihilating 178 German divisions in the east. Hopkins was also encouraged by Stalin's affirmation that the Red Army would join the war against Japan after the defeat of Germany. "If there was any supreme peak in Roosevelt's career," Robert Sherwood observed, "I believe it might well be fixed at this moment, at the end of the Teheran Conference. It certainly represented the peak for Harry Hopkins."[74]

Those who loyally served Roosevelt often observed that he rarely expressed his appreciation to those around him. Thus, it was something of a surprise when, during one of the dinners during the conference, Churchill magnanimously proposed to Stalin and Roosevelt that the three leaders toast Hopkins for his contributions to the war effort. Glass in hand, the president leaned across the table, looked him in the eye and said, "Dear Harry, what would we do without you."[75]

# CHAPTER SIX

~

# Catalyst of the Grand Alliance

We simply cannot organize the world between the British and ourselves without bringing the Russians in as equal partners. For that matter, if things go well with Chiang Kai-shek, I would surely include the Chinese too.

*—Harry Hopkins to John Winant in June 1942.[1]*

"I believe just as we can have a total victory in war, so we can win an abiding and just peace," Harry Hopkins told an enormous Madison Square Garden rally in June 1942. "Just as we can fight with Russia, England and China as military allies, so we can win the peace, with their cooperation and lasting friendship."[2] Hopkins anticipated that the postwar world would be shaped by the enormous changes wrought by the war. The Soviet Union and the rising nations of Asia would inevitably seek to play a larger role in the world, with China and India gradually emerging as important regional powers. He recognized that the American people did not want a postwar relationship with Great Britain to the exclusion of Russia.[3] "We simply cannot organize the world between the British and ourselves without bringing the Russians in as equal partners," he wrote to the U.S. ambassador to Britain, John Winant, in June 1942. "For that matter, if things go well with Chiang Kai-shek, I would surely include the Chinese too."[4]

The strategic importance of the Red Army's Eastern Front against the Germans remained central to Hopkins's thinking about how Hitler might be defeated. He also shared with Roosevelt the belief that it would be absolutely essential that the USSR play a constructive role in the postwar world.[5] Hopkins found, however, that with the exception of persistent pressure for an Anglo-American Second Front in France, Stalin and Molotov remained single-mindedly focused on the challenges before them on the Russian-German Front. Efforts to remind Stalin or Molotov of the American struggle in the Pacific, or of American efforts to aid China, elicited negligible interest from Soviet officials facing the brunt of German military might.[6]

Throughout his engagements with British officials, Hopkins noted that American military objectives in the Pacific and Asia, vital to his own broader conception of the war, were of only secondary interest. Despite frequent promptings, these topics did not feature prominently in their discussions, and the Pacific war was of only marginal interest to the prime minister. When he sought to remind Churchill that the United States also was carrying enormous burdens in the Pacific and China, the latter often changed the subject. He found that senior British officials had little interest in the fate of China and thus did not seriously concern themselves with the enormous challenge of supplying China and keeping it in the war against Japan. Nor, Hopkins found, did Churchill give priority to the American determination to establish a genuine Second Front in France, and certainly not until the prime minister was forced by the combined efforts of Roosevelt, Hopkins, and General Marshall to abandon his evasive penchant for "eccentric operations" in the Balkans and Eastern Mediterranean.

Hopkins also understood that there was no way to reconcile Roosevelt and Churchill's fundamentally divergent views of the postwar future. He concluded that the prime minister had an essentially obsolete worldview. Churchill's wartime objectives frequently emphasized Britain's imperial dimension. The prime minister remained convinced that an important factor in the postwar world would be the restoration of European imperial possessions lost to the Japanese in the early months of the war. Hopkins concluded that the prime minister maintained a primary interest in restoring British (and even French and Dutch) rule over enormous, and perhaps even enlarged, global empires.[7]

Hopkins anticipated, however, that profound changes had occurred during the war and that the postwar world would be fundamentally different from what had come before, with the gradual displacement of the European empires by emerging nation-states rising out of colonial servitude. He foresaw that throughout the European possessions there would continue to be a worldwide movement of the "awakening of peoples."[8]

These British imperial objectives often troubled Hopkins. He understood that Churchill did not want British troops in the Far East serving under an

American commander and instead preferred to focus on reestablishing former British positions throughout Asia as well as those of the Dutch and the French. The Americans remained single-mindedly focused on the earliest defeat of Japan and had little interest in the restoration of European possessions in Asia.[9] Roosevelt and Hopkins thought that restoration of European possessions in the region might destroy any hope of postwar harmony. Hopkins thought Churchill's comments about preserving the empire ill conceived, particularly when many Americans were looking for any reason to distrust the British and many suspected that American boys were dying in far-off lands merely to restore the British Empire. Despite the Anglo-American alliance, he well understood that the American people "simply do not like the British Colonial Policy."[10]

Unlike other members of the administration such as Vice President Henry Wallace and Undersecretary of State Sumner Welles, Hopkins did not publicly criticize European colonialism, and he never aggressively pushed Churchill on the issue. As with Soviet objectives in the Baltic and Eastern Europe, he was ambivalent about the usefulness of the United States pressuring its allies on matters that were clearly their primary interests but of secondary national interest to Washington. He also understood that Anglo-American clashes over matters such as the role of China and the future status of India had the potential to undermine the war effort and distract the Allies from what should be the primary goal of defeating the Axis powers.[11]

Yet Hopkins was never Churchill's passive enabler on the issue. He sought to find a middle ground between those who desired immediate decolonization and the British, some of whom actually believed the war might result in enlarged European empires. Churchill instinctively sensed that Hopkins was less hostile to his objectives than Roosevelt, and the prime minister often turned to Hopkins when he felt anxious about imperial matters. Owing to the sensitivity of the India question, both Churchill and Roosevelt informally used Hopkins as their go-between.[12] He found himself pinioned between an often-exasperated Roosevelt, who sought to compel Churchill to allow reforms in India, and the prime minister, who looked to Hopkins for rescue from the president's pressure. Hopkins also understood that confusion and deep divisions beset British officials over India and that Churchill represented an extreme view that was not necessarily shared by all of his cabinet colleagues or military officials.

Hopkins was in London with General Marshall in April 1942 during a period of particular tension between the president and the prime minister over India.[13] Roosevelt went so far as warning Churchill that he could not comprehend "the unwillingness of the British Government to concede to the Indians the right of self-government."[14] A panicked Churchill, upon later hearing rumors that the president planned to invite Indian independence leader Jawaharlal Nehru to Washington, wrote to Hopkins in May 1942: "We are fighting to defend this vast mass of helpless Indians from imminent invasion. I know you will remember my many difficulties."[15]

Despite his efforts to reassure Churchill, Hopkins nonetheless believed that, with the conflict increasingly characterized as a United Nations war, featuring so much rhetoric about the Four Freedoms and the Atlantic Charter, every step should be taken to make the subject peoples of the world aware that the United States supported their aspirations. He thought the United States should make it clear that it embraced alternatives to Churchill's outdated worldview by giving tacit support for political and economic self-determination of all peoples.[16]

Hopkins reflected in an unpublished political testament in July 1945 that the United States should encourage those around the world who desired freedom from imperial control. "Now, you can say that that spells the doom of all the Colonial Empires," Hopkins said. "Well, it probably does." He believed that, ultimately, most of those living in the colonial empires would achieve their freedom because none of the European imperial powers had sufficient military strength to stop the inevitable drive toward independence. He thought decolonization was inevitable. "You cannot dilute this business of freedom," he continued. "Either you believe in it, or you don't. . . . You can think of a hundred and one reasons why this and that colonial country . . . should not be free, but none of those reasons have ever made sense to me."[17]

Hopkins also became entangled in Anglo-American disagreements over China. Churchill and the British never shared Roosevelt and Hopkins's emphasis on the importance of China's role in the Far East war. To the British, China became psychologically linked to the fate of the European empires. Hopkins suspected that Churchill resented Generalissimo Chiang Kai-shek, in part, because of Chinese enthusiasm for nationalist aspirations in Asia and, in particular, Chinese sympathy for the Indian struggle for Home Rule. The British hoped to recover postwar control over their many possessions in Asia and thus saw China as a dangerous example for Asian nationalists. Hopkins suspected that British hostility to Chiang had nothing to do with China's military weakness and everything to do with reestablishing European empires in Asia after the war. The prospect of an empowered China, acting in harmony with the other, completely white, Great Powers, troubled British officials such as Churchill who worried about the postwar status of the British Empire in Asia.[18]

In his effort to assist China, Hopkins and his Lend-Lease staff confronted enormous obstacles from the British. He thought the prime minister's attitude toward China misguided but, worse still, Churchill's antipathy filtered down to all levels of the British war effort, fostering a hostility characteristic of the British policy toward China. Hopkins and his staff were dismayed that British officials sought to impede efforts to deliver Lend-Lease to China. He doubted the British much cared if the Burma Road route into China remained open, and he suspected that many British officials preferred to lose Burma to the Japanese rather than receive Chinese assistance, which might result in concessions to Burmese nationalists. Hopkins worried that deterioration in the China theater could play into Churchill's desire to abandon the generalissimo altogether. A weakened China might embolden British efforts to focus on the reclamation of European colonial possessions. Hopkins suspected that some British officials might prefer that China be defeated to prevent it from having any role in the peace settlement or giving future inspiration to Asian nationalists. Warned by members of his Lend-Lease staff in Burma, as well as other officials in both Chungking and Washington, Hopkins suspected that many British officials preferred a disunited China with the southern half of the country remaining a de facto British sphere of influence.[19]

Wartime China confronted Hopkins with enormous challenges that could not easily be solved by his trademark pragmatism. Nor would China's problems be solved, as he suspected Churchill preferred, simply by ignoring them. In fact, he appreciated that the many challenges in China may not have had any satisfactory outcomes, but the odds did not deter him from striving for solutions.[20]

Hopkins attained a growing influence on China policy even prior to U.S. entry into the war. At the time of the passage of the Lend-Lease Act in March 1941, he grew concerned about the plight of China and explored ways that assistance might also be dispatched to Chiang's regime in Chungking. Even during the earliest days of Lend-Lease he understood that if China capitulated the consequences would prove catastrophic to American interests worldwide. He also appreciated the absolute necessity of precluding any Chinese settlement with Japan that might free up Japanese forces for redeployment elsewhere.[21]

Like Roosevelt, he grasped that China's vast manpower and territorial depth—much like the USSR's—played an enormous, if underappreciated, role in the war. He understood that American support for China had both military and political dimensions. On the military side, strengthening China would occupy enormous numbers of Japanese troops on the Asian continent, forces that otherwise might be redirected elsewhere. Hopkins always kept uppermost in his mind that several million Japanese troops remained trapped in a quagmire in China, consuming preciously scarce Japanese manpower and resources. He emphasized this vital contribution by China, recognizing the enormous consequences for the Allies should China collapse, and instinctively understood that everything should be done to keep China in the war. Chiang Kai-shek, whatever his shortcomings, still offered the best hope of holding China together and maintaining resistance to Japan's barbarous war and occupation.[22]

After Pearl Harbor, Hopkins concurred with American military officials that Japan might eventually be attacked from bases in China much as Germany was being attacked from Great Britain. "The second phase of the China business is to get a springboard from which to bomb Japan itself," Hopkins reminded the president in March 1942, and, even if only for upholding Chinese morale, "this is extremely important and the sooner it can be done the better."[23]

In his dealings with Chinese officials, Hopkins appreciated that they thought little about other theaters of the war beyond China. He also found that the Chinese had only a marginal interest in the American struggle in the Pacific against their common Japanese adversary. The generalissimo's wife, Soong Mei-ling, then widely known as Madam Chiang Kai-shek, went so far as to imply to Hopkins that a truce with Hitler might allow for a more concentrated focus on the war against Japan in China.[24]

Hopkins also valued China's geopolitical importance. He believed that postwar stability in Asia required an independent, unified, and gradually more prosperous China, which also might provide the United States with a postwar counterbalance to the future ambitions of the USSR, Great Britain, and even a revived Japan.[25] He understood that the postwar role of Britain in Asia posed an area of potential conflict. A weak China had created opportunities for European and Japanese imperial expansion in Asia. A strong China might blunt European, Japanese, and even Soviet ambitions. With Japan eventually defeated and disarmed and the Soviet Union emerging as a Far Eastern power, China might provide the United States with a rising postwar ally in Asia.[26]

Chinese officials recognized Hopkins as a genuine friend of China and valued his ties to the president. With the United States formally in the war as of December 1941, he stressed the contributions China could make to Allied war objectives. He intervened when supply problems emerged, and Chinese officials did not hesitate to appeal to him when they felt their needs were not being adequately met.[27] He emerged as the de facto liaison with officials such as the influential Foreign Minister T. V. Soong, the brother of Madam Chiang and thus the brother-in-law of the generalissimo.[28]

Roosevelt wanted Hopkins to manage Soong Mei-ling as he did Churchill. Hopkins assisted with her visits to America in 1942 and 1943, including for medical treatments for a variety of ailments. She assured Hopkins she had come to the United States solely for medical reasons, but "in the same breath she proceeded to raise many questions relating to China and the United States."[29] She later reassured him that China would "line up with us at the peace table" with the Americans and urged him to make an official mission to Chungking as he had previously to London and Moscow.[30]

Hopkins also sought to raise the plight of China with the other members of the Grand Alliance. Whether with the Russians or the British, he pressed for military assistance to Chunking and fought against Churchill's proclivity for diversions that would come at the expense of supplying China. Hopkins, Marshall, and King shared the concern that the logistical and supply drain of Churchill's preferred diversions would come at the expense of China.[31]

Seeking to obtain a clearer picture of developments in China, Hopkins established his own intelligence sources. He communicated with the newspaperman Joseph Alsop, temporarily assigned to the staff of Clair Chennault, the American general given responsibility for organizing Chinese air power, as well as with the perceptive Foreign Service Officer John Paton Davies. Both served as his de facto eyes and ears in China. These sources warned him that the generalissimo possessed only nominal authority over his own forces and none over the regional armies under warlord control. Hopkins feared a split in the Chinese government or a coup and the establishment of a puppet government making peace on Japanese terms. Worse still, the Chinese might yet collapse militarily and be forced out of the war.[32]

General Chennault warned Hopkins that airpower diversions to support the Burma Road would inevitably delay and perhaps even prevent his plans to create offensive air power in China to strike against the heart of Japan. Chennault's plan offered the possibility of faster results and had other positive aspects such as bypassing British obstructionism. Hopkins understood that the president, increasingly horrified by the carnage of the campaigns in the Pacific, was interested in the notion that China might provide a springboard for carrying the war to Japan.[33]

Hopkins thought the Chungking government had legitimate concerns of their own, and he urged Roosevelt to meet with Soong Mei-ling. He nonetheless also suspected, from his various sources, that Chinese officials were not doing enough to address their many problems, such as rampant corruption, and that some of the criticism leveled at the generalissimo and his coterie was probably valid. He wanted the Chinese to be alerted that Washington had serious concerns about their shortcomings.[34]

The generalissimo had made clear to Hopkins China's interests when they met in Cairo in late November 1943, but dissension among senior

American officials only added to the challenges in China.[35] The president's two chief commanders in that theater, General Joseph Stilwell and General Chennault, remained at cross purposes, and Hopkins inevitably became embroiled in the controversy. Chennault believed that his Fourteenth Air Force should attack Japanese forces, and eventually Japan itself, from bases in China, whereas Stilwell wanted Chennault's air force to assist in opening the Burma Road supply route into southern China. The generalissimo, aware of Britain's hostility to him and opposed to future British control over Burma, favored Chennault's strategy. The dispute between Stilwell and the generalissimo went beyond these strategic differences, however, as Stilwell made no effort to conceal his disdain for the generalissimo. Hopkins listened patiently to the concerns of Chinese officials, but he did not immediately commit himself to any particular course of action regarding Stilwell. He understood, through his meetings with Soong Mei-ling and other Chinese officials, the depths of the Chinese dislike of Stilwell and, conversely, their admiration for Chennault.[36]

Hopkins certainly had a hand in Stilwell's eventual removal, but he did not recommend such action carelessly. In fact, it was an extraordinarily difficult decision, one that placed him in the unfamiliar position of opposing General Marshall, who backed Stilwell in his disagreements with Chennault. The Army Chief of Staff later acknowledged that the Stilwell-Chennault controversy provoked his only serious disagreement with Hopkins. Marshall agreed that Stilwell was indiscreet, too tactless for his own good, and sometimes lacking the skills necessary to work well with others. But Marshall supported Stilwell's strategy and, he added, Stilwell was also the only high-ranking American officer who spoke Chinese.[37]

Hopkins agreed with Marshall that Stilwell was his own worst enemy, and he grew increasingly exasperated by his attitudes toward the Chinese. He had little patience for American officials who failed to demonstrate self-control during their assignments and who personalized their differences with foreign officials. He concluded from his investigations that Stilwell had been thoroughly impolitic in his dealings with the Chinese. He arranged a special meeting on China in the president's bedroom in July 1943, with Marshall and Admiral Leahy also in attendance. The president began by expressing his strong dissatisfaction, noting, according to Hopkins's notes of the meeting: "Our whole business in China was an awful mess and ought to be straightened out at once." Roosevelt voiced his concerns about Stilwell's disrespectful tone. He told the assemblage, Hopkins recorded, that "Stilwell obviously hated the Chinese and that his cablegrams are sarcastic about the Chinese and this feeling is undoubtedly known to the Chinese and the Generalissimo. Furthermore, the president said that it is quite clear the Generalissimo does not like Stilwell." The American general may have had legitimate grievances against the Chinese premier, but Chiang Kai-shek was still the head of state of a nation of five hundred million people and needed to be afforded respect. Little would be gained by gratuitously antagonizing the generalissimo.[38]

The president ultimately relieved the unrepentant Stilwell in October 1944. The general's supporters portrayed Hopkins as one of the villains behind the decision, too ready to appease the generalissimo's desire to rid himself of the obstreperous "Vinegar Joe."[39] Despite Hopkins's disavowals, Chungking credited him with disposing of Stilwell and guaranteeing that the president's special envoy to China, General Patrick Hurley, remained behind as ambassador. Hurley, along with Stilwell's replacement, General Albert C. Wedemeyer, both proved better able to work with Chiang and his regime.[40]

Throughout 1944 and 1945, American officials in China expressed to Hopkins their growing concerns about the corruption and deterioration of the generalissimo's government. Hopkins heard reports of factionalism in China, dissention in the Nationalist armed forces, rumors of a possible coup d'etat against Chiang, and Chinese Communist gains.[41]

While Hopkins never wavered in his support for China's postwar aspirations, his confidence in China's military potential began to falter by 1945. He recognized that China had already provided a vital contribution to the Allied war effort by holding down an enormous number of Japanese troops after 1937. But Chungking could contribute little beyond that because of its military weakness. Hopkins lost confidence in the Chinese military's ability to function as an effective offensive instrument. Moreover, with American progress in the Pacific and, in particular, the establishment of B-29 bases in the Marianas from which to bomb Japan, he further explored the possibilities of the Red Army providing the final assault on the Japanese in Manchuria and Northern China.[42]

Hopkins understood the implications of John Davies's insightful reports from China, but these mattered little to him. He recognized the hazards identified by such observers, but he subordinated such issues to his single-minded emphasis on winning the war. China would certainly have a say in the postwar peace as a permanent member of the new Security Council of the United Nations, but its military contributions, beyond tying down large numbers of Japanese troops, would remain limited.

Hopkins worried about the "appalling economic differences between the masses of people in China and those who rule it from an economic point of view." He shrewdly anticipated that enormous changes were long overdue, and "there will be great revolutionary forces that work in China to reform their economic system." He remained uncertain whether Chinese leaders were prepared to implement the kinds of social, political, and economic reforms necessary for China's modernization. "It is ridiculous," he observed, "to assume China is not going to have great problems—internal political and economic problems—after this war is over."[43]

Like Roosevelt, Hopkins sought the objective of an enduring relationship with China. In his unpublished political testament, dictated only weeks before the end of the war in Asia, Hopkins revealed his feelings on the future of the U.S.-China relationship. "If I were to indicate a country in which the United States, for the next hundred years, had the greatest interest from a political and economic point of view, I would name the Republic of China. With the defeat of Japan, China will become one of the greatest land powers on earth. I do not say that she will become one of the most powerful for many years to come, but . . . we hope that there will arise out of the welter of war a unified China."[44]

Roosevelt and Hopkins often disagreed over policy toward General Charles de Gaulle and the Free French. Roosevelt developed a deep dislike of de Gaulle, whom the president saw as an apprentice dictator, and sought to exclude him from wartime decisions. Furthermore, the factionalism and infighting among the French exiles dismayed American officials, including Hopkins. Yet he found himself more often in alignment with Churchill than the president. With the president, Hull, and Welles hostile to de Gaulle and often reluctant to parlay with Free French representatives, Hopkins offered a sympathetic ear and provided ballast for Franco-American relations.[45]

He saw the French general, despite his difficult temperament, as a strong leader, perhaps, like Churchill, even a man of destiny who might expunge the humiliation of the defeat of 1940 and help lead France proudly into the postwar years. He understood that de Gaulle devoted nearly all of his energy to staying atop the scrum of French exiles. De Gaulle and his officials had little latitude to contemplate much about the war other than their persistent desire for the Free French to be recognized as legitimate members of the Grand Alliance and that France be acknowledged as a world power after the war. Hopkins believed that U.S. "foreign policy toward France should not be governed by the personalities of the people who happen for the moment to be in executive power in either of our countries."[46]

Roosevelt likely thought Hopkins was being too solicitous of de Gaulle and the Free French, but Hopkins operated from an entirely different set of goals from his detractors. His relations with de Gaulle were linked to his broader objective of harmonious Alliance relations. Hopkins's support for

France was consistent with his support for Great Britain, the USSR, or even China. With his innate pragmatism, he put aside whatever personal feelings he had toward de Gaulle and focused only on the need to maximize potential French contributions, particularly in the postwar period. Just as with his approach to Churchill, Stalin, or Chiang Kai-shek, Hopkins believed in subordinating potential areas of conflict for the larger objective of defeating the Axis powers. Anything that contributed to that goal, even the cultivation of the difficult de Gaulle, should be pursued.[47]

Perhaps Hopkins's biggest contribution to the future of France, and one where he was in sharp disagreement with Churchill, was his persistent determination to open a Second Front in northern Europe, thus precipitating France's earlier liberation from Nazi occupation, perhaps many months, even years, before this likely would have occurred had the Allies followed Churchill's preferred path of Balkan operations. The president, General Marshall, Admiral King, and even de Gaulle himself all fully shared Hopkins's single-minded desire to secure a Second Front in France as quickly as logistically possible.[48]

Hopkins's challenges over France came to a head at the January 1943 Casablanca Conference, where matters related to French exile movements consumed much of his time.[49] Roosevelt had been none too happy with de Gaulle, but Hopkins urged him not to disavow the disagreeable French general. He "urged the President to be conciliatory and not beat de Gaulle too hard."[50] Hopkins also suggested that Churchill insist upon de Gaulle coming to Casablanca to meet with the American-backed French exiled General Henri Giraud.[51] He brought Giraud and de Gaulle together with Roosevelt and Churchill. "Churchill walked in and I went after Giraud believing that if the four of them could get together we could get an agreement," Hopkins recorded. "The President was surprised at seeing Giraud but took it in his stride. De Gaulle was a little bewildered. Churchill grunted. But the president went to work on them with Churchill backing him up vigorously. De Gaulle finally agreed to a joint statement and, before he could catch his breath, the President suggested a photograph."[52]

Hopkins observed that de Gaulle arrived at his Casablanca meeting with FDR "cold and austere." He surmised that de Gaulle had valid reasons for his demeanor. During the president's discussions with the French leader, Hopkins noted the unusual presence of the president's Secret Service entourage, "armed to the teeth" with a dozen Tommy guns, posted at every doorway behind the curtains around the room, even in the gallery above de Gaulle. He thought it stranger still that no such show of force had been so obvious during Roosevelt's earlier meeting with Giraud. He lamented that this was typical of the atmosphere de Gaulle endured at Casablanca. "To me, the armed Secret Service was unbelievably funny and nothing in Gilbert and Sullivan could have beaten it." Hopkins observed sympathetically: "Poor General de Gaulle . . . was covered by guns throughout his whole visit."[53]

Hopkins grew annoyed at Roosevelt's tendency to exaggerate de Gaulle's eccentricities. He derided as "apocryphal" Roosevelt's later retelling of stories about de Gaulle's megalomania and perceptions of himself as part Clemenceau and part Joan of Arc. "This story is pure fiction," Hopkins lamented. He observed that it was typical of Roosevelt to concoct unflattering anecdotes about those he disliked. He later heard the president retell this story numerous times and concluded that this may have been the sort of impression Roosevelt took away from his first meeting with de Gaulle. Hopkins suspected that, with every retelling, "I have no doubt it took on more authenticity and finally come to be accepted as a fact." He regretted that Roosevelt told this apocryphal story to reporters because it was soon published very widely in the American press and General de Gaulle no doubt became aware of it. Such behavior only made more difficult Hopkins's efforts to promote harmony with and among the French.[54]

Contrary to Roosevelt, Hopkins respected de Gaulle and even admired him for his calm and confidence under extraordinarily difficult circumstances.[55] Hopkins not only sought to balance the president's hostility toward France, he also often found himself standing between France and wrathful Soviet officials who deemed France not a defeated nation, but rather an active supporter of Germany that should be held accountable.[56] Hopkins disagreed. He had nothing but sympathy for the French people and believed they had faced a tragic national catastrophe in 1940 with admirable stoicism. He acknowledged that de Gaulle, like Stalin and even Churchill, was not necessarily the easiest leader with whom to work, but he thought the focus should be on the welfare of forty million French people and not on the eccentricities of one Charles de Gaulle.[57]

In early 1945, Roosevelt delegated to Hopkins the impossible task of somehow including France in the Yalta meeting without physically including de Gaulle. The place of France in European and world affairs was uncertain as he flew to Paris in January to meet with General de Gaulle. The pro–Free French Hopkins endured de Gaulle's wrath so that the anti–Free French Roosevelt did not have to.[58] "The interview was really astonishing," recalled one of the few witnesses to the scene, Etienne Burin des Roziers, General de Gaulle's interpreter for his meeting with Hopkins. "It began badly because it was taking place at a very difficult period. . . . De Gaulle was willing to believe that Mr. Hopkins was playing a decisive role but he was ill at ease

An exhausted looking Hopkins looks on as President Roosevelt is about to cut into birthday cake while returning from the Casablanca Conference. At his right is his chief military adviser, Admiral William D. Leahy. Captain Howard Cone, the captain of the plane, is at Hopkins's left. Credit: Office of War Information.

with him nonetheless. . . . A long silence followed. Nobody said anything. . . . After a long moment (especially for me, having nothing to translate), the conversation finally began and it was very interesting because it had the pretention, justified I believe, of dealing with the essential questions."

Hopkins told de Gaulle: "I would like to talk about what seems to me the fundamental reason for the 'malaise' (this was the word he used), that has existed for so long between our two countries.' And he went on: 'The truth is that in June '40, the defeat of the French army, the institution of the Vichy government under German control, was for America and for President Roosevelt in particular, a painful surprise. And we have never gotten over it. It is at that time that we decided to deal with Vichy, and many things followed from this."[59]

General de Gaulle replied by challenging Hopkins: "If you really mean that you believe that relations between the United States and France are not all that they should be, why don't you do something about it?"[60] De Gaulle then added: "There is also something else. You have a choice to make. Either you believe that France still has a great role to play in the world, or you consider that after what my country went through, France is on the decline and can no longer be one of the leaders. If it is the second case, you are right. I believe, however, that France will come back stronger, and that France has an important role to play. And if that is the case, your behavior is regrettable and ill-inspired."[61]

Hopkins was in no way discouraged by de Gaulle's comments. Rather, he accepted the logic of the general's argument, not only openly at Yalta but also, more remarkably, in his private thoughts and musings. At Yalta, Hopkins often defended the interests of France, seeking to secure it a place in the UN Security Council as well as a zone in the Allied Control Commission for Germany. The president mostly followed Hopkins's suggestions, often only on the basis of a note handed to him.[62] After the conference Hopkins again struck a blow for Free France when he successfully persuaded Roosevelt to tone down an angry draft cable to de Gaulle.

Hopkins believed a democratic Europe absolutely essential to postwar stability and a democratic France central to that objective. France would have to be included in a matrix of international institutions, and he believed there was no reason for Washington and Paris not to share close relations and become strong postwar allies. As a harbinger of the Marshall Plan, Hopkins thought the United States was the only nation in the world that could provide France with sufficient economic support and that Washington had every interest in doing so. Although General Marshall later became renowned for the eponymous Marshall Plan, or European Recovery Program, in 1948, Hopkins had been thinking along these lines as early as 1943, contemplating the human consequences of what would likely be a series of brutal postwar winters in Europe. He feared that without massive emergency relief, millions of Europeans might starve or freeze. He also feared that such further distress, following on the heels of a catastrophic war, might undermine democracy and lead to totalitarianism.[63] Just as he had worried whether millions of Americans enduring the Great Depression would survive the winter of 1933 to 1934 and came up with the novel solution of the Civil Works Administration, and later the Works Progress Administration, he contemplated something akin to a CWA or WPA for the world to provide basic relief to the Europeans to get them through the first postwar winters, aspects of which later evolved into the Marshall Plan. One can imagine, had Hopkins remained healthy and succeeded in his goal of becoming postwar proconsul in Berlin, he might have been in a strong position to oversee the implementation of postwar relief.[64]

# CHAPTER SEVEN

~

# Defeating Fascism

We really believed in our hearts that this was the dawn of a new day we had all been praying for and talking about for so many years. The Russians had proved they could be reasonable and farseeing and there wasn't any doubt in the minds of the President or any of us that we could live with them and get along with them peacefully for as far into the future as any of us could imagine.[1]

—*Harry Hopkins on Yalta*

"You know you need not have told me what a terrible correspondent I am," Harry Hopkins acknowledged to one his more dedicated correspondents, Pamela Churchill. "I never write letters."[2] His extraordinary intuition must have compelled him, however, to write to each of his three sons at the beginning of February 1944. "The attack on the Marshalls has taken place," Hopkins wrote to his son, Robert, on February 2, 1944, "and the Division Stephen is in is one of the two divisions that are making the landings and I know David is on one of the aircraft carriers that is out there. They will both have great stories to tell about it later."[3] To his youngest son, Stephen, on February 2, 1944, Harry wrote: "You can imagine how much my thoughts have been with you during the last few days and I hope that all has gone well. I am sure it has. . . . David is on an aircraft carrier somewhere in that show and it may be you have already seen him."[4]

Stephen never received his father's letter. He was killed in action in the Pacific the day before Harry wrote his letter, February 1. En route to Florida as part of his recovery from his post-Teheran exhaustion, Harry learned of his youngest son's death in a telegram from FDR: "I am terribly sorry to tell you that Stephen was killed in action at Kwajalein. We have no details as yet other than that he was buried at sea. His mother has been notified. I am confident that when we get details we will all be even prouder of him than ever. I am thinking of you much, FDR."[5]

Harry wrote to his son, Robert: "There is so little we can say to each other about Stephen. And yet this is everything—events, incidents, remembrances that made both of us love him so much. . . . I am sure he went to war very proudly—and I know enough about the end to know that he died gallantly."[6]

Stephen's death was a blow to Harry and may have contributed to his physical relapse that spring. He returned to Room 301 at the Mayo Clinic for the third time in seven years, for yet another stomach operation. A year earlier, shortly after returning from Casablanca, an exhausted Hopkins told Churchill that he dreaded going under the knife again for "a look at my innards by the surgeons. I am none too pleased at the prospect but only because it will take me out of the war at such a critical time, but no matter what I will meet you in Berlin!"[7]

Hopkins put up a brave face, but friends thought he was feeling low and may have been more depressed about Stephen's death than he let on. Those close to him remained unsure if they should raise the subject. Close friends Robert and Florence Kerr found Hopkins in bed holding a parchment of a Shakespeare quotation Churchill had sent him upon learning of Stephen's death.[8]

> Stephen Peter Hopkins.
> Age 18
> To Harry Hopkins from Winston S. Churchill
> 13 February, 1944
> Your son, my lord, has paid a soldier's debt;
> He only liv'd but till he was a man;
> The which no sooner had his prowess confirm'd
> In the unshrinking station where he fought,
> But like a man he died.

Hopkins shared the parchment with Florence and Robert, and then, unexpectedly, began to open up about Stephen's death, recounting the minute-by-minute details of everything he had been able to learn about Stephen's final hours.[9] A month later he acknowledged: "Stephen's death still hangs heavily over my heart and mind."[10]

Hopkins wrote to Averell Harriman in March. "There is not much to be said about a son who is killed in the war. Life was very good for him so far as it went. I know he died very gallantly for his country and I get great satisfaction and pride out of this."[11] "It is tough to lose your nice boy," wrote Frances Perkins. "You were sporting about it and I thought you said just the right thing—right for the public reaction, but more than that, I mean right as an attitude toward life and death. It is hard to remember it, but of course it is true nonetheless, that the people we love are only loaned to us for a few brief years. . . . I think about you a great deal and I say an occasional prayer for you, not only because I miss you but because I think you have had a hard winter."[12]

Harry's health continued to falter during the first months of 1944. So long as he took his medications, he kept going. On trips he often forgot. After the London and Moscow missions he had to be rushed to the naval hospital in Bethesda. He returned from Teheran and Cairo worn down and ailing and ended up back at the Mayo Clinic. "My prayers are for your early and complete recovery," General Marshall wrote to Harry in March 1944. "I know you have one great reserve in your favor and that is cold nerve and great courage."[13] Roosevelt inquired about Harry's health and sought to encourage him. If Hopkins was discouraged about ending up back at the Mayo Clinic, he did not reveal it in his correspondence with the president. But Hopkins's post-Teheran relapse could not have come at a worse time for the Grand Alliance. In August 1944, Hopkins shared with Churchill that he was too ill to attend the Second Quebec Conference, alerting the PM that he would "not risk the dangers of a setback by fighting the Battle of Quebec. Better men than I have been killed there."[14] Hopkins's adviser on Soviet matters, the State Department Russia specialist Charles "Chip" Bohlen, felt that the controversial Morgenthau Plan, proposing the permanent deindustrialization and fragmentation of Germany, would have never seen the light of day at Quebec had Hopkins remained at the White House. Bohlen recalled that the president felt Hopkins's absence acutely and that the consequences were revealed in subsequent policy problems, particularly during Churchill's solo mission to Moscow in October 1944.[15]

Roosevelt's health also began to flag as the war dragged on. Hopkins thought the president's health, against all odds, had held up astonishingly well for the first two years of the war. At the beginning of 1944, FDR began to undergo a noticeable physical decline. As Roosevelt's health faltered throughout 1944, Hopkins increasingly took on greater responsibility fielding Churchill's many requests, concerns, and complaints. When Hopkins's health problems took him away from the war, there was no one to answer the prime minister.[16] An April 1944 *Time* magazine story on Hopkins's latest illness observed: "When Harry Hopkins, who comes closest to being the real Assistant president of the U.S., is not at work, the president has more visitors, more decisions to make, more troubles. Hopkins, besides being the one real Roosevelt confidant, holds a dazzling combination of official posts. . . . If Hopkins now needs several months to recover, the president will have lost the valuable services of his closest friend at a time when he needs him most."[17] Both military and civilian officials observed that they could always tell when Hopkins was absent from the White House by the slow pace with which orders moved. George Marshall wrote to an absent Hopkins: "We have been deeply concerned for you personally and, quite selfishly, as much concerned over your absence from Washington."[18] Perkins wrote to Hopkins in June 1944, only ten days after the Overlord landings at Normandy, which Hopkins had done so much to bring about: "I can't tell you how much I miss you these days, or how hard it is to do business without you. . . . The President seems just about three times as inaccessible as he did when you were there . . . I think of you every time I read of a gun going off the way it ought to, and a shipload of soldiers being where they ought to be when they are needed. And when I see the ships come rolling off and the supplies going where they ought to go, I say 'Bless Harry Hopkins for that.' I do know what a load you carried. I do know what you accomplished. It was magnificent!"[19]

By October 1944, Hopkins, still gaunt from his recent convalescence, was finally back on his old six-day workweek at the White House. He returned just in time to confront the fires started by Churchill during his controversial mission to Moscow in October 1944. The prime minister had grown increasingly frustrated over Great Britain's gradual marginalization within the Grand Alliance. He grew anxious to take the lead in negotiations between the Western allies and Moscow and establish himself as a go-between. But Roosevelt had made it abundantly clear that he thought the Big Three should meet after the November 1944 election, rather than a hastily arranged Churchill-Stalin meeting. Churchill nevertheless insisted on going to Moscow in October 1944.[20]

Churchill's actual record on Anglo-Soviet relations is sharply at odds with the popular image he did so much, particularly with his voluminous memoirs, to cultivate. This was never more so than during the controversial October 1944 Churchill-Stalin bilateral meetings in Moscow—code-named "Tolstoy." Enormously consequential decisions would be reached without Roosevelt, or Hopkins, present. Action would be taken for territorial and spheres of influence deals that would contribute toward determining the configuration of postwar Europe. Both Roosevelt and Hopkins worried about the enormous amount of mischief Churchill would get up to in the absence of American supervision.

Back at the White House by October 1944, Hopkins reasserted his influence at the time of the Moscow Conference. His preferred Russia expert, Charles Bohlen, advised that it would be preferable if Stalin and Churchill not meet until it was possible for a tripartite meeting including the president. He warned Hopkins that Churchill might seek to use the bilateral Moscow meetings to take actions in the name of both London and Washington. He cautioned that such a Churchill-Stalin meeting might result in a division of Europe into spheres of influence. "At the present juncture of the war in Europe," Bohlen wrote to Hopkins, "it is almost certain that any decisions reached between the Prime Minister and Stalin at the proposed meeting will set the pattern, without American participation, for the future structure of Europe."[21]

Hopkins had grown concerned by Churchill's tendency to freelance with Stalin in the president's absence. Hopkins recalled with dismay that, after Roosevelt had turned in for the evening at Teheran, Churchill had raised the Polish question with Stalin. In the absence of the president, the prime minister told the Soviet leader that he had no attachment to any particular frontier between Poland and the Soviet Union and that the Kremlin's concerns about Soviet security should be the primary factor. This was done without the participation of Polish representatives. Churchill had suggested that the Big Three work out some kind of understanding about Polish frontiers and then offer it as a fait accompli to the Polish government in London.[22] During his discussions with Hopkins two days later, Eden had sheepishly acknowledged this "indiscrete conversation" between Churchill and Stalin over Poland.[23]

Hopkins wanted to prevent further "indiscrete conversations" between Churchill and Stalin about borders, territorial deals, or spheres of influence. Hopkins and Bohlen worried that Churchill would not genuinely attempt to address the Polish problem at Moscow. They presciently feared the prime minister might instead bargain with Stalin over the Balkans, particularly over the status of Greece—a nation the prime minister saw as essential to Great Britain's postwar status in the Eastern Mediterranean and the Middle East. Hopkins also worried that Churchill had a tendency to minimize the importance of the war against Japan, whereas the Americans were seeking to persuade the Russians to intervene in the Far East as soon as possible.[24]

Prompted by Bohlen, Hopkins acted immediately. He called Bohlen to the White House on the morning of October 3 and shared with him Churchill's message to the president hinting that he would speak for both Western Allies at Moscow. A concerned Hopkins shared the president's cable merely wishing Churchill "good luck" at Moscow. Hopkins suspected that Roosevelt had inadvertently implied that Churchill would speak for him. Hopkins knew Churchill well enough to suspect that the president's vague message might give the prime minister the opening he desired to represent both Washington and London.[25]

Hopkins then took the extraordinary action of countermanding the president's message and drafting follow-up cables to both Stalin and Churchill. He clarified that Washington remained interested in all questions related to the war but that no one except the president, and only the president, could represent the United States. The messages also suggested that Ambassador Harriman should attend the meetings as an observer, but only as an observer, for the United States. Hopkins then went to the White House living quarters and met with the president. He urged FDR to inform Churchill and Stalin that no one but the president could speak for the United States. To Bohlen, who witnessed most of this incident, it revealed that the president would reverse himself entirely on Hopkins's recommendation.[26]

Hopkins then drafted Roosevelt's cable to Harriman, warning the ambassador: "I would have very much preferred to have the next conference between the three of us for the very reasons that I have stated to the marshal. I should hope that this bi-lateral conference be nothing more than a preliminary exploration by the British and the Russians leading up to a full dress meeting between the three of us. You, therefore, should bear in mind that there are no subjects of discussion that I can anticipate between the Prime Minister and Stalin in which I will not be greatly interested. It is of importance, therefore, that when this conference is over Mr. Hull and I have complete freedom of action."[27]

Hopkins's simultaneous October 4 draft of Roosevelt's follow-up message to Stalin read: "You, naturally, understand that in this global war there is literally no question, political or military, in which the United States is not interested. I am firmly convinced that the three of us, and only the three of us, can find the solution to the still unresolved questions. In this sense, while appreciating the necessity for the meeting, I prefer to regard your forthcoming talks with Churchill as preliminary to a meeting of the three of us, which, so far as I am concerned, can take place any time after the elections here."[28]

After Harriman delivered the revised message to Stalin, the Soviet leader cabled Roosevelt expressing his appreciation for the clarification. As Hopkins had feared, Churchill left Stalin with the impression that he had been authorized to speak on behalf of the president.[29] Stalin replied: "Your message of October 5 somewhat embarrassed me. I supposed that Mr. Churchill was going to Moscow in accordance with the agreement reached at Quebec. It happened, however, that this supposition of mine does not seem to correspond in reality. It is unknown to me with what questions Mr. Churchill and Mr. Eden are going to Moscow. So far, I have not been informed about this by either one. Mr. Churchill, in his message to me, expressed a desire to come to Moscow, if there would not be any objections on my part. I, of course, gave my consent. Such is the matter in connection with Mr. Churchill's trip to Moscow."[30]

Churchill arrived in Moscow on October 9. The prime minister told Harriman that he merely thought he might engender good feelings by coming to Moscow to see Stalin. Harriman cabled the president that Churchill's stated objective was to explore the Polish question and Yugoslavia "while he wanted to talk out with Stalin the Greeks, etc." Churchill was disappointed that the president would not make this Tolstoy conference a de facto tripartite meeting by empowering Harriman to validate decisions made by Stalin and Churchill. Most troubling was Churchill's desire that Harriman "not participate in his tête-à-têtes with Stalin." While Churchill told Harriman he would keep him "fully informed of all his conferences," Hopkins was troubled to learn that the prime minister would "have most of his important talks with Stalin alone" and that Harriman would only be kept appraised of what Churchill wanted him to know.[31]

Churchill vaguely hinted that he would do the real dealing with Stalin bilaterally.[32] Hopkins worried that Harriman did not seem sufficiently concerned that Churchill desired to reach some sort of arrangement with Stalin to determine the postwar fate of nations from Hungary to Greece. "On Matters in the Balkans," Harriman reported, "Churchill and Eden will try to work out some sort of spheres of influence with the Russians, the British to have a free hand in Greece and the Russians in Rumania and perhaps other countries."[33]

"My desire," Roosevelt cabled Harriman, "is that you attend those conferences to which you are invited, where you should be in the position of a listener in preparation for giving me an accurate report and estimate of the results of the conference when you come to Washington."[34] Harriman did his best to keep Hopkins and the president informed, but he struggled under the critical disadvantage of not being privy to all of the discussions. Harriman warned Hopkins and the president that the prime minister had been using the controversial term *spheres of influence* to discuss the fate of Hungary and the Balkan countries. Churchill sought a Soviet sphere of influence in Eastern Europe in exchange for a British sphere of influence in the southern Balkans and Eastern Mediterranean. These spheres would be defined by percentages, granting the USSR 90 percent in Romania, 75 percent in Bulgaria, and 50 percent in Hungary and Yugoslavia in exchange for 90 percent for Great Britain in Greece. Harriman reported that Churchill had secured Stalin's pledge not to come to the aid of the Greek communists.[35]

The prime minister claimed to be spending an appropriate amount of time on the Polish question, but his messages to Hopkins during the Tolstoy conference omitted much that he did not want the Americans to know.[36] "Everything is most friendly here but the Balkans are in a sad tangle," he cryptically told Hopkins. "Russian attitude [toward Bulgaria] is . . . in the spirit of a loving parent, 'This hurts me more than it does you.' They are taking great interest in Hungary which they mentioned erroneously, was their neighbor. They claim fullest responsibility in Roumania but are prepared largely to disinterest themselves in Greece."[37]

The prime minister then deliberately misled Hopkins: "All these matters are being flogged out by Mr. Eden and Mr. Molotov"—concealing from Hopkins the Churchill-Stalin bilateral "percentages agreement" that sought to establish an Anglo-Soviet sphere of influence understanding for Eastern Europe and the Balkans. Churchill promised to include Harriman in discussions about the future of Germany as well as "the Polish conversations when they begin." He added: "We have so many bones to pick about the Balkans at the present time that we would rather carry the matter a little further *a deux* in order to be able to talk more bluntly than at a larger gathering. I will cable fully to the President about this in a day or two." Churchill evasively cabled to Hopkins: "Balkan affairs are being straightened out."[38]

Harriman confirmed Hopkins's concerns about the results of the Tolstoy discussions. Churchill's negotiations with Stalin had avoided the Far East, and Hopkins suspected that Harriman had failed to grasp the deeper consequences of the Stalin-Churchill negotiations over the Balkans. Having observed Churchill more perceptively than any other American, Hopkins could also sense that the prime minister was shading his messages from Moscow. Hopkins shrewdly suspected that, whatever had actually occurred at Tolstoy, vital information was being deliberately left out of Churchill's reports to Washington.[39] Hopkins did not have to wait long to confront the consequences of Tolstoy: the first place would be Greece, the second Poland.

The president's reelection also preoccupied Hopkins in the autumn of 1944. Worried about the president's chances, as well as the possible succession, Hopkins urged the president to consider replacing Vice President Henry A. Wallace as his running mate with the 1940 Republican presidential candidate Wendell Willkie. In fact, considerations of health aside, the president hinted to several intimates his intention not to serve out a full fourth term if reelected.[40] Some had even begun to think of Willkie as a possible Democratic nominee for president in 1944, but Hopkins suspected that the former 1940 Republican candidate would never be able to swing the base of the party at a Democratic Convention. If the president insisted upon

Willkie as his running mate, however, just as he had insisted upon Wallace in 1940, he might get his way. Harry stressed to the president that when Lincoln ran in 1864 he replaced his 1860 Republican party running mate, Hannibal Hamlin, with a Democratic Unionist, Andrew Johnson.[41]

But in light of the controversy over Wallace's nomination in 1940, FDR hinted that he desired to avoid the appearance of dictating the selection of a running mate in 1944. Roosevelt explained to Hopkins that he had little hope that any vice presidential candidate would gain him votes, but he did expect his running mate not to cost him any votes, which the president assumed Wallace might. The president confided to Hopkins his dismay that Wallace's four years as vice president had exposed his lack of political skills, and that while presiding over the Senate he had failed to make significant political allies on Capitol Hill.[42]

Thus, the biggest political news of the summer of 1944 was the selection of Missouri senator Harry Truman as Roosevelt's running mate. With the president en route to the Pacific at the time of the Convention, Hopkins spoke with Democratic Party leaders and helped from behind the scenes to engineer Truman's ascent. Despite trying to avoid the spotlight, Hopkins also found himself to be a frequent target of Republican nominee Thomas E. Dewey, who called for a "house cleaning" in Washington, which would begin with the firing of Harry Hopkins.[43]

Making matters more difficult for Hopkins, his adversaries in the administration also had the knives out for him. Ickes arranged an impressive lineup of officials to persuade the president to fire Hopkins as a liability to his reelection in 1944.[44] Along with Ickes and Wallace, another disgruntled official was Jimmy Byrnes, who had anticipated replacing Wallace on the ticket, thus putting him one increasingly frail heartbeat away from his lifelong quest for the presidency. Byrnes would forever blame Hopkins for the selection of Truman, but Hopkins reassured Roosevelt that Byrnes likely would not make trouble during the campaign.[45]

Hopkins also sought to mollify a worried Churchill and his political coterie about the election.[46] "I am most anxious to be kept informed," Churchill cabled Hopkins on election night. "I shall certainly be awake at 2:00 A.M. GMT, and anyhow shall be most grateful for the news as it comes in."[47] Hopkins cabled an anxious Churchill that night: "No reason to change opinion that it will be landslide for Roosevelt . . . Very heavy voting in industrial centers. I do not think we will know until 10:00 o'clock our time which is pretty late for even you to stay up."[48] A few hours later, as Hopkins learned of FDR's taking of thirty-seven states to Dewey's twelve, he added: "It's in the bag."[49]

"The election went very much as I had expected," Harry shared with his son, Robert. "Dewey just wasn't good enough and the American people didn't fall for his campaign. I think they decided he had no convictions about anything and was too young and too short for the job. . . . I don't feel particularly elated because I well know the great difficulties ahead, both in war and peace, so I think [the President] is going to have a pretty tough four years."[50]

Despite Roosevelt's reelection, Harry was ambivalent about the future. He realized that the challenges of the peace would prove every bit as difficult as those during the war. "I cannot bring myself to feel boastful about this election," Hopkins shared with Vice President Wallace. "Elated as I am, personally, for the President's victory, I realize that the four years ahead are going to be the most difficult ones this country has ever faced."[51] Hopkins warned Vice President-elect Truman: "The next 4 years are going to be, in many ways, the most difficult that our country has ever seen and we must be sure that the American people understand that the war and the peace must be won in their interest. There is no such thing as a settled American foreign policy that does not have the full strength of the American people behind it."[52]

Hopkins demonstrated his enduring influence by spearheading a postelection reorganization of the State Department. He fashioned a new diplomatic team headed by another of his protégés, Edward Stettinius, whose replacement of Cordell Hull as Secretary of State was seen as reinforcing Hopkins's growing control over foreign policy. Characterized in the press as Stettinius's "patron," Hopkins's critics understood that he was the instigator of the selection and that he had further enhanced and consolidated his power with the reorganization. Having served as Undersecretary of State for the previous year and, prior to that, chairman of the War Resources Board and administrator of Lend-Lease, Stettinius was certainly qualified for the post. Yet many observers suspected that Hopkins, working through Stettinius, had made himself the de facto secretary of state.[53]

The president's reelection provided no respite from the crises of the war. Adding to the strain, just as Hopkins had feared, the October 1944 Churchill-Stalin Tolstoy conference had done little to advance the issues of most vital importance to Hopkins, such as the future of Germany, the war against Japan, and the formation of the United Nations Organization. To the contrary, in dealing with Churchill's focus on Greece, the bilateral agreements reached at Moscow may have jeopardized American objectives by giving Stalin the impression that he had been granted a free hand in Eastern Europe and the Balkans.[54]

Hopkins grew alarmed over subsequent British actions in Italy and Greece. In Italy, Churchill's opposition to the American-supported antifascist Italian exile, Carlo Sforza, revealed divergent Anglo-American views on the future of Italy. The British blocked the pro-American Sforza from becoming Foreign Minister, and the Americans opposed Churchill's desire to maintain the profascist King Victor Emmanuel on the Italian throne. Hopkins urged that the United States should boldly pursue its objectives in Italy and not meekly acquiesce to Churchill's. Ultimately, the Churchill-backed Victor Emmanuel, indelibly tainted by his backing of Mussolini's fascist regime, sought to rescue his monarchy by nominating his son, Umberto, as successor. The Italian people responded in June 1946 by voting for a constitutional referendum, thus creating a republic and abolishing the monarchy entirely.[55]

Provoking even greater headaches was Greece, where Anglo-American disagreement arose over Churchill's desire to restore the monarchy and crush the antifascist resistance. Hopkins worried that the Greek crisis would cause irreparable injury to the Alliance. The newspapers and members of Congress began asking why Lend-Lease supplies should be used to kill heroic Greek resistors to fascism. Following the controversial killing of Greek civilians by British forces, Hopkins sent Churchill a series of sharp warnings that the Greek entanglement was establishing a dangerous precedent and alienating American public opinion. Hopkins feared that Churchill's actions in Greece might come back to haunt the Grand Alliance, perhaps with regard to the USSR's neighbors.[56] Britain's crushing of the Greek resistance might create the impression of equivalency between British actions in Greece and Soviet actions in areas where the Red Army was entering. In fact, during Hopkins's May 1945 mission to Moscow, Stalin adopted precisely that track by favorably comparing Soviet actions in Poland to British repression in Greece.[57]

Hopkins grew concerned that British actions in Greece might shatter the Grand Alliance before Hitler could be defeated. He anxiously monitored the Kremlin for its reaction to the situation in Greece. Would Moscow merely stand aside while British troops crushed the Greek resistance, which included a substantial number of Greek communists? To Hopkins's enormous relief, the Kremlin scrupulously adhered to the agreements made by Stalin and Churchill at the October 1944 Moscow meeting.[58]

Still, Hopkins had to handle a furious Churchill. The prime minister angrily cabled Hopkins insisting upon Roosevelt's support for British actions in Greece.[59] "I hope you will tell our friend," Churchill wrote to Hopkins, referring to the president, "that the establishment of law and order in and around Athens is essential to all future measures of magnanimity and consolation towards Greece." Churchill argued that after the Greek resistance was crushed there would be "time for talking." He then asserted: "I consider we have a right to the President's support in the policy we are following. If it can be said in the streets of Athens that the United States are against us, then more British blood will be shed and much more Greek. It grieves me very much to see signs of our drifting apart at a time when unity becomes even more important, as danger recedes and faction arises."[60]

Churchill subsequently phoned Hopkins in a "very angry" and "stirred up" mood. The prime minister denounced the American navy for opposing the shipping of supplies to the British in Greece. Hopkins worked with admirals Leahy and King to resolve the crisis. American troops, Hopkins believed, should stay clear of the Greek fiasco. But denying the British shipping was "like walking out on a member of your family who was in trouble."[61]

Hopkins warned Churchill on December 16: "Public opinion here deteriorating because of Greek situation."[62] Churchill replied: "I am distressed and puzzled by your message. . . . I hope you will not hesitate to telegraph me on any points on which you think we, or I personally, have been in error and what you would advise, because I have great trust in your judgment and friendship even if I may at times look at matters from a different angle."[63]

A few days later, Hopkins sought to repair the shaken relations with a distraught Churchill. "I want you to know, on this fateful Christmas, that I am well aware of the heavy burdens you carry. Since our first meeting I have tried to share them with you. I would share them now."[64] Hopkins nevertheless remained sharply critical of British actions in Greece and Italy. He felt that the Greek controversy should have been handled with much more skill and that the British should stop aggressively meddling in the affairs of liberated countries.[65]

Hopkins also faced problems with Stalin. Throughout 1944 Hopkins feared that growing antagonisms between the Kremlin and the Polish government-in-exile made relations between them impossible. The crisis over Poland was obvious well before Yalta, as both Bohlen and Harriman had warned Hopkins of growing Soviet intransigence over the composition of the Polish government. Hopkins wanted the administration to take a more hands-on approach to Poland and create a set of achievable, realistic objectives.[66]

As part of this, he felt the need for another meeting of the Big Three.

The 1944 campaign had distracted Roosevelt from Big Three matters. Nevertheless, by the middle of September 1944 the president, too, sensed that a variety of pressing challenges necessitated another Big Three gathering. At Teheran in November 1943, Stalin had made a firm commitment on Soviet participation in the war against Japan. The precise dates and the extent of Soviet participation needed to be confirmed. Moreover, the situation in Asia needed a thoroughgoing understanding, particularly with regard to Soviet aims and objectives. Hopkins knew from Teheran that the Russians wanted concessions in the Far East as a condition of going to war with Japan. Hopkins thought it necessary that the United States protect China's interests in discussions with the other powers. Matters tentatively negotiated previously, such as the next steps in the war against Germany and Japan, the future disposition of Germany, the configuration of the United Nations Organization, and the role of France, also needed to be clarified.

Hopkins considered a wide variety of locations for the conference, none of which initially included Russia. He warned the president that it was unlikely that Stalin would leave Russia in light of the war situation. If the president were not careful, Hopkins advised, he would wind up with, in apparent reference to Churchill, "a lot of long-winded, irritating cables back and forth getting exactly nowhere."[67] Hopkins assumed the Big Three would have little choice but to meet somewhere in the USSR and suggested that a meeting might take place in the more salubrious region of the Crimea. The president did not object to this but, with the upcoming elections in mind, he considered any pre-November meeting impossible. Roosevelt also suspected that Dewey would exploit any announcement that Russia might host the next meeting of the Big Three. The president thus postponed all such planning until after the election.

Hopkins talked to Andrei Gromyko, the Soviet ambassador in Washington, who confirmed that Stalin would never leave Russia at such a critical time in the war. Hopkins inquired whether there was any place in the Crimea where a conference might be held. A couple of weeks later the president received a message from Stalin saying he understood the president might be willing to go to the Crimea and suggested Yalta as a possibility. "Ambassador Gromyko has informed me about his recent conversation with Mr. Hopkins," Stalin wrote to Roosevelt in October, "in which Mr. Hopkins expressed an idea that you could arrive in the Black Sea at the end of November and meet with me on the Soviet Black Sea coast. I would extremely welcome the realization of this intention."[68]

All of the president's close advisers, save Hopkins, reacted with varying degrees of apprehension to his going to Russia. Hopkins later observed, "Most did not like or trust the Russians anyway and could not understand why the president of the United States should cart himself all over the world to meet Stalin. This argument carried no weight with me. The all-important thing was to get the meeting. There was not a chance of getting that meeting outside of the Crimea." Knowing Roosevelt as well as he did, Hopkins remained confident that the president, always a curious and intrepid traveler, would gamely go to the Crimea, because "it was a part of the world he had never visited and his adventurous spirit was forever leading him to go to unusual places and, on his part, the election being over, he would no longer be disturbed about it for political reasons."[69]

To outward observers, Hopkins appeared to have reclaimed his position of influence with FDR. A series of *Time* magazine profiles of Hopkins observed: "After eleven years of the kaleidoscopic changes of the New Deal, Harry Hopkins was still the man Franklin Roosevelt most trusts. . . . As the Roosevelt Administration enters its fourth term this week, Hopkins is, more than ever, the President's right arm."[70] Yet the reality was more complicated. Throughout 1944 and 1945, there was growing evidence suggesting that Hopkins's influence was gradually waning. His lengthy absences from Washington, coupled with the president's steady physical decline, meant that Hopkins did not have the substantive influence over policy that he had enjoyed as recently as the Teheran Conference.[71]

The president nevertheless dispatched Hopkins on a short advance exploratory trip by air to Britain, France, and Italy to obtain the latest information from these three countries and to help prepare for the upcoming conference.[72] Hopkins flew to Britain on January 21 and remained there for three days, conferring mostly with Churchill and Eden.[73] "Have had very satisfactory visit," Hopkins cabled the president on January 24. "Leaving for Paris tomorrow. Churchill well. He says that if we had spent ten years on research, we could not have found a worse place in the world than [Yalta] but that he feels that he can survive it by bringing an adequate supply of whiskey. He claims it is good for typhus and deadly on lice which thrive in those parts."[74]

At Yalta, Hopkins's precarious health prevented him from playing as large a role as he had at Teheran the year before. Moreover, Hopkins's hand-picked surrogate, Secretary of State Stettinius, was at the conference, and thus Hopkins could remain in the background. Stettinius remembered Hopkins "was so weak that it was remarkable that he could be as active as he was. He fought his way through difficult and trying conferences on coffee, cigarettes, an amazingly small amount of food . . . and sheer fortitude. He was so exhausted by the time we reached Yalta, for instance, that he was confined to bed almost all of the time except when Roosevelt, Churchill, and Stalin were in session."[75]

The president's daughter, Anna Roosevelt, now serving as FDR's unofficial gatekeeper, learned from Stettinius that Hopkins was very ill. She noted in the diary she kept during the conference: "So, after dinner I went in to see Harry, and found him in a stew. He gave me a long song and dance that

FDR <u>must</u> see Churchill in the morning for a long meeting to dope out how those two are going to map out the Conf.; made a few insulting remarks to the effect that after all FDR had asked for this job and that now, whether he liked it or not, he had to do the work, and that it was imperative that FDR and Churchill have some prearrangements before the big Conf. started. I asked him if he didn't think this course might stir up some distrust among our Russian brethren, and Harry passed me off very lightly." Dr. Howard Bruenn, the president's cardiologist, explained to Anna that Hopkins's health greatly worried him and that he feared Harry might be developing an immunity to his medications. "Certainly it didn't seem to me that his mind was clicking or his judgment good," Anna observed, "or maybe it's just that I had never quite realized how pro-British Harry is." Anna went to see Hopkins the next morning. "Found him much more calm. It's quite obvious that he thinks I'm trying to save FDR too much, so I'm augmenting my 'buttering' process in this direction, and Harry seems to be responding nicely! He said he didn't think a long meeting was necessary with Churchill."[76]

The minutes of the Yalta sessions nevertheless reveal Hopkins's behind-the-scenes influence, frequently passing handwritten notes to the president and reminding him of obscure details. Churchill's personal physician, the conniving Charles McMoran Wilson, observed that Hopkins "knows the President's moods like a wife watching the domestic climate. He will sit patiently for hours, blinking like a cat, waiting for the right moment to put his point; and if it never comes he is content to leave it to another time."[77]

Aside from the substance of the conference, Harry had his own challenges at Yalta. He sought to marginalize the disgruntled Jimmy Byrnes, whom the president hoped might help sell agreements made at Yalta to the Congress and the conservative wing of the Democratic Party. Yet by all accounts, Byrnes sulked and threw childlike tantrums throughout the conference and departed early in an angry huff. A furious Byrnes complained to anyone who would listen with charges that Hopkins was being granted too much access to the president.[78] Harry also had to address a minor family crisis. A delighted Robert Hopkins shocked his father with news that he had obtained permission from Stalin to accompany the Red Army as it fought its way into the heart of Berlin. When Robert bounded into his father's room with the news, Harry threw cold water on the idea. "If you go," Harry curtly told Robert, "the Russians will never let you near the front. If you managed to get to the front, they would never let you take any pictures. If you were clever enough to take some pictures, they would never let them out of their control—so why go?" Robert protested that it had all already been cleared with General Marshall and Stalin. Robert asked: "What should I tell them?"

"That's your problem!" Harry impatiently replied.[79]

Harry spent much of the conference plenary sessions working to reach agreements over the composition of the United Nations, the postwar role of France, the ultimate disposition of Germany, as well as attempting to discern the true meaning of Churchill's frequently off-topic comments. During one plenary session, Hopkins warned the president that Churchill was opposing an early meeting of the United Nations Organization. Roosevelt replied to Hopkins: "All this is rot! Local politics," to which Hopkins replied: "I am quite sure now he is thinking about the next election in Britain."[80]

Regarding Poland, Hopkins understood that Stalin sought to create a Polish government exclusively from the Warsaw communist group previously based in Lublin. Hopkins and Bohlen collaborated in drafting a letter for the president to be dispatched at once to Stalin, summarizing and clarifying the American position that the future Polish government should be more diverse and include elements other than the Lublin group.[81] Hopkins understood the seriousness of the Polish question. If not resolved, it threatened to shape American and British perceptions of Soviet behavior and thus had the potential to undermine Moscow's relations with the Western powers.[82]

Roosevelt, too, certainly realized the seriousness of the Polish question, but perhaps took some encouragement in public opinion polls in the weeks after the Yalta Conference revealing that the public overwhelmingly supported the administration's foreign policy. Back in January, public opinion polling had revealed that the public supported the administration's policies by a margin of only 3 percent. By late February, following Yalta, that margin of support had grown to an astonishing 56 percent.[83] Hopkins nevertheless understood, however, that American policy toward Poland might not have been viable or sustainable in the longer term.[84]

On the matter of the postwar treatment of Germany, Hopkins advised the president to postpone a decision on dismemberment. Hopkins suggested that the most contentious issues be referred to the foreign ministers.[85] Hopkins told the president: "The Russians have given in so much at this conference that I don't think we should let them down. Let the British disagree if they want to—and continue their disagreement [later]."[86]

To Harry's relief, and in light of the desire of American military chiefs, Stalin confirmed his pledge to enter the Far East war before the assault on the main Japanese islands. The Americans feared that Stalin might have insisted upon acquiring Manchuria, but he did not. Bohlen later reflected that the Far East decisions were "a diplomatic price for a military objective

"I can never forget him as he was at Yalta," General Marshall recalled after the war, "wrestling with all those problems, day and night, on his sickbed."[89]

then regarded as of vital importance to the saving of American lives in the war against Japan . . . I find it difficult to believe that the President did this for any reason other than the military importance of having Russia in before we attempted to land in Japan proper."[87]

The president planned to give an address about the results of the Yalta Conference to a joint session of Congress upon his return, and he wanted Hopkins to remain with him on his sea journey back to the United States to assist with its preparation. Hopkins let Roosevelt know that he preferred to leave the ship at Algiers. Unfortunately, for all that they had achieved together in peace and war, Roosevelt and Hopkins's final parting was somewhat curt and abrupt. He would never see the president again.[88]

Hopkins felt that the Soviets had given more than the Americans or British. In this view, he was strongly supported by General Marshall and Secretary Stettinius. Hopkins was optimistic upon leaving Yalta. "We really

At the Livadia Palace during the Yalta Conference. Left to right: Secretary of State Edward Stettinius, Major General L. S. Kuter, Admiral E. J. King, General George C. Marshall, Ambassador Averill Harriman, Admiral William Leahy, and President Roosevelt, February 4, 1945. Souce: Signal Corps.

believed in our hearts that this was the dawn of a new day we had all been praying for and talking about for so many years," Hopkins told Bob Sherwood. "The Russians had proved they could be reasonable and farseeing and there wasn't any doubt in the minds of the president or any of us that we could live with them and get along with them peacefully for as far into the future as any of us could imagine."[90]

~

# CHAPTER EIGHT

# The Final Mission to Moscow

Practically every time Harry had to be carried out on a stretcher, I thought time and time again that he was finished insofar as any further work was concerned. But always, when he was really needed, he was there.

—*George Marshall*[1]

On April 12, 1945, Hopkins was back in his room at the Mayo Clinic, convalescing from his post-Yalta physical collapse, when the phone rang. His friend Chip Bohlen was on the other end calling from Washington. Chip stunned Hopkins with the news that FDR had suddenly died earlier that day in Warm Springs, Georgia. After a long silence on the other end of the line, Hopkins finally said, "I guess I better be going to Washington."[2]

"I cannot tell you what goes through my mind and heart," Hopkins cabled a stunned Winston Churchill. "All I know is that we lost one of our greatest friends, and the world its most outstanding champion of human freedom and justice. I still find it difficult to believe that our gallant friend has gone."[3] Churchill cabled back to Hopkins: "I understand how deep your feelings of grief must be. . . . I feel with you we have lost one of our greatest friends and one of the most valiant champions of the causes for which we fight. I feel a very painful personal loss quite apart from the times of public action, which bound us so closely together. I had a true affection for Franklin."[4]

To Clementine Churchill, Hopkins cabled: "I feel so proud that I had some part in the development of the devoted friendship between Winston and the President."[5] Churchill's closest confidant, Brendan Bracken, observed to Hopkins: "No one can overestimate the world's debt to Roosevelt. It is no exaggeration to say the president was one of the saviors of civilization. Himself he would not save."[6]

Cabling Stalin, Hopkins said: "I feel that Russia has lost her greatest friend in America. The president was ever deeply impressed by your determination and confidence that the Nazi tyrants of the world will be driven from power forever."[7] And, to Chiang Kai-shek: "You can be sure that those of us who remain behind will do everything in our power to promote the cause of a free China but the oppressed people throughout the world have lost their greatest champion."[8]

Hopkins telephoned Bob Sherwood the day after Roosevelt's death. He spoke with little sentiment. "You and I have got something great that we can take with us all the rest of our lives," he told Sherwood. "It's a great realization. Because we know it's true what so many people believed about him and what made them love him. The president never let them down. That's what you and I can remember. Oh, we all know he could be exasperating, and he could seem to be temporizing and delaying, and he'd get us all worked up when we thought he was making too many concessions to expediency. But all of that was in the little things, the unimportant things—and he knew exactly how little and how unimportant they really were. But in the big things—all of the things that were of real, permanent importance—he never let the people down."[9]

After the White House service, Hopkins asked Sherwood and his wife to come home with him to his house in Georgetown. Sherwood sat up with him as Hopkins talked. "God damn it," Hopkins said to Sherwood. "Now we've got to get to work on our own. This is where we've really got to begin. We've had it too easy all this time. Whatever we thought was the matter with the world, whatever we felt ought to be done about it, we could take our ideas to him, and if he thought there was any merit in them, or if anything that we said got him started on a train of thought of his own, then we'd see him go ahead and do it, and no matter how tremendous it might be or how idealistic he wasn't scared of it. Well—he isn't there now, and we've got to find a way to do things by ourselves."[10]

The new president knew more fully than most the role Hopkins played in the war. In fact, immediately after Truman took the oath of office at 7:09 p.m. on the day Roosevelt died, he suddenly looked around the room and asked: "Where's Harry Hopkins?"[11] In his former capacity as head of the

Senate's so-called wartime watchdog Truman Committee, he understood that Hopkins had been Roosevelt's wartime eyes and ears, taking on sensitive missions and attending wartime conferences, and he asked Hopkins to brief him "on all phases of the job" of president. Truman told Hopkins he desired to appoint him to his cabinet to have him close at hand. Hopkins demurred and instead suggested that other old New Dealers should resign to give the new president a free hand to choose his own people and enjoy a fresh start. "Truman should have his own people around him, not Roosevelt's," Hopkins advised Truman's political handler, Missouri political boss Bob Hannegan. "If we were around, we'd always be looking at him and he'd know we were thinking, 'The President wouldn't do it that way!' "[12]

When Germany surrendered at the beginning of May, congratulations poured in to the surviving member of the Roosevelt-Hopkins partnership. From the San Francisco Conference, Molotov, Eden, and Stettinius dispatched a joint toast to Hopkins. "At dinner last night," they cabled from San Francisco, "we three drank a special toast to you in sincere recognition of the outstanding part you personally have played in bringing our three countries together in the common cause. We regret that you are not with us at this moment of victory."[13] Churchill graciously wrote to Hopkins: "Among all those in the Grand Alliance, warriors or statesmen, who struck deadly blows at the enemy and brought peace nearer, you will ever hold an honoured place."[14]

"For myself," George Marshall wrote, "I wish to tell you this, that you personally have been of invaluable service to me in the discharge of my duties in this war. Time after time you have done for me things I was finding it exceedingly difficult to do for myself and always in matters of the gravest import. You have been utterly selfless as well as courageous and purely objective in your contribution to the war effort."[15] Hopkins nonetheless felt it a cruel fate that FDR was buried in "that little garden in Hyde Park" while "no man in the world contributed more to victory and freedom." Commemorating the day of Germany's final capitulation, he emotionally told a national radio audience: "I believe that the free people of the earth will forever bless his name."[16]

Privately, Hopkins grew concerned that the opportunity for an enduring peace had been jeopardized with Roosevelt's death.[17] He thus took an intense interest in the post-Yalta U.S.-Soviet relations.[18] Hopkins had long believed that it was imperative to avoid postwar conflict with the Soviet Union. "It is in our self-interest to play ball with Russia," Hopkins had written back in November 1943. "The logical thing is to cooperate with Russia, do business with Russia, be friends with Russia, make the maintenance of armaments by her and by us for defense against one another unnecessary."[19]

In the wake of the president's death, Hopkins seemed to be the only remaining American official in whom Stalin had confidence.[20] Urged on by Stettinius and Harriman, Truman decided that Hopkins might achieve more in Moscow to rescue U.S.-Soviet relations than anyone else. "I believe that Stalin's feelings for Hopkins went back to July 1941," Harriman recalled. "Hopkins was the first Western visitor to Moscow after the German attack, when things were going pretty badly. Stalin evidently saw in Hopkins a man who, in spite of ill health, had made that long, exhausting and hazardous journey to bring help. It was an example of courage and determination that impressed Stalin deeply. He had not forgotten."[21]

By sending one of the leading proponents of the policy of cooperation with the Soviet Union, Truman would convey a clear message about his desire for frank talk with Stalin. The Soviets would respect this gesture. Charles Bohlen thought Hopkins a smart choice because he was "esteemed by the Bolsheviks because of his forthright honesty and his refusal to indulge in any diplomatic subterfuge or ambiguity." Bohlen later revealed that Stalin once confided that Harry Hopkins was the first American to whom he had spoken *po dushe*—"from the soul."[22]

Hopkins understood he would face enormous challenges at Moscow. Relations between Moscow and Washington had rapidly deteriorated since Roosevelt's death on April 12. Hopkins's agenda included rescuing the faltering United Nations Conference, salvaging the increasingly doubtful upcoming meeting of the Big Three in Berlin, reaffirming the Kremlin's previous pledge to intervene against Japan in the Far East, clearing up the growing discord over Poland, and, time permitting, discussing the fate of a defeated Germany.[23]

It was an ambitious agenda, but Hopkins was realistic. He had long thought it best to lower expectations with regard to relations with the Russians, work hard for the best outcome you could possibly achieve, keep matters in perspective, and strive to mitigate the inevitable misunderstandings. Churchill you could manage, Hopkins thought. The prime minister's eccentricities and self-absorption were tolerable, even typical of men of his stature. But the enigmas of Stalin and the Soviet system always remained slightly beyond his comprehension.[24]

In his book *Roosevelt's Lost Alliances*, historian Frank Costigliola makes the case that Hopkins began gravitating at this time toward Harriman's more skeptical view of U.S.-Soviet relations. Indeed, Hopkins certainly held out hope that he would continue to be relevant to the new Truman administration, and thus the perception of a harder line may be evidence that Hopkins intuitively understood that, with the death of Roosevelt, the spirit of cooperation might be subject to adjustments. Another plausible explanation for Hopkins's altered perspective was his hope to persuade Stalin to accept the blunt reality that future relations would be constantly influenced by "perceptions" of Soviet behavior and that Poland currently represented the biggest symbol of that behavior. Moreover, Hopkins's private views, expressed in a political testament six weeks after the mission, indicate that he continued to see cooperation and mutual understanding as the only hope of avoiding future conflict.[25]

General Marshall was astonished that Hopkins would assent to take on another mission to negotiate with Stalin, writing to him: "You have literally given of your physical strength during the past three years to a degree that has been, in my opinion, heroic and will never be appreciated except by your intimates."[26] Marshall later recalled: "Practically every time Harry had to be carried out on a stretcher, I thought time and time again that he was finished insofar as any further work was concerned. But always, when he was really needed, he was there."[27] Others such as Harold Ickes felt otherwise. "I am very sorry that Truman is hanging on to Harry and I am surprised, too. Apparently, Hopkins has been able to persuade Truman that he knows all that there is to know about the intricacies of Stalin's mind."[28]

No British representative was present during any of Hopkins's meetings with Stalin. Hopkins learned from the British ambassador, Archibald Clark Kerr, that Churchill was "obviously quite disturbed about the whole business but there was not very much he could say because it was probably to his political interest to get agreement on the Polish question before the British elections."[29] Truman thus dispatched Joseph E. Davies to London to partially mollify Churchill and further demonstrate that he was relying on FDR's trusted advisers on U.S.-Soviet relations. He also cabled Stalin explaining that Hopkins would confidentially discuss "the complicated and important questions with which we are faced" and then "return immediately to Washington in order to report personally to me."[30]

Prior to Hopkins's departure, Truman shared with him his great anxiety at the state of U.S.-Soviet relations. Truman expressed to Hopkins his sincere hope to continue Roosevelt's policy of cooperation with the Soviet Union as well as all wartime arrangements, both formal and informal, which Roosevelt and Stalin had worked out together.[31]

During his opening meeting with Stalin, Hopkins shrewdly played upon the recent death of FDR and ties of trust dating back to the establishment of his relationship with Stalin from the dark days of July 1941. Hopkins began by explaining Roosevelt's state of mind just prior to his death. He told Stalin that, on the return trip from Yalta, it had become clear to him that the president was dangerously exhausted and that his life force was slipping away. On the other hand, Hopkins continued, on the very morning of the president's death, he had plunged into his work with enthusiasm and was preparing his upcoming address to the United Nations Conference in San Francisco. Hopkins shared with Stalin that Roosevelt never regained consciousness after his collapse. He died, as far as anyone knew, without much suffering. A quick, easy death, Hopkins perhaps knowingly observed, was certainly preferable to lingering as an invalid in a state of slow decline.[32]

Hopkins allowed that he, too, was gravely ill, and that he would never have agreed to make such a mission had he not grasped the seriousness of the current impasse. Nor would he have come to Moscow had he not been convinced that the current troubling trends in relations could be reversed and that a common basis could be found to resume moving forward. He emphasized that President Truman would find it impossible to continue Roosevelt's policies without the support of public opinion and, equally important, the late president's network of supporters.

Hopkins also recalled for Stalin their first meeting in the Kremlin in July 1941 during the early weeks of the German offensive. He reminded Stalin of that earlier mission, coming at a time when many in Moscow and Washington predicted an inevitable German victory, and Roosevelt's conviction to the contrary that the USSR would survive. Hopkins told Stalin that Yalta had given the president a renewed hope that the United States and the Soviet Union could work out their differences in peacetime as they had in war. He remembered that Roosevelt deeply appreciated the Big Three's toast at Yalta that their next meeting would take place upon the ruins of Hitler's Berlin.

Hopkins emphasized that the primary reason President Truman had dispatched him to Moscow was to discuss questions of the fundamental relationship between the United States and the Soviet Union. Only two months before, there had been overwhelming sympathy among the American people for the USSR and complete support for President Roosevelt's policies toward the Soviet Union. Such admiration came easily because of the heroic achievements of the Soviet people but also from Roosevelt's leadership and the magnificent way the two nations had worked together to defeat nazism.

Hopkins suggested they not focus on the minority of Roosevelt haters and Red baiters in America. They should instead consider the millions of Americans who had supported Roosevelt's policies and believed that, despite different political and economic ideologies, the United States and the Soviet Union could work together after the war to bring about a genuine peace for future generations. Hopkins assured Stalin "with all the earnestness at his command" that the large body of American opinion that had supported Roosevelt's Russia policy had recently grown concerned about relations with Russia. In the six weeks since Roosevelt's death, the deterioration of public opinion had become so dire as to jeopardize future relations between Russia and America.

Hopkins sought to explain American public opinion to Stalin. He suspected that Stalin might not grasp the genuine sense of disillusionment with U.S.-Soviet relations slowly settling over America. Hopkins acknowledged that there had always been a "small minority, the Hearsts and the McCormicks, who had been against the policy of cooperation with the Soviet Union. These men had also been bitter political enemies of President Roosevelt but had never had any backing from the American people as was shown by the fact that against their opposition President Roosevelt had been four times elected President." Hopkins underscored, however, that there was also a discernable change of heart among many of the very people who had supported Roosevelt's policy of U.S.-Soviet cooperation. Even the allies of Roosevelt's policy had grown alarmed at the present trend of relations and did not understand what had changed so abruptly. Yet it was obvious that if present trends continued, the entire structure of world cooperation and relations with the Soviet Union—which President Roosevelt and Stalin had labored so hard to build—would be destroyed.

Hopkins emphasized that both Washington and Moscow had worldwide interests but that the two nations could still work out almost all of the political or economic differences between them. At Yalta, the United States and the USSR appeared to have found a formula for resolving their differences. His goal during his current mission, he explained, was to return to that formula to resolve the current difficulties. He concluded his opening comments by explaining that public opinion in the United States was influenced by specific incidents. He emphasized the ongoing Polish entanglement as the chief culprit for the deterioration of relations between the United States and the USSR since the president's death.

After a brief pause, Stalin replied to Hopkins's opening statement by asserting that the Soviet Union desired a friendly Poland, whereas Great Britain sought to revive the system of the cordon sanitaire on and around the USSR's borders. Hopkins immediately interjected that neither the U.S. government nor its people had any such designs, and Washington desired friendly states on the USSR's borders. Hopkins understood that Stalin would stubbornly insist that the USSR's borders were protected from what the Soviet leader perceived as states hostile to Soviet interests that, in light of the recent war, was probably unavoidable. Moreover, Hopkins remained unconvinced that Russia's historic interests in Eastern Europe posed a sufficient threat to American primary interests to justify a confrontation.[33]

Somewhat taken aback by Hopkins's abrupt retort, Stalin explained that he was speaking only of the hostile designs of Great Britain, not the United States. Hopkins again interjected that he wanted to firmly emphasize the importance that he, personally, attached to the present trend of events with regard to Poland, which absolutely needed to be addressed. He had therefore been glad to hear Stalin say that he thought the question could be settled.[34]

Hopkins said the other important questions he wished to discuss involved the Pacific War and China. He candidly told Stalin that he desired to bring back to the American military chiefs a clearer idea of the approximate date of Soviet entry into the Pacific War. Hopkins concluded their first meeting by reemphasizing that he would never have dragged himself out of his sick-bed to come all the way to Moscow had he not believed that the future relationship of the United States and the Soviet Union would determine the fate of hundreds of millions of people. Nor would he have journeyed so far had he not believed that the current difficulties could ultimately be reconciled.

Stalin surprised Hopkins with his sudden agreeableness, telling the envoy that he was "entirely at Mr. Hopkins's service and now that war in Europe was over he had more time at his disposal than he had, for example, a year ago." Seeking to conclude their first day on a friendlier note, Hopkins told Stalin that he hoped Soviet authorities would soon find Hitler's body. Stalin, knowing full well that Hitler's remains had been recovered in Berlin, lied to Hopkins by asserting that Hitler was not dead but likely hiding somewhere. Whatever his reasons, Stalin persisted in his subterfuge by suggesting to Hopkins that Hitler probably fled to Japan in a German submarine.[35]

Hours after the first meeting, an exhausted Hopkins cabled President Truman. "Stalin listened with the utmost attention to our description of the present state of American public opinion and gave us the impression that the drift of events disturbed him also."[36]

The discussions grew heated on the second day when Stalin told Hopkins that Kremlin officials felt alarm over Washington's change of tone toward them. It was Stalin's impression that, with Hitler now defeated, the Americans no longer needed the USSR's enormous sacrifices. Stalin confronted Hopkins with several examples, but his biggest grievance remained Poland.[37] Hopkins knew the extent of Stalin's hatred for the London Poles. He had been subjected to Stalin's forceful exposition on the subject only a few months before at Yalta.

Stalin contended that the Yalta Agreement provided that the existing Polish government was to be reconstructed and that anyone with common sense could see this meant that the present government was to form the basis of the new. He said no other understanding of the Yalta discussions could be possible. It is true, Stalin continued, that the Russians are patient in the interest of a common cause, but their patience had clearly reached its limits. He emphatically told Hopkins that, although the Russians are "simple people," they should never be regarded as fools, a mistake the West always made about them. Nor were the Russians so blind that they could not see what was going on before their eyes.

Hopkins replied that the Polish question had grown into a symbol of Moscow and Washington's ability to work collaboratively. The United States had no "special interests in Poland and no special desire to see any particular kind of government" and "would accept any government in Poland which was desired by the Polish people and was at the same time friendly to the Soviet Government." Hopkins further said that the Polish people should be given the right to free elections to choose their own government and that Poland should be genuinely independent. What Hopkins seems to have had in mind for Poland was a solution that more closely resembled the ultimate outcome in Finland, where the Finns enjoyed self-determination and an open society while their nonaligned stance posed no threat to the security of the USSR. With regard to Poland, Hopkins explained to Stalin, the U.S. government and the American people had grown concerned because Moscow seemed to be working unilaterally to achieve its narrow objectives without regard to the will of the Polish people or global opinion.

Stalin parried Hopkins by reminding him that the USSR insisted upon a "friendly Poland" because, in the past quarter-century, the Germans had twice invaded Russia through Poland. Stalin emphasized that historical precedents had revealed that a Poland hostile to the Soviet Union was essential to constructing a *cordon sanitaire* to isolate the USSR. It was thus in Moscow's "vital interest" that Poland be both strong and friendly. Reassuring Hopkins that "the Soviet system was not exportable," Stalin claimed that he had no desire to Sovietize Poland. Poland's uniqueness precluded such a policy, but he reaffirmed his insistence upon a "friendly Poland" as a "vital interest" of the USSR. Stalin also "recognized the right of the United States as a world power to participate in the Polish question" and that Soviet interests in Poland did "not in any way exclude those of England and the United States." But, Stalin added, the Red Army's march across Poland had necessitated the establishment of a Polish government, and the Moscow-bred Lublin group was the logical choice. To Hopkins's dismay, Stalin further pointed out "that Soviet action in Poland had been more successful than British action in Greece and at no time had they been compelled to undertake the measures which [the British] had done in Greece." Stalin then presented his proposed solution to the Polish question: the current Warsaw government might be diversified to include four members from other groups. Of course, they had to be friendly to the USSR and the other Allies.[38]

On day three, Hopkins turned to the U.S. military's desire to secure the Red Army's entry into the war against Japan. This issue had been at the very top of General Marshall's priorities for Hopkins to raise with Stalin. Hopkins always envisioned the potentially enormous impact from Russian entry on the war against Japan. He understood just how the Japanese leadership feared this and how devastating a Soviet intervention in the Far East would prove to Japanese morale.[39] Stalin pledged to an elated Hopkins that the Soviet Union would make good on the Yalta agreements and enter the war against Japan within two to three months after the surrender of Germany. He estimated that Soviet intervention would occur on or around August 8, 1945.[40]

Hopkins expressed his concern about Japanese peace feelers toward Moscow. There had been much alarm in Washington that Tokyo would seek to obtain a "conditional" surrender through the good offices of Moscow. Hopkins was relieved to hear Stalin reaffirm his commitment to the unconditional surrender of Japan. Stalin observed that Japan would indeed do everything it could to preserve its military as a basis for a future war of revenge. The Russian leader indicated that he desired the elimination of the imperial house, fearing it might serve as a postwar inspiration for Japanese ultranationalists. Stalin thought the war, which he described as a once-in-one-hundred-year event, offered a rare opportunity to put Japan on a new course to guarantee decades of postwar peace.

Hopkins also raised the future of China. Stalin encouragingly told Hopkins that he supported postwar Chinese unity and that China needed genuine economic assistance "which could only come from the United States." He emphasized that "the United States must play the largest part in helping China to get on their feet; the Soviet Union would be preoccupied with its own reconstruction and Great Britain would be uninterested." Stalin said he knew little of the Chinese leader but that he felt "Chiang Kai-shek was the best of the lot and would be the one to undertake the unification of China." Stalin added that he "saw no other possible leader and that for example he did not believe that the Chinese communist leaders were as good or would be able to bring about unification of China." Hopkins also understood that Stalin held no affection for fellow communists such as China's Mao Zedong or Joseph Broz Tito of Yugoslavia, both of whom were seen by the Soviet leader as dangerously independent of Kremlin influence.

After the meeting, an elated Hopkins cabled President Truman. "We were very encouraged by the conference on the Far East," he reported. "By August 8 the Soviet Army will be properly deployed on the Manchurian positions. . . . Stalin left no doubt in our mind that he intends to attack during August. . . . He made the categorical statement that he would do everything he could to promote unification of China under the leadership of Chiang Kai Shek."[41] Yet Stalin sought a price for his cooperation. Hopkins warned the president: "The marshal expects that Russia will share in the actual occupation of Japan and wants an agreement with the British and us as to occupation zones."[42]

Hopkins took the deepest satisfaction from the fact that the meetings had achieved his primary goal of securing Red Army cooperation in the Far East. "There is no doubt in the minds of any competent authorities," Hopkins noted to himself after his return, "that if Russia enters the war and Japan intends to fight it out that she will be conquered much more rapidly than with Russia out of the war. I have heard some people say that they would like to see us win the Japanese War without the help of Russia for political reasons, but anyone who takes this position must accept the logic of their premise, namely, that tens of thousands more American boys will lose their lives than would be the case if the Soviet Union joins the war."[43] To Hopkins, who had already lost one son in the Pacific, and had two more in harm's way, this point was more than an abstract argument.

During their fourth session, on May 30, Hopkins and Stalin discussed the anticipated Berlin meeting among the Big Three. Stalin suspected that Churchill desired to hold the meeting earlier, perhaps in June rather than July, to give himself a boost in the upcoming British elections in June. Hopkins abruptly returned to the issue of Poland, however. He sought to reassure Stalin that the United States had no interest in reestablishing a *cordon sanitaire* around Russia. He recognized the historic enmities between Poland and Russia and suggested that, if the Soviet Union persisted in acting unilaterally with Poland, the Poles would likely prove less cooperative. Citing the concerns of American public and media opinion, Hopkins emphasized the importance of freedom of speech in Poland, a multiparty system, the rule of law, and a functioning system of justice. He explained that when the president left Yalta he had presumed the Polish question had been largely settled and was more optimistic about the situation than previously. Hopkins added that he and all of the other American representatives felt the same. Hopkins confessed to being "bewildered and disturbed," and he bluntly told Stalin "there was a strong feeling among the American people that the Soviet Union wished to dominate Poland." He added: "It was widely held in the United States and that friends of international collaboration were wondering how it would be possible to work things out with the Soviet Union if we could not agree on the Polish question."[44]

During his fifth discussion with Stalin on May 31, Hopkins encountered a new and troubling degree of obstructionism. Debating the composition of the Polish government, Hopkins found Stalin more truculent. Citing the recent arrest of a group of Polish leaders by Soviet secret police, Hopkins asserted that the controversy, coming on top of the inability to agree on the larger Polish question, had provoked an understandably negative reaction from American public opinion. To Hopkins's dismay, Stalin once again defended the Red Army's actions in Poland by comparing them favorably to what the British had been doing in Greece.[45] Hopkins told President Truman that he would link the plight of the detained Poles to the American desire to compromise on the composition of the Polish government.[46] Hopkins assumed that "the best plan would be that at the dinner which Stalin is giving for me tonight I should find an appropriate occasion to press hard for the release of the majority of the arrested Polish political leaders."[47]

Hopkins met with Stalin alone, with only an interpreter, during dinner on June 1. He used the privacy of their meeting to return to the sensitive subject of the arrested Poles, hoping that Stalin might be more lenient. Hopkins candidly told Stalin that their disagreements over Poland threatened everything the two sides had achieved since 1941. He patiently explained that American public opinion had to remain friendly to the Soviet Union for the new president to continue Roosevelt's policies. "I reminded him again," Hopkins wrote later that night in his notes on the conversation, "and told him very forcefully that he must believe me when I told him that our whole relationship was threatened by the impasse of Poland. I made it clear again to Stalin that Poland was only a symbol, . . . I told Stalin further that I personally felt that our relations were threatened and that I frankly had many misgivings about it and . . . was, frankly, bewildered with some of the things that were going on."[48]

Stalin replied to Hopkins that he did not intend to let the British dominate the affairs of Poland because, he argued, "that is exactly what they want to do." Stalin nonetheless pledged that the arrested Poles would receive a fair trial and that they would be treated humanely. "I closed the conversation by telling him that I thought the real solution lay in his releasing these men entirely so that we could clear the atmosphere not only for the immediate discussions about Poland but in preparation for the Berlin Conference."[49]

Truman briefed Churchill on Hopkins's progress in Moscow with the Polish controversy, particularly the composition of the Polish government. Truman was effusively pleased with Hopkins's achievements.[50] Churchill replied to Truman: "Harry Hopkins has made very remarkable progress at Moscow, and I am entirely in sympathy with what he has already achieved."[51] "You are doing splendid work," Churchill cabled Hopkins.[52] Hopkins responded to Churchill on June 3: "I am doing everything under Heaven to get these people out of the Jug, but the more important things it seems to me is to get these Poles together in Moscow right away."[53]

The State Department and the president pleaded with Hopkins to address the San Francisco controversies with Stalin.[54] During their final discussion, which took place several days later on June 6, Hopkins successfully persuaded Stalin to drop Soviet obstructionism at the ongoing UN conference at San Francisco. For good measure, an unaccountably agreeable Stalin also agreed to cooperate with Red Cross efforts in Poland. Hopkins concluded this, their final meeting, on a friendly note by mentioning that he was stopping in Berlin before returning to Washington, joking that, while he was there, he "might even be able to find Hitler's body." Stalin morosely replied that he was sure that Hitler was still alive somewhere.[55]

Hopkins had nonetheless succeeded in wringing important concessions from Stalin on Red Army intervention against Japan, the progress of the United Nations Conference, and the upcoming Berlin Conference. Hopkins recognized that Poland, certainly of primary interest to Stalin, would continue to be a vexing problem, but he had largely resolved the other issues. He secured the meeting between Truman and Stalin at Berlin, the Potsdam Conference, which Truman acknowledged Hopkins had single-handedly saved. Stalin even agreed to a specific date, July 15.[56] Truman also publicly credited Hopkins with rescuing the San Francisco Conference.[57] Hopkins had done what he had to do to untangle the messes that had occurred since FDR's death, but it would be up to Truman and his advisers to make a long-term success of things. Many senior American officials, both civilian and military, felt a great deal of optimism that Hopkins's talks with Stalin had placed relations back on track and would better enable the possibility of continued cooperation with Moscow.[58]

When Hopkins arrived in Frankfurt, he received an urgent telephone message from Churchill. The prime minister insisted that Hopkins see him in London at once, but Hopkins had no desire to demonstrate Anglo-American solidarity when Washington's relations with Russia had been so strained. "I stalled about this," Hopkins wrote. "I felt it unwise for me to go to England and see Churchill before reporting to Truman, so I gave Churchill no encouragement." Churchill then wired Truman, but the president insisted that Hopkins return to Washington.[59]

Truman continued to solicit Hopkins's views during the early months of his presidency.[60] He urged Hopkins to accompany him to Potsdam, but Hopkins understood that his longtime rival Jimmy Byrnes was going to be

A fatigued-looking Hopkins touring the ruins of Hitler's Berlin with his wife, Louise, and Chip Bohlen after spending two punishing weeks in Moscow negotiating with Stalin.

appointed Secretary of State and thus would be accompanying the president to Potsdam. He declined the invitation on the grounds of ill health.[61] "I am sorry that I cannot persuade you to remain in government any longer," President Truman wrote to Hopkins on July 3. "It would have given me great pleasure to have you associated with my Administration. However, I understand fully the reasons which prompted your decision and I do not feel that I can justifiably ignore them. . . . There are few people in the United States who know more fully than I the substantial role which you have played in the prosecution of our war."[62]

"The time has come when I must take a rest," Hopkins replied to the president. "I have, therefore, reached the decision that I should now retire from the Government Service and, hence, not be able to accompany you to the Berlin area for your impending conference with Mr. Churchill and Mr. Stalin."[63] Hopkins felt he needed a rest. "Had I gone to Berlin," he wrote to Lord Beaverbrook, "I surely would have been asked to do something else and if I keep that kind of merry-go-round going I have no chance in the world of ever regaining my health."[64]

Hopkins suspected that General Marshall was behind Truman's decision to award him the Distinguished Service Medal in July.[65] "That you have carried on as long as you have done is a remarkable example of the principle of mind over matter," Marshall wrote, "or to put it more crudely—of sheer guts. I wonder if you have any idea of the immense comfort that it has been to our Chief, and indeed to all of us to have had you at the President's right hand through all these grim years."[66] Lord Beaverbrook added: "You are the greatest diplomat of our age. There are also the many millions in Britain, in America and in Europe too, who have reason to call you blessed."[67]

Nearly everyone, with the exception of the McCormick and Hearst press, cheered the outcome of the Hopkins-Stalin Moscow negotiations, relieved that U.S.-Soviet relations seemed back on course. Hopkins had suddenly achieved a kind of near-universal acclaim that had eluded him during the previous twelve years. Praise also came from unexpected quarters as even many of his adversaries felt compelled to say something complimentary. His old nemesis, Arthur Krock of the New York Times, wrote appreciatively on July 4: "This correspondent has heard a general statement from several of the chief military and civil administrators of the war program which can be published, and follows: No man did more, if as much to assure the vigor and success of high policy directed toward the conduct of the war and to the maintenance of the national interest of the United States among the allied nations. No man more firmly and constantly made this the test of every proposal—will it help to win the war as quickly and constructively as possible?"[68]

~

# Conclusion
## *The Lost Peace*

> He rendered a service to his country which will never even vaguely be appreciated.
>
> —*George Marshall on Harry Hopkins*[1]

Despite his failing health, Hopkins had ambitious plans for the future. Upon his return from Moscow, he pursued a multitrack effort of maintaining harmonious U.S.-Soviet relations. He urged Eleanor Roosevelt to sojourn to the USSR on a goodwill mission, and he lobbied President Truman and General Marshall to encourage General Eisenhower to make a courtesy visit to Moscow, as well as allowing Red Army general Georgy Zhukov to reciprocate by visiting Washington.[2] Hopkins also hoped to recuperate sufficiently to make himself available to Truman as a special envoy should the president require his services.[3] He also may have held out hope that he would obtain appointment as High Commissioner in Berlin.[4]

He told friends and family that he needed to remain healthy long enough to write about all the remarkable things he had experienced in the previous twelve years, and he set out to write a multivolume memoir, anticipating that the first two volumes would cover the war and the third would explore the enigmatic FDR. "I don't want to do any slipshod job on Roosevelt," he wrote to Lord Beaverbrook in July 1945.[5] At the end of July, months after the defeat of nazism but just weeks before the surrender of Japan, he began dictating his recollections in anticipation of producing the memoir.[6]

When people marveled at his capacity for physical punishment, they did not take into account his loathing for the life of the sickbed, his disgust with his body's inability to sustain his goals, his life. He'd rather die imbibing late at night with Churchill, or the Russians, or even on a miserably cold flight to Archangel, than in a sickbed at the Mayo Clinic. Frances Perkins recalled his heroic struggles with his failing body. "He knew pain, grief, frustration, weakness, political and personal animosity and misrepresentation. These he managed to bear, not like a saint but like a man."[7] His physician brother Lewis speculated that the war might have prolonged Harry's tenuous hold on life. "He understood his situation," Lewis reflected after the war, "but an iron will to live and to help defeat Germany made his latter years possible. He told me once that he had to live in order to write of what he had experienced."[8]

Hopkins was in no way resigned to returning to his sickbed or to the life of a semi-invalid. To provide himself with an income, he took a position as the chairman of the cloak and suit industry. Optimistic about postwar America, he believed that American workers, already more technologically skilled than workers in most other countries as a result of millions of jobs in the wartime industries, would provide the United States with the largest skilled workforce in world history and would spur postwar prosperity.[9] As for himself, he once shared with Brendan Bracken that he hoped to live long enough after the war "to never again speak of wars or threats of wars, but only of good books and beautiful women."[10] As he entered a period of gradual physical decline after the Moscow mission, he must have realized that that was not likely to happen.

"I wish I could tell you how I'm getting along," he wrote to his son, Robert, from his room in Manhattan's Memorial Hospital, near the end of January 1946, "but I don't know myself so there is no way of telling you, nor do I think the doctors could. I am here for, I think, an indefinite stay, which may be several weeks or several months. I have felt better the last couple of days but that does not mean very much because I go downhill just as fast as I go up, but I am hoping for the best."[11]

"All I can say about myself at the moment," he wrote to Churchill on January 22, "is that I am getting excellent care, while the doctors are struggling over a very bad case of cirrhosis of the liver—not due, I regret to say, from taking too much alcohol. But I must say that I dislike having the effect of a long life of congenial and useful drinking and neither deserve the reputation nor enjoy its pleasures."[12] It would be his final letter. Shortly thereafter he slipped into a coma, and, a few days later, on January 29, 1946, he died. He was fifty-five. George Marshall, mediating the Chinese Civil War, cabled a public statement from Chungking: "He rendered a service to his country which will never even vaguely be appreciated."[13]

In a perceptive obituary, Frances Perkins echoed General Marshall's sentiments and added that the history of American Progressivism and World War II would not be fully understood without appreciating Hopkins's contributions. Perkins observed: "His own character and almost every act of his short, heroic life expressed the deep-rooted conviction that 'It is what happens to people that matters.' In his last years he did work of such enormous importance to his country and to mankind, under circumstances of such extreme confidence, that it is doubtful whether the world will ever know the full debt of gratitude it owes him."[14]

"To be sure," the *Washington Post* obituary read, "his word was respected because of his closeness to Mr. Roosevelt. But the military chiefs valued his judgment, too. No man did greater service in the prosecution of the war than Mr. Hopkins did. His health, frail even before the war, broke down repeatedly under the strain. Administrator, expediter, secretary, fixer, errand boy, idea man, boon companion, alter ego—he was all these to Mr. Roosevelt, and the President never wavered in his attachment to him."[15]

Perhaps out of deference to the dead, even some of his longtime critics softened toward him. Henry Luce's *Time* felt compelled to acknowledge his contributions in a lengthy paean: "There had never been anyone quite like him in U.S. history. The tall, gaunt youth from the Middle West, the harness maker's son who rose to be the second most powerful man in the land. . . . Above all he would be remembered for his work during the war years when, as FDR's agent, he was the confidential troubleshooter sent to fix the hotboxes and burnt-out bearings of the worldwide coalition which won World War II. He was the prodder and pusher for more war production, the passionate pleader for unity, the go-between from Roosevelt to Churchill and Stalin. He was and regarded himself as an instrument, with the selflessness of an instrument."[16] Even his most persistent critic, Arthur Krock of the *New York Times*, later recalled Hopkins's dictum with a newfound admiration: "Will it help us win the war? If not, to hell with it, let it wait. This to my mind is his epitaph. It's a great thing."[17]

A few months after Harry's death, his friends and admirers gathered together on May 22—the thirteenth anniversary of his entry into the administration—for an outdoor memorial service at the base of the Washington Monument. Presided over by former vice president Henry Wallace, the highlight of the service was a eulogy written by the author John Steinbeck and read by the actor Burgess Meredith. "It is customary when a man dies to tell the great bells to obscure personality and purpose in the splendor of ceremony," Meredith intoned. "It is customary for a man's enemies to forgive him once he is dead for he has ceased to be dangerous. These things are usual and possible, except when the man was also an idea. Ideas are not mortal but can become stronger with the death of the man."[18] Harry's first wife, Ethel, wrote to Bob Sherwood: "The more I thumb through these old papers, I realize, more than ever, how heavily the burdens of the world lay on Harry's shoulders and what a consuming desire he had to do something, personally, about it."[19] Churchill recalled: "From 1941 to 1943, when his health broke a lot, he was a vital spring in the whole machine. No one can ever measure, and neither America nor England can ever repay, what he did to make things go well."[20]

The collective power and coordination of the Grand Alliance afforded the Allies an enormous advantage over the Axis, and Hopkins deserves much credit for this achievement. It was his primary goal throughout the war and explains his reactions in 1944 and 1945 to controversies such as British intervention in Greece and Soviet unilateralism in Poland. Despite misgivings about the nature of the Soviet regime, he pushed for harmonious relations. He had few illusions about the future of the Soviet-American relationship. He understood it would be a challenge to maintain U.S.-Soviet relations after the war, certainly a far greater challenge than sustaining the alliance during the war when the common goal of destroying Hitler encouraged the subordination of disputes. He understood, and even anticipated, that negotiations with the Russians always had the potential to "blow up at the last minute."[21] At the Teheran Conference in November 1943, Hopkins had emphasized to V. M. Molotov and Anthony Eden that Roosevelt felt it essential to world peace that Russia, Great Britain, and the United States work out postwar matters in a fashion that would preclude any of the three arming against each other following the war.[22]

Shortly after the war, Anthony Eden reflected on the question of how things might have been different had Roosevelt lived. He maintained that the turning point in relations might have occurred with FDR's death in April 1945. He recalled that FDR emphasized the importance of the Great Powers cooperating in making the postwar organization a success. Eden believed the gradual deterioration in relations following Yalta should not have proven fatal to the alliance and could have been rectified by skillful handling, just as previous crises had been managed during the war. Eden recalled Roosevelt's extraordinary ability to manage relations with Moscow, as well as the genuine respect the Soviets had for the president. He believed this stemmed from Stalin's respect for Roosevelt himself, as much as for the office he held and the nation he represented. Eden further said he had no doubt that Stalin

Hopkins and Anthony Eden at Yalta, February 1945.

respected Roosevelt because of the enormous moral influence as well as the political and military power he exerted throughout the world. That, Eden thought, was the real basis of the exceptional fairness that Stalin displayed in making concessions and reaching agreements in all sorts of negotiations with Roosevelt and also with Hopkins. Stalin demonstrated a pragmatism and willingness to compromise, Eden recalled, that he certainly did not display in dealings with others.[23]

Another official with close proximity to wartime relations, ambassador to the USSR Averell Harriman, reflected that Roosevelt was optimistic about the long-term prospects of U.S.-Soviet relations. The president did not think that the communist ideology would ultimately survive in Russia and, if Washington and Moscow could achieve a postwar period of working together and establish a basis on which to work for peace, it would encourage a progressive change from the rigidities of the Soviet system. Harriman later observed: "I've often thought of certain things which I feel very deeply about. One is this canard on Roosevelt, that he was naïve about Stalin, that

Hopkins and Averell Harriman at Teheran, December 1943.

he was taken in by Stalin. It's a lot of nonsense. The facts of the matter are that he thought that the intimacies that were developed during the war with the Russians should be used to attempt to come to an understanding for postwar collaboration. . . . [FDR] was always a little bit concerned about the way Stalin and Churchill would get along. But he was concerned that Churchill was so unsympathetic with the Russians, the Revolution, and so skeptical about it that he would get into difficulties. Now, people have said that Churchill was right and Roosevelt was naïve. He wasn't naïve at all. He was attempting to achieve an objective, and I was one of the tools that he used. Hopkins was another."[24]

In Hopkins's private political testament dictated in late July 1945, nearly two months after his final return from Moscow, he expressed his thoughts about the future of U.S.-Soviet relations. He emphasized that the United States had just fought in a coalition with the Russians in the greatest war in history and that this should be used to establish a foundation for postwar relations. He observed that the "great enigma" about the Soviet Union in the years to come would be Russia's postwar foreign policies. "True, they are going to see to it that their borders are protected from unfriendly states and I, for one, do not blame them for that." Yet he confidently predicted: "Russia's interests, so far as we can anticipate them, do not afford an opportunity for a major difference with us in foreign affairs. . . . The Russians undoubtedly like the American people, they like the United States. They trust the United States more than they trust any power in the world. I believe they not only fight with us, but are determined to take their place in world affairs in an international organization, and above all, they want to maintain friendly relations with us."[25]

Hopkins nonetheless anticipated that there would be future challenges to U.S.-Soviet relations, just as there had been during the war. "There can be no question that the United States' permanent long-time relations with the Soviet Union are going to be seriously handicapped, not so much by our fundamental differences in ideology as between a capitalist economy and a socialist state, but between our fundamental notions of human liberty—freedom of speech, freedom of the press and freedom of worship. The American people want not only freedom for themselves, but they want freedom throughout the world for other people as well, as they simply do not like the notion that you cannot say what you like when you want to say it."

Hopkins had once told Vice President-elect Truman: "There is no such thing as a settled American foreign policy that does not have the full strength of the American people behind it."[26] Hopkins believed that President Truman and his foreign policy team would need to make a genuine effort to avoid an unnecessary conflict with Moscow. Moreover, he understood that there were powerful people in the United States who desired postwar confrontation with the Soviet Union. "The thing the American people must look out for is that there is a minority in America who, for a variety of reasons, would just as soon have seen Russia defeated in the war and who said publicly before we got into the war that it did not make any difference which one—Russia or Germany—won. That small, vociferous minority can take advantage of every rift between ourselves and Russia to make trouble between our two countries. There are plenty of people in America who would have been perfectly willing to see your armies go right on through Germany and fight with Russia after Germany was defeated. They represent nobody but themselves and no government worth its salt in control of our country would ever permit that group to influence our official actions."[27]

There might be greater tensions with the USSR after the war, and Hopkins anticipated that a degree of misunderstanding was probably inevitable given the vast differences between America and Russia, but it need not have resulted in decades of the Cold War. Having spent most of the war seeking to achieve Alliance harmony and having devoted considerable energy to laying the groundwork for a durable postwar relationship between Moscow and Washington, Hopkins likely would have had deep misgivings over the advent of the Cold War in 1946.

Judging by their wartime record, Hopkins and Roosevelt would have been less credulous about Churchill's erratic efforts to stir conflict with the Soviet Union than Truman and Byrnes proved to be. Moreover, Roosevelt and Hopkins would never have reacted with as much alarm to Stalin's actions and comments, nor would they have accepted at face value the pessimistic and alarmist premonitions of Russia hands such as George Kennan. In fact, when Kennan implored Hopkins not to negotiate with Stalin during his Moscow mission in 1945, Hopkins impatiently retorted: "Then you think it's just sin, and we should be agin it?" Kennan replied: "That's just about right." To which Hopkins shot back: "I respect your opinion, but I'm not at liberty to accept it."[28] When another Russia hand, Chip Bohlen, shared with Hopkins some of the challenges the Americans had encountered with the Russians at the recent Potsdam Conference, Bohlen expressed his growing pessimism about the future of U.S.-Soviet relations. Hopkins acknowledged that such difficulties would no doubt arise but, speaking from personal experience, he observed that it was important to downplay ideological differences and instead pursue a course of patient, careful dealings with the Kremlin. Experience had taught Hopkins not to see most matters as deterministically inevitable or unsolvable.[29]

He thought the United States could continue to do business with Stalin and use the relationship to achieve its own objectives, even though there might always be some degree of uncertainty about relations. Hopkins believed relations with Moscow need not necessarily pose problems any greater than those created by Great Britain. He recognized that America's global strategic interests certainly intersected to a greater extent with Britain's interests, particularly in areas such as the Middle East and Asia, than would likely be the case with Moscow's chief interests in areas such as the Baltic, Eastern Europe, and the Balkans. Those latter areas had never previously been of primary interest to the United States, nor did Hopkins anticipate that they should become so in the future. The Cold War obscured the reality that many wartime officials such as Hopkins worried just as much about the postwar objectives of the British Empire as they did about the establishment of Soviet satellites.

Hopkins believed the world would prove large enough for diversity, but he also concluded that both Churchill's and Stalin's objectives revealed their essentially antiquated thinking about the changes coming to the postwar world. Given time, enormous changes would occur in the postwar decades that would overwhelm both the Soviet and British imperial efforts to control millions of people contrary to their desires. "There are those who believe it Utopian for us to fight for anything else," Hopkins optimistically proclaimed in June 1942, "but I believe that we are fighting for a new world. Because there can be no real freedom without economic freedom. The world can be freed from the economic oppressions that have nourished misery among hundreds of millions of people. There is enough wheat to feed the world; there is enough stone and brick and lumber to house the world; there is enough cotton and wool to clothe the whole human family. Among the United Nations there is room for differences of opinion as to how this should be achieved and each one of us can dwell within the particular economic environment that suits his purpose."[30]

Hopkins was confident that Truman would prove worthy of the challenge. And indeed, Truman initially, if haphazardly, pursued Roosevelt's objectives, even to the point of sending Hopkins to Moscow after FDR's death. However, Truman eventually diverged from Hopkins's approach. The relative ease with which Truman, after fits and starts, abandoned the Roosevelt-Hopkins course for postwar relations with the USSR reveals how their objectives had never been securely anchored in institutions such as the War and State departments or Congress.

Throughout the war, Hopkins often left an enormous void during his long convalescences. He may have worked himself into ineffectiveness, and his frequent illnesses led to the neglect of his many portfolios. During his absences, FDR often found himself relying upon less able advisers such as Henry Morgenthau or Jimmy Byrnes. When Hopkins departed, the Grand Alliance began to falter. There was no one left with sole responsibility of ensuring the harmony of the Alliance.

Roosevelt and Hopkins were the two crucial parts of the Grand Design. With both of them removed, replaced by officials who were in no way committed to their objectives, their policy foundered. There is ample evidence that Hopkins sought to create an architecture that would outlast his tenure. Much as he had while seeking to institutionalize a new architecture of personal security with the New Deal, he sought to solidify his efforts to create a more secure world strategically. In November 1944 Hopkins had sought to introduce an organizational system in the State Department that would survive his, and the president's, departure. He enjoyed some success, at least initially, as the State Department reorganization of November 1944 placed Hopkins's protégé, Ed Stettinius, in charge. But this was easily overturned when Truman decided to appoint Byrnes to head the State Department and began the process of abandoning the Yalta formula. An informal combination of Byrnes, Leahy, and Harriman took on the various roles Hopkins had once played as troubleshooter and counselor.

The diplomacy of the Second World War was highly personalized, and much depended upon the tenor of relations among Roosevelt, Churchill, and Stalin. One of the most remarkable aspects of the war, however, was how the United States succeeded in achieving so much diplomatically when it often had so little leverage, particularly in its relations with the Soviet Union. At both Teheran and Yalta, Roosevelt and Hopkins, and later Hopkins alone in Moscow, wrung significant concessions from Stalin. The Soviet leader kept his military agreements, stayed in the war until the defeat of Hitler, provided an offensive to keep the pressure off the landings in France, carried out his pledge to attack Japanese forces in the Far East, and largely conceded to FDR and Churchill's desires on matters related to France and the postwar organization.[31]

Hopkins had become the embodiment of FDR's personal diplomatic style of using close associates and special envoys to conduct sensitive diplomacy while bypassing the more hidebound traditional institutions such as the State and the Army and Navy departments. This led to innumerable problems, as the president grew increasingly dependent on the one official in the administration whose health was perhaps more precarious than his own. The structural impermanence of FDR's and Hopkins's policy toward the USSR was exposed after they departed the stage. When FDR died in April 1945 and Hopkins entered the final stages of his own illness, this diplomatic "grand design" lost its two most important advocates and would be abandoned by their successors.

In private observations revealing his thoughts about the future of U.S.-Soviet relations, Hopkins felt it would be essential to emphasize the commonalities and subordinate the differences. "The Soviet Union is made up of a hundred and eighty million hard-working, proud people. They are not an uncivilized people. They are a tenacious, determined people who think and act just like you and I do. Our Russia policy must not be dictated by people who have already made up their minds that there is no possibility of working with the Russians, and that our interests are bound to conflict and ultimately lead to war. From my point of view, that is an untenable position and can but lead to disaster."[32]

# Bibliographic Essay

## Unpublished Primary Sources

A study of Harry Hopkins's life and career is supported by an abundance of source material, including an enormous amount of unpublished and published primary sources, scores of memoirs, and thousands of secondary works. What follows is thus, by necessity, a select bibliography.

Starting with unpublished primary sources, Hopkins's papers are divided between the Franklin D. Roosevelt Library (FDRL) in Hyde Park, New York, and the Special Collections Research Center at the Lauinger Library at Georgetown University. The Hopkins materials at the Roosevelt Library consist of a vast amount of material in 353 boxes. This collection includes family and health records, private and official correspondence, speech and article files, materials related to his various New Deal assignments, but also scores of containers on his wartime service, including Lend-Lease, his missions to London and Moscow, and his attendance at wartime conferences. Also at the FDRL are several collections in President Roosevelt's papers essential to understanding Hopkins's role, such as the President's Secretary's Files, the Official Files, and the Map Room Files. The papers of two of the president's children, Anna Roosevelt Halstead and James Roosevelt, also contain materials pertaining to Hopkins.

The Hopkins collections in the Lauinger Library at Georgetown are also essential. They consist of approximately seventy-eight boxes in four parts (Part I comprises sixty-two boxes, Part II seven boxes, Part III seven boxes, and Part IV has two boxes), which include family papers, correspondence, unpublished manuscripts, and speech files. Also at Georgetown is the Robert Hopkins collection, which includes correspondence with his father, thousands of photographs, and several early drafts of a manuscript about his life and wartime experiences, much of which overlapped with his father's.

Other collections essential for understanding Hopkins's wartime role include the Robert E. Sherwood Papers at the Houghton Library at Harvard University. This collection contains hundreds of files of correspondence related to Sherwood's research for his 1948 Pulitzer Prize–winning book about Roosevelt and Hopkins. More remarkable are his notes from scores of interviews with figures from the New Deal and the war. These interview notes, which were conducted shortly after the war in 1946 to 1947, contain fresh and proximate revelations, making the collection a must see for anyone interested in the period.

The Manuscript Collection at the Library of Congress includes the papers of Interior Secretary Harold Ickes, Ambassador Charles Bohlen, Ambassador W. Averell Harriman, Ambassador Joseph E. Davies, Ambassador Laurence Steinhardt, Admiral William Leahy, and Navy Secretary Frank Knox. The Ickes Papers are an important source of information about Hopkins, not only the correspondence files but also particularly the thousands of deleted pages of the Ickes diaries that did not make it into the published versions. The Bohlen and Steinhardt Papers include correspondence with Hopkins and materials related to his service at wartime conferences and his 1945 mission to Moscow, as do the W. Averell Harriman Papers.

In Great Britain, the British National Archives at Kew Gardens hold materials touching upon Hopkins's missions to London between 1941 and 1945 spread out over the Foreign Office, Premiership files, as well as cabinet minutes and memoranda of conversations about Hopkins's relationship with Churchill. The Churchill Papers, reposing in the Churchill Centre at Cambridge University, include Hopkins-Churchill correspondence. Other useful collections include the George C. Marshall Papers at the Marshall Foundation, Virginia Military Institute, Lexington, Virginia; the James Forrestal Papers at the Mudd Library at Princeton; the Henry L. Stimson Papers at Yale University; and the Hallie Flanagan collection at the New York Public Library. The Oral History Collection at Columbia University includes relevant interviews with Claude Wickard, Frances Perkins, Averell Harriman, Arthur Krock, Samuel Rosenman, Eleanor Roosevelt, Anna Roosevelt, Jerome Frank, Florence Kerr, and Frank Bane.

# Published Primary Sources

The published primary sources touching upon Hopkins and wartime diplomacy are also substantial, but several works stand out, starting with relevant volumes of *Foreign Relations of the United States* (*FRUS*), 1941–1945 (Washington, DC: Government Printing Office, 1956–1972). The thirty-seven *FRUS* volumes covering the war years include thousands of documents on Hopkins's wartime involvement with issues related to Lend-Lease, Great Britain, the USSR, China, and Poland, among other matters. These volumes also include documents on Hopkins's two missions to London in 1941, and his missions to Moscow in 1941 and 1945. The State Department also published six additional volumes focusing on the wartime conferences, which include hundreds of documents on Hopkins's participation at the Atlantic Conference in 1941, the Washington Conference of 1941 to 1942, Casablanca 1943, Quebec I 1943, Cairo and Teheran 1943, and Yalta in February 1945. Where there is little difference between *FRUS* and the published originals, *FRUS* has been used and cited for its greater accessibility. With regard to documents in which there are significant differences between the original and the published *FRUS* version, the original, if available, has been preferred and cited.

Another essential source for understanding Hopkins's wartime role is Warren Kimball, ed., *Churchill and Roosevelt: The Complete Correspondence* (Princeton: Princeton University Press, 1984). This award-winning three-volume work is essential to understanding wartime diplomacy and includes an introduction on the Churchill-FDR relationship as well as extensive commentaries on the major issues of the war, which serve to contextualize the correspondence. In a similar vein, Susan Butler, ed., *My Dear Mr. Stalin: The Complete Correspondence of Franklin D. Roosevelt and Joseph V. Stalin* (New Haven: Yale University Press, 2006) is a valuable source, a useful accompaniment to Kimball's collection and, like Kimball, contextualizes the correspondence with extensive commentaries.

Robert Sherwood, *Roosevelt and Hopkins: An Intimate History* (New York: Enigma Books, reprint 2008) is the most important single source on Harry Hopkins. Beyond its literary merits, it contains hundreds of reproduced documents and, at nearly eight hundred pages, it represents an enormous compendium of the events of World War II. As neither Roosevelt nor Hopkins lived to write memoirs, this may be the closest we will ever come. In fact, after Hopkins's death in January 1946 his widow turned to Sherwood to complete the work he had begun on his three-volume memoirs. Sherwood won his fourth Pulitzer Prize (his previous three were for drama) with this work, and it remains a classic by one of America's leading writers who also happened to be a presidential speechwriter and developed a close relationship with both men. Sherwood's account stands alone as straddling both primary and secondary sources. It remains a valued primary source because he lived through much of these events, knew the participants socially, and enjoyed conversations with them for which there is no other source, particularly scores of verbatim conversations between Hopkins and the author that are simply unobtainable elsewhere. He reproduces hundreds of documents throughout the book. It also remains an essential secondary source because Sherwood did not merely rely upon his memory of events but also did substantial research in Hopkins's papers. Finally, he also maintained a two-year correspondence with officials during the 1946 to 1947 years while he was working on the book, and he conducted scores of meticulous interviews throughout 1946 to 1947.

Other important memoirs include Edward Stettinius, *Roosevelt and the Russians: The Yalta Conference* (Garden City: Doubleday, 1949); Averell Harriman and Elie Abel, *Special Envoy to Churchill and Stalin, 1941–1946* (New York: Random House, 1975); Charles Bohlen, *Witness to History, 1929–1969* (New York: W.W. Norton, 1973); and *The Stilwell Papers*, Theodore H. White, ed. (New York: W. Sloan Associates, 1948). The multivolume Churchill memoirs, while filled with interesting reconstructions of wartime conversations, are problematic at best, unreliable at worst, and should be used with extreme caution.

## Published Secondary Works

The secondary sources touching on wartime diplomacy are also substantial. For a thorough bibliography of published primary and secondary works on FDR's wartime diplomacy, readers should refer to the detailed bibliographic essay by Mark Stoler, "The United States and Wartime Diplomacy, 1940–1945," in *American Foreign Relations since 1600*, Robert L. Beisner, ed. (Santa Barbara: ABC-CLIO, 2003), 933–1078.

Several secondary works stand out. Starting with biographies, the best are George McJimsey, *Harry Hopkins: Ally of the Poor and Defender of Democracy* (Cambridge: Harvard University Press, 1987), with equal parts devoted to the New Deal and the war; and David L. Roll's more recent *The Hopkins Touch: Harry Hopkins and the Forging of the Alliance to Defeat Hitler* (Oxford: Oxford University Press, 2012). McJimsey balances Hopkins's New Deal years with the war years while Roll has done an admirable job exploring Hopkins's critical role in the Grand Alliance. Matthew B. Wills, *The Wartime Missions of Harry*

*Hopkins* (Raleigh, NC: Ivy House, 1996), is an excellent resource, focusing exclusively on Hopkins's many wartime missions, including those he made with General Marshall and Admiral King in 1942. For the various aspects of Hopkins's experience during the New Deal, biographies such as George McJimsey's can be supplemented with works specifically exploring this period, such as June Hopkins, *Harry Hopkins: Sudden Hero, Brash Reformer* (New York: Palgrave Macmillan, 1999) and works about WPA such as Nick Taylor, *American-Made: The Enduring Legacy of the WPA* (New York: Bantam, 2008).

On the controversial subject of Hopkins and the Soviet Union, Mary E. Glantz, *FDR and the Soviet Union: The President's Battles over Foreign Policy* (Lawrence: University Press of Kansas, 2005) is particularly good and offers a fresh retelling of Roosevelt's efforts to hold the alliance together in the face of opposition from many of his own officials. Important secondary works using Soviet sources include Geoffrey Roberts's *Stalin's Wars: From World War to Cold War* (New Haven: Yale University Press, 2008) and his *Molotov: Stalin's Cold Warrior* (Washington: Potomac Books, 2011).

As for the larger story of wartime politics, an earlier generation of works should be supplemented with newer works. A good place to start is Warren Kimball, *The Juggler: Franklin Roosevelt as Wartime Statesman* (Princeton: Princeton University Press, 1991); *Forged in War: Roosevelt, Churchill, and the Second World War* (New York: William Morrow, 1997); and Lloyd Gardner, *Spheres of Influence: The Great Powers Partition Europe, from Munich to Yalta* (Chicago: Ivan R. Dee, 1993). More recent works include Frank Costigliola's *Roosevelt's Lost Alliances: How Personal Politics Helped Start the Cold War* (Princeton: Princeton University Press, 2011), in which he has taken a familiar story and made it fresh by focusing on issues of personality, psychology, emotions, and health. Also useful are Mark Stoler, *Allies and Adversaries: The Joint Chiefs of Staff, the Grand Alliance, and the U.S. Strategy in World War II* (Chapel Hill: University of North Carolina Press, 2000); and Joseph Persico, *Roosevelt's Centurions: FDR and the Commanders He Led to Victory in World War II* (New York: Random House, 2013).

# Notes

## Introduction

1. Winston Churchill to Harry Hopkins, July 7, 1945, CHAR 20/222/36, Winston S. Churchill Papers, Churchill College, Cambridge, United Kingdom.

2. Interview with George Marshall, July 23, 1947, File 1899, Robert E. Sherwood Papers, Manuscript Collection, Houghton Library, Harvard; General George C. Marshall to Robert Sherwood, February 25, 1947, File 548, Sherwood Papers, Harvard.

3. Arthur Krock, Columbia Center for Oral History, Butler Library, Columbia University, 31–32.

4. Churchill to Hopkins, July 7, 1945, CHAR 20/222/36, Churchill Papers.

5. Sidney Hyman interview with General Burns, located in conversations with Paul Appleby, October 8, 1946, File 2415, Robert E. Sherwood Papers, Houghton Library, Harvard.

6. Harry L. Hopkins, Speech at Madison Square Garden, June 22, 1942, Box 12, of Harry L. Hopkins Papers, Franklin D. Roosevelt Library, Hyde Park, New York (hereafter referred to as FDRL).

7. There have been several very fine biographies of Hopkins, including ones by Robert E. Sherwood, *Roosevelt and Hopkins: An Intimate History* (New York: Enigma Books, reprint 2008), George McJimsey, *Harry Hopkins: Ally of the Poor and Defender of Democracy* (Cambridge: Harvard University Press, 1987), and, more recently, David L. Roll, *The Hopkins Touch: Harry Hopkins and the Forging of the Alliance to Defeat Hitler* (Oxford: Oxford University Press, 2012).

8. This point has been made by scholars such as Warren Kimball, *The Juggler: Franklin Roosevelt as Wartime Statesman* (Princeton: Princeton University Press,

1991), and, most recently, Frank Costigliola's *Roosevelt's Lost Alliances: How Personal Politics Helped Start the Cold War* (Princeton: Princeton University Press, 2011).

9. See, for example, the standard neoconvervative accounts by Robert Nisbet, *Roosevelt and Stalin: The Failed Courtship* (Washington: Regnery, 1988), and Amos Perlmutter, *FDR and Stalin: The Not So Grand Alliance* (Columbia: University Press of Missouri, 1991).

10. Ickes Diaries, May 23, 1943, 7769, Harold L. Ickes Papers, Library of Congress.

11. Interview with John G. Winant, September 13, 1946, File 1907, Robert E. Sherwood Papers, Manuscript Collection, Houghton Library, Harvard.

12. Samuel I. Rosenman, Columbia Center for Oral History, Butler Library, Columbia University, 173; Interview with Vannevar Bush, October 31, 1946, File 1876, Sherwood Papers, Harvard.

13. Interview with George Marshall, July 23, 1947, File 1899, Sherwood Papers, Harvard.

14. Hopkins to Winant, June 12, 1942, Hopkins Papers, Box 311, Molotov Visit file, 1942, FDRL.

15. Hopkins to Roosevelt, February 7, 1945, *FRUS, Yalta*, III, 729.

16. Sumner Welles to Robert Sherwood, November 10, 1948, File 865, Sherwood Papers, Harvard.

17. The most recent example of these accusations is seen in Diana West, *American Betrayal: The Secret Assault on Our Nation's Character* (New York: St. Martin's Press, 2013). A review of West's book from a conservative perspective is Ronald Radosh, "McCarthy on Steriods," *Front Page Magazine*. See: http://www.frontpagemag.com/2013/ronald-radosh/mccarthy-on-steroids/print/.

18. Also instructive is John Earl Haynes and Harvey Klehr, "Was Harry Hopkins a Soviet Spy?" *Front Page Magazine*. See: http://www.frontpagemag.com/2013/john-earl-haynes-and-harvey-klehr/was-harry-hopkins-a-soviet-spy/print/.

19. An analysis of some of the Russian documents in question can be found at "Harry Hopkins: A Glimpse into the Russian Records" at DocumentsTalk.com. See: http://www.documentstalk.com/wp/harry-hopkins-a-glimpse-into-the-russian-records.

20. "The Stalin-Hitler Grudge Fight," by Harry Hopkins, Hopkins Papers, Part I, Box 56, Folder 18, Special Collections Research Center, Lauinger Library, Georgetown University.

21. Hopkins Notes on Conversation between the President, Molotov, Hopkins, and Hull, May 29, 1942, *FRUS, The Soviet Union, 1942*, Vol. III, 571–72.

22. Dictation by Harry Hopkins, July 20, 1945, Hopkins Papers, Part I, Box 57, Folder 12, Georgetown University.

23. A refreshing exception is the works of Warren Kimball, who established early in his scholarship that relations between Roosevelt and Churchill featured frequent incidents of tension that the surface bonhomie may have obscured. See Warren Kimball, ed., *Churchill and Roosevelt: The Complete Correspondence* (Princeton: Princeton University Press, 1984).

24. Interview with Louis Brownlow, February 15, 1947, File 1874, Sherwood Papers, Harvard.

25. Recollections of Sidney Hyman conversation with Harry Hopkins can be found in his interview with Paul Appleby, October 8, 1946, File 2415, Sherwood Papers, Harvard.

## Chapter 1

1. Hopkins to Morgenthau, September 6, 1940, Hopkins Papers, Part I, Box 15, Folder 25, Special Collections Research Center, Lauinger Library, Georgetown University.

2. Frances Perkins to Hopkins, not dated [c. September 1940], Hopkins Papers, Box 94, Franklin D. Roosevelt Library, Hyde Park, New York (hereafter referred to as FDRL).

3. Harry L. Hopkins, *What Is the American Way?* (Washington, DC: Works Progress Administration, 1938).

4. Hopkins to Morgenthau, September 6, 1940, Hopkins Papers, Part I, Box 15, Folder 25, Special Collections Research Center, Lauinger Library, Georgetown University.

5. Hopkins, *What Is the American Way?*

6. Hopkins Address at WPA Luncheon, Los Angeles, September 19, 1936, Hopkins Papers, Box 9, FDRL; Robert Humphreys, "The Man Who Knows Roosevelt," *American Mercury*, December 1943.

7. Sidney Hyman Interview with Aubrey Williams, March 13, 1947, File 2430, Robert E. Sherwood Papers, Houghton Library, Harvard.

8. Address by Harry Hopkins, June 17, 1933, National Conference of Social Work, Hopkins Papers, Box 9, FDRL; Interview with Leon Henderson, October 11, 1947, File 1889, Sherwood Papers, Harvard.

9. Interview with Wayne Coy, March 12, 1947, File 1878, Sherwood Papers, Harvard.

10. FDR to Hopkins, August 24, 1940, Hopkins Papers, Box 96; Hopkins to Roosevelt, August 19, 1940, Hopkins Papers, Box 96, FDRL.

11. Florence Kerr, Columbia Center for Oral History, Butler Library, Columbia University, 34–35.

12. Charles Hurd, "Hopkins: Right-Hand Man," *New York Times Magazine*, August 11, 1940; Frank L. Kluckhohn, "Washington Success Story," *New York Times Magazine*, July 26, 1942; Ickes Diaries, May 23, 1943, 7768, Papers of Harold L. Ickes, Library of Congress.

13. Hopkins to Roosevelt, August 19, 1940, Hopkins Papers, Box 96, FDRL.

14. Interview with George Marshall, July 23, 1947, File 1899, Sherwood Papers, Harvard.

15. Ickes Diaries, January 2, 1939, 3340, Harold L. Ickes Papers, Library of Congress.

16. Conversation between Sidney Hyman and Howard Hunter, November 21, 1946, File 2423, Sherwood Papers, Harvard.

17. Clarke Beach, "Harry Hopkins: The President's Right Hand," *Washington Post*, April 20, 1941.

18. Interview with James Forrestal, January 17, 1947, File 1885, Sherwood Papers, Harvard.

19. Interview with Felix Frankfurter, May 25, 1946, File 1886, Sherwood Papers, Harvard University.

20. Ernest K. Lindley, "It's Harry L. Hopkins," *Washington Post*, October 26, 1938.

21. "Presidential Agent," *Time*, January 22, 1945.

22. Interview with Bernard Baruch, January 27–31, 1947, File 1872, Sherwood Papers, Harvard.

23. Frances Perkins, "The People Mattered," *Survey Midmonthly*, February 1946, 38–39.

24. Hopkins to FDR, April 18, 1937, Hopkins Papers, Part I, Box 19, Folder 3, Georgetown University.

25. Interview with Harold Ickes, December 10, 1947, File 1890, Sherwood Papers, Harvard.

26. Kluckhohn, "Washington Success Story."

27. Interview between Robert Sherwood and James Forrestal, January 17, 1947, File 1885, Sherwood Papers, Harvard.

28. Interview with Robert Kerr, October 12, 1947, File 1893, Sherwood Papers, Harvard.

29. Interview with Adah Aime, November 13, 1947, File 1871, Sherwood Papers, Harvard.

30. Interview with Robert Kerr, October 12, 1947, File 1893, Sherwood Papers, Harvard.

31. Lewis Hopkins to Robert Sherwood, November 5, 1947, File 389, Sherwood Papers, Harvard.

32. Interview with Robert Kerr, October 12, 1947, File 1893, Sherwood Papers, Harvard.

33. "It Never Could Happen," by Harry Hopkins, Hopkins Papers, Part III, Box 6, Folder 3, Georgetown University.

34. Ethel Hopkins to Robert Sherwood, September 13, 1947, File 386, Sherwood Papers, Harvard.

35. Glotzbach to Kerr, July 22, 1940, Hopkins Papers, Box 299, FDRL; Harry Hopkins to Ethel Hopkins, July 17, 1928, in Ethel Hopkins to Robert Sherwood, September 23, 1947, File 368, Sherwood Papers, Harvard.

36. Perkins's recollections of these events can be found in Frances Perkins to Hopkins, not dated [c. September 1940], Hopkins Papers, Box 94, FDRL; 1933, Hopkins Diaries, Entry for May 19, Hopkins Papers, Part I, Box 51a, Georgetown University.

37. Arthur Krock, Columbia Center for Oral History, Butler Library, Columbia University, 64.

38. Interview with Adah Aime, November 13, 1947, File 1871, Sherwood Papers, Harvard.

39. Interview with Aubrey Williams, March 18, 1947, File 1906, 2430, Sherwood Papers, Harvard.

40. Hopkins to Hellman, June 5, 1943, Hopkins Papers, Box 299, FDRL.

41. Frances Perkins to Hopkins, June 17, 1944, Hopkins Papers, Part I, Box 17, Folder 33, Georgetown University.

42. Jerome Frank, Columbia Center for Oral History, Butler Library, Columbia University, 36.

43. "Personality Profile Harry L. Hopkins," by Harry H. Balkin, December 29, 1934, Hopkins Papers, Part IV, Box 1, Folder 46, Georgetown University.

44. Adah Aime to Robert Sherwood, December 14, 1948, File 10, Robert E. Sherwood Papers, Harvard.

45. Hurd, "Hopkins: Right-Hand Man."

46. Conversation between Sidney Hyman and Howard Hunter, March 18, 1947, File 2423, Sherwood Papers, Harvard.

47. Harry Hopkins, "Churchill-Roosevelt First Rough Draft," c. September 1941, Hopkins Papers, Box 306, FDRL.

48. Conversation between Sidney Hyman and Howard Hunter, March 18, 1947, File 2423, Sherwood Papers, Harvard.

49. Perkins, "The People Mattered."

50. Notes of Sidney Hyman Conversations with John Hazzard, September 16–18, 1946, File 2422, Sherwood Papers, Harvard.

51. "Memorandum of Telephone Call of Secretary Perkins to Harry L. Hopkins," June 28, 1935, Hopkins Papers, Box 94, FDRL.

52. Hopkins to Farley, November 8, 1935, Confidential Political Files, Hopkins Papers, Box 37, FDRL.

53. Interview with Aubrey Williams, January 18, 1947, File 2430, Sherwood Papers, Harvard.

54. "John Steinbeck's Memorial to Harry Hopkins," Read by Burgess Meredith, May 22, 1946, Hopkins Papers, Part IV, Box 1, Folder 45, Georgetown University.

# Chapter 2

1. Notes of Conversation between Sidney Hyman and Paul Appleby, October 8, 1946, File 2415, Robert E. Sherwood Papers, Houghton Library, Harvard.

2. "What Price Recovery," by Harry Hopkins, December 1936, Hopkins Papers, Part I, Box 56, Folder 5, Special Collections Research Center, Lauinger Library, Georgetown University.

3. Interview with Louis Brownlow, February 15, 1947, File 1874, Sherwood Papers, Harvard.

4. Sidney Hyman Interview with Rex Tugwell, April 5, 1947, File 2429, Sherwood Papers, Harvard.

5. Address by Harry Hopkins, "Dollars and Sense," October 9, 1936, Hopkins Papers, Box 9, FDRL; Harry L. Hopkins, *What Is the American Way?* (Washington, DC: Works Progress Administration, 1938).

6. "What Price Recovery"; Address by Harry Hopkins, "Jobs vs. Jibes," October 19, 1936, Hopkins Papers, Box 9, FDRL.

7. Interview with Leon Henderson, October 11, 1947, File 1889, Sherwood Papers, Harvard.

8. Federal Civil Works Administration, Proceedings of General and Executive Meeting, November 15, 1933, Hopkins Papers, Box 9, FDRL.

9. Sidney Hyman Interview with Frank Bane, April 7, 1947, File 2417, Sherwood Papers, Harvard.

10. Howard Hunter to Sherwood, June 25, 1948, File 399, Sherwood Papers, Harvard.

11. "Causes of the Recession," no date, Hopkins Papers, Box 96, FDRL.

12. Conversation between Sidney Hyman and Jerome Frank, January 13, 1947, File 2420, Sherwood Papers, Harvard; Sidney Hyman Interview with Frank Bane, April 7, 1947, File 2417, Sherwood Papers, Harvard.

13. Hopkins to FDR, July 25, 1934, Hopkins Papers, Part I, Box 19, Folder 3, Georgetown University. Also see Sidney Hyman Interview with Rexford Guy Tugwell, April 5, 1947, File 2429, Sherwood Papers, Harvard.

14. Interview with Louis Brownlow, February 15, 1947, File 1874, Sherwood Papers, Harvard.

15. Frank Bane, Columbia Center for Oral History, Butler Library, Columbia University, 168.

16. Address by Harry Hopkins, June 17, 1933, National Conference of Social Work, Hopkins Papers, Box 9, FDRL.

17. Hopkins, *What Is the American Way?*; "Jobs vs. Jibes."

18. Frances Perkins to Hopkins, not dated [c. September 1940], Hopkins Papers, Box 94, FDRL.

19. "What Price Recovery."

20. Charles Hurd, "Hopkins: Right-Hand Man," *New York Times Magazine*, August 11, 1940.

21. Henry Wallace Interview, Small Collections, FDRL.

22. Ickes Diaries, February 19, 1934, 444, Library of Congress.

23. Ickes to Hopkins, November 21, 1938, Hopkins Papers, Box 91, FDRL; Ickes to FDR, November 22, 1938, Hopkins Papers, Box 91, FDRL.

24. Harold Ickes Diary, Deletions for Publication, June–July 1940, Library of Congress, 4482; Ickes Diaries, September 15, 1940, 4816, Library of Congress; Ickes Diaries Extracts, Harry Hopkins File, 32, Harold L. Ickes Papers, Library of Congress.

25. Hopkins to Ickes, September 6, 1940, Hopkins Papers, Part I, Box 10, Folder 8, Georgetown University.

26. Recollections of Sidney Hyman conversation with Harry Hopkins are in his conservations with Paul Appleby, October 8, 1946, File 2415, Sherwood Papers, Harvard.

27. Harold Ickes to Hopkins, August 26, 1940, Hopkins Papers, Part I, Box 10, Folder 8, Georgetown University.

28. Interview with Aubrey Williams, March 16, 1947, File 2430, Sherwood Papers, Harvard.

29. Interview with Charles Merriam, January 1, 1947, File 2426, Sherwood Papers, Harvard.

30. Interview with Harold L. Ickes, December 10, 1947, File 1890, Sherwood Papers, Harvard.

31. Interview with Rex Tugwell, April 5, 1947, File 2429, Sherwood Papers, Harvard.

32. Lewis A. Hopkins to Robert Sherwood, November 5, 1947, File 389, Sherwood Papers, Harvard.

33. Robert Hopkins to Sherwood, January 28, 1948, File 391, Sherwood Papers, Harvard.

34. Ickes Diaries Excerpts, Harry Hopkins, Entry for September 9, 1939, Harold L. Ickes Papers, Library of Congress.

35. Interview with Admiral Ross McIntire, March 14, 1947, File 1898, Sherwood Papers, Harvard; Hopkins to Admiral Grayson, January 20, 1938, Hopkins Papers, Box 6, Personal Health file, 1937–1940, FDRL.

36. Robert Humphreys, "The Man Who Knows Roosevelt," *American Mercury*, December 1943.

37. Diana Hopkins to President Roosevelt, January 31, 1939, PPF 4096, FDRL; Eleanor Roosevelt to Harry Hopkins, July 20, 1941, Hopkins Papers, Box 1, Family Correspondence, FDRL.

38. Interview with Robert Kerr, October 12, 1947, File 1893, Sherwood Papers, Harvard.

39. Hopkins to LeHand, June 29, 1943, Hopkins Papers, Part I, Box 12, Folder 27, Georgetown University.

40. Lewis A. Hopkins to President Roosevelt, March 6, 1939, PPF 4096, FDRL.

41. Roosevelt to Dr. George Eusterman, January 27, 1938, PPF 4096, FDRL; Dr. George Eusterman to President Roosevelt, January 15, 1938, PPF 4096, FDRL.

42. Roosevelt to Hopkins, January 11, 1938, PSF, Box 138, FDRL.

43. Turner Catledge, "It's 'Send for Harry,'" *New York Times*, March 16, 1941.

44. Ickes Diaries, August 10, 1940, 4703, Harold L. Ickes Papers, Library of Congress.

45. "We Left Washington Early in the Afternoon," April 3, 1939, Hopkins Papers, Part I, Box 56, Folder 8, Georgetown University; Hopkins to LeHand, September 11, 1942, Hopkins Papers, Part I, Box 12, Folder 27, Georgetown University.

46. Roosevelt to Hopkins, October 26, 1937, Hopkins Papers, Box 96, FDRL.

47. Interview with Leon Henderson, October 11, 1947, File 1889, Sherwood Papers, Harvard.

48. Hopkins Diary, Box 6, Hopkins Papers, FDRL; Bernard M. Baruch to Hopkins, September 28, 1937, Hopkins Papers, Box 85, FDRL.

49. "Causes of the Recession," no date, Hopkins Papers, Box 96, FDRL; "The Expansion of Productive Capacity," Hopkins Papers, Box 299, FDRL.

50. Conversation between Sidney Hyman and Howard Hunter, November 21, 1946, File 2423, Sherwood Papers, Harvard.

51. Roosevelt to Hopkins, June 20, 1938, Hopkins Papers, Box 96, FDRL.

52. FDR to Secretary of Commerce Hopkins, January 21, 1939, Hopkins Papers, Box 96, FDRL.

53. Leon Henderson to Hopkins, June 9, 1938, Papers of James Roosevelt, Box 29, FDRL.

54. Statement of Harry Hopkins before the Special Committee to Investigate Unemployment and Relief, April 8, 1938, Hopkins Papers, Box 11, FDRL.

55. Arthur Krock, "The Reemergence of Admininstrator Harry Hopkins," *New York Times*, June 22, 1937; "The Ubiquity and Influence of Mr. Hopkins," *New York Times*, October 18, 1938.

56. Conversation between Sidney Hyman and Jerome Frank, January 13, 1947, File 2420, Sherwood Papers, Harvard.

57. Hopkins to Roosevelt, September 15, 1936, PSF Box 138, Harry Hopkins File, FDRL; Roosevelt to Barbara Hopkins, November 9, 1936, PPF 4096, FDRL.

58. Walter Lippmann, "The New Secretary of Commerce," *Washington Post*, December 31, 1938.

59. Sam Rosenman, Columbia Center for Oral History, Butler Library, Columbia University, 168.

60. "The Cabinet: Second Stocking," *Time*, December 26, 1938.

61. "Cabinet: Restoration in Iowa," *Time*, March 6, 1939.

62. "The Cabinet: Second Stocking," *Time*, December 26, 1938.

63. Humphreys, "The Man Who Knows Roosevelt."

64. Eleanor Roosevelt, Columbia Center for Oral History, Butler Library, Columbia University, 5.

65. "Roosevelt Holding Favor of Democrats," *New York Times*, September 13, 1939.

66. Ickes Diaries for January 15, 1939, 3163, Library of Congress.

67. Notes of Conversation between Sidney Hyman and Paul Appleby, October 8, 1946, File 2415, Sherwood Papers, Harvard.

68. Samuel Rosenman, Columbia Center for Oral History, Butler Library, Columbia University, 168.

69. Interview with Victor Sholis, January 15, 1947, File 1904, Sherwood Papers, Harvard.

70. Ickes Diaries, March 12, 1939, 3286, Library of Congress.

71. Notes of Conversation between Sidney Hyman and Howard Hunter, November 21, 1946, File 2423, Sherwood Papers, Harvard.

72. Arthur Krock, Columbia Center for Oral History, Butler Library, Columbia University, 64–65.

73. Arthur Krock, ""The Ubiquity and Influence of Mr. Hopkins," *New York Times*, October 18, 1938.

74. Mark Sullivan, "Hopkins Build Up," *Washington Post*, January 8, 1939.

75. Telegram to Harry Hopkins from Betsey, Missy, FDR, May 25, 1939, PPF 4096, FDRL.

76. Interview with Robert Kerr, October 12, 1947, File 1893, Sherwood Papers, Harvard.

77. Ickes Diaries, June 17, 1939, Harold L. Ickes Papers, Library of Congress.

78. Speech at Des Moines, February 24, 1939, Hopkins Papers, Box 12, FDRL; Florence Kerr, Columbia Center for Oral History, Butler Library, Columbia University, 61–64.

79. "Cabinet: Restoration in Iowa," *Time*, March 6, 1939.

80. Charles Hurd, "Hopkins: Right-Hand Man," *New York Times Magazine*, August 11, 1940.

81. Interview with Admiral Ross McIntire, March 14, 1947, File 1898, Sherwood Papers, Harvard.

82. Lewis Hopkins to Sherwood, November 5, 1947, Sherwood Papers, Harvard.

83. Robert Hopkins to Sherwood, January 28, 1948, Sherwood Papers, Harvard.

84. Roosevelt to Hopkins, August 25, 1939, PPF 4096, FDRL.

85. Catledge, "It's 'Send for Harry.'"

## Chapter 3

1. Winston Churchill to Joseph Stalin, July 28, 1941, CHAR 20/41/63, Winston S. Churchill Papers, Churchill College, Cambridge, United Kingdom.

2. Turner Catledge, "It's 'Send for Harry,'" *New York Times*, March 16, 1941.

3. Interview with Samuel I. Rosenman, Columbia Center for Oral History, Butler Library, Columbia University, 97–98.

4. "Roosevelt, Churchill and Stalin: Personal Recollections and Photographs," by Robert Hopkins, Draft of December 24, 1995, Robert Hopkins Papers, Box 5, Special Collections Research Center, Lauinger Library, Georgetown University.

5. Gen. George Marshall Memorandum for Harry Hopkins, January 14, 1942, George Marshall Papers, George C. Marshall Foundation, Virginia Military Institute, Lexington, Virginia.

6. Excerpts from Ickes Diaries for June 23, 1940, November 5, 1940, Box 25; Ickes Diaries, February 22, 1941, 5248, Harold L. Ickes Papers, Manuscript Division, Library of Congress, Washington D.C.

7. Hopkins to Hellman, June 5, 1943, Harry L. Hopkins Papers, Box 299, Franklin D. Roosevelt Library, Hyde Park, New York (hereafter referred to as FDRL).

8. Catledge, "It's 'Send for Harry.'"

9. Harry Hopkins, "Churchill-Roosevelt First Rough Draft," c. September 1941, Hopkins Papers, Atlantic Conference File, Box 306, FDRL.

10. Interview with Leon Henderson, October 11, 1947, File 1889, Robert E. Sherwood Papers, Manuscript Collection, Houghton Library, Harvard.

11. Interview with Arthur Krock, Columbia Center for Oral History, Butler Library, Columbia University, 31.

12. Notes of Conversation between Sidney Hyman and Howard Hunter, November 21, 1946, File 2423, Sherwood Papers, Harvard.

13. Frances Perkins, "The People Mattered," *Survey Midmonthly*, February 1946, 38–39.

14. Harry Hopkins to Robert Hopkins, June 7, 1940, File 391, Sherwood Papers, Harvard.

15. Charles Hurd, "Hopkins: Right-Hand Man," *New York Times Magazine*, August 11, 1940.

16. Interview with Samuel I. Rosenman, Columbia Center for Oral History, 181–82.

17. Sidney Hyman Interview with Rexford Guy Tugwell, April 5, 1947, File 2429, Sherwood Papers, Harvard.

18. Ickes Diaries, July 19, 1940, 4593, Library of Congress.

19. "Campaign: By Acclamation," *Time*, July 29, 1940; Interview with Victor Sholis, January 15, 1947, File 1904, Sherwood Papers, Harvard.

20. Interview with Robert Kerr, October 12, 1947, File 1893, Sherwood Papers, Harvard.

21. "Campaign: By Acclamation."

22. Henry Wallace "Guru" Letters File, Hopkins Papers, Box 99, FDRL; Convention Notes, 1940, Box 123, Hopkins Papers, FDRL; Interview with Victor Sholis, January 15, 1947, File 1904, Sherwood Papers, Harvard.

23. Sherwood to Hopkins, July 30, 1940, Hopkins Papers, Box 97, FDRL.

24. Harry Hopkins Resignation Statement, August 24, 1940, PPF 4096, FDRL.

25. Frances Perkins to Hopkins, not dated [c. September 1940], Hopkins Papers, Box 94, FDRL.

26. Roosevelt to Hopkins, January 4, 1941, Franklin D. Roosevelt Papers, President's Personal Files, 1933–1945, (PPF) 4096, FDRL.

27. Roosevelt to King George VI, January 4, 1941, PPF 4096, FDRL.

28. Interview with Edward R. Murrow, September 16, 1946, File 1902, Sherwood Papers, Harvard.

29. Hopkins notes on London meetings, January 10, 1941, Hopkins Papers, Part I, Box 56, Folder 12, Georgetown University; Hopkins to Roosevelt, January 25, 1941, PREM 4/25/3, Visit of Mr. Harry Hopkins, British National Archives, Kew Gardens, United Kingdom.

30. Winston S. Churchill, *The Grand Alliance* (New York: Rosetta Books, 1948, reprint 2002) 19; Hopkins notes on London meetings, January 10, 1941, Hopkins Papers, Part I, Box 56, Folder 12, Georgetown University; Churchill to Roosevelt, January 13, 1941, in Warren Kimball, ed., *Churchill and Roosevelt: The Complete Correspondence*, vol. I, Princeton: Princeton University Press, 1984, 129.

31. Hopkins notes on London meetings, January 10, 1941, Hopkins Papers, Part I, Box 56, Folder 12, Georgetown University; Hopkins to Roosevelt, January 25, 1941, PREM 4/25/3, Visit of Mr. Harry Hopkins, British National Archives.

32. Anthony Biddle to Hopkins, February 18, 1941, Hopkins Papers, Part I, Box 2, Folder 14, Georgetown University; Memorandum of conversation with Their Majesties the King and Queen at Buckingham Palace, January 30, 1941, Hopkins Papers, Part I, Box 56, Folder 13, Georgetown University.

33. Ickes Diaries, February 8, 1941, 5205, Library of Congress.

34. Hopkins to Churchill, January 27, 1941, PREM 4/25/3, Visit of Mr. Harry Hopkins, British National Archives.

35. Hopkins to Churchill, not dated, February 1941, Visit of Mr. Harry Hopkins, January–February 1941, PREM 4/25/3, British National Archives.

36. Hopkins to Churchill, February 17, 1941, PPF 4096, FDRL.

37. Hopkins to Churchill, March 6, 1941, Hopkins Papers 136, FDRL; Hopkins to Roosevelt, January 14, 1941, President's Secretary's Files (PSF) Safe Files, Box 3, FDRL.

38. "National Affairs: Assistant President," *Time*, April 28, 1941.

39. Roosevelt to Hopkins, July 19, 1941, PPF 4096, FDRL; Hopkins to Roosevelt, July 23, 1941, PSF Safe Files, Box 3, FDRL.

40. Minutes of the 71st Meeting of the War Cabinet, July 17, 1941, CAB 65/19/7, 71 (41), July 17, 1941, British National Archives.

41. Harry Hopkins, "Churchill-Roosevelt First Rough Draft," c. September 1941, Hopkins Papers, Atlantic Conference File, Box 306, FDRL.

42. See Hamilton to Hopkins, August 14, 1943, Hopkins Papers, Box 132, Atlantic Charter File, FDRL; Harry Hopkins, "Churchill-Roosevelt First Rough Draft," c. September 1941, Hopkins Papers, Atlantic Conference File, Box 306, FDRL.

43. Hopkins to Churchill, August 9, 1941, Hopkins Papers, Atlantic Conference File, Box 306, FDRL.

44. Reminiscences of Frances Perkins, Columbia Center for Oral History, 23–24.

45. Churchill, *The Grand Alliance*, 19.

46. Memorandum by Harry Hopkins, January 3, 1942, Hopkins Papers, Box 136, FDRL; Ickes Diaries, May 23, 1943, 7768, Ickes Papers, Library of Congress.

47. Hopkins Memorandum on Churchill's medication, December 19, 1941, Hopkins Papers, Part I, Box 4, Folder 5, Georgetown University. Hopkins learned from the naval hospital that Churchill was taking barbital (a hypnotic), barbitonum, phenacetin (a pain remedy), urotropin (a powerful urinary antiseptic), phenyldimethylpyrar, lactylphenetidin (a fever reducer), hexamine (for treatment of urinary tract infections), amylum, magnesium peroxide (an antacid and laxative), and stearin, all washed down with liberal amounts of brandy, whiskey, champagne, and red wine. See John Harper to Hopkins, December 8, 1941, Hopkins Papers, Part I, Box 4, Folder 5, Georgetown University.

48. Churchill to Hopkins August 28, 1941, CHAR 20/42A/35, Churchill Papers.

49. Hopkins to Churchill, September 10, 1941, CHAR 20/42B/120-122, Churchill Papers.

50. Hopkins to Churchill, September 29, 1941, Hopkins Papers, Box 136, FDRL.

51. Hopkins to Churchill, December 23, 1944, CHAR 20/178/23, Churchill Papers.

52. Churchill to Hopkins, February 27, 1943, CHAR 20/107/37-39, Churchill Papers.

53. Hopkins to Churchill, February 3, 1943, CHAR 20/142A/76, Churchill Papers.

54. Hopkins to Churchill, December 23, 1944, CHAR 20/178/23, Churchill Papers.

55. First Draft of "The Stalin-Hitler Grudge Fight," by Harry L. Hopkins, Hopkins Papers, Part I, Box 56, Folder 18, Georgetown University.

56. Roosevelt to Hopkins, not dated, January 1941, PPF 4096, FDRL.

57. Harry Hopkins, "Churchill-Roosevelt 1st Draft," Hopkins Papers, Atlantic Conference File, Box 306, FDRL.

58. Interview with Averell Harriman, Columbia Center for Oral History, 89.

59. Churchill, *The Grand Alliance*, 18.

60. Reminiscences of Frances Perkins, Columbia Oral History, 23–24.

61. Brendan Bracken to Sherwood, June 5, 1946, File 106, Sherwood Papers, Harvard.

62. Interview with General Eisenhower, January 14, 1947, File 1884, Sherwood Papers, Harvard.

63. Interview with Admiral Ernest J. King, Part I, May 24–25, 1946, File 1894, Sherwood Papers, Harvard.

64. Churchill, *The Grand Alliance*, 20.

65. Interview with Admiral Ernest J. King, Part I, May 24-25, 1946, File 1894, Sherwood Papers, Harvard.

66. Churchill to Hopkins, October 8, 1941, Hopkins Papers, Box 136, FDRL.

67. Beaverbrook to Hopkins, October 23, 1944, Hopkins Papers, Part I, Box 1, Folder 33, Georgetown University; Churchill to Robert Sherwood, August 17, 1946, File 168, Sherwood Papers, Harvard.

68. Churchill to Hopkins, September 25, 1941, Hopkins Papers, Box 136, FDRL; Sydney Hyman to Robert Sherwood, July 22, 1946, File 411, Sherwood Papers, Harvard.

69. Churchill to Hopkins, January 21, 1943, Hopkins Papers, Box 330, FDRL.

70. Hopkins Notes on Casablanca, January 22, 1943, Casablanca File II, Box 330, FDRL.

71. Interview with Admiral Ernest King, Part I, May 24–25, 1946, File 1894, Sherwood Papers, Harvard.

72. Interview with George Marshall, July 23, 1947, File 1899, Sherwood Papers, Harvard.

73. "What Victory Will Bring Us," by Harry Hopkins, November 4, 1943, Hopkins Papers, Part I, Box 57, Folder 4, Georgetown University.

# Chapter 4

1. Harry Hopkins, "Churchill-Roosevelt First Rough Draft," c. September 1941, not published, Harry L. Hopkins Papers, Atlantic Conference File, Box 306, Franklin D. Roosevelt Library, Hyde Park, New York (hereafter referred to as FDRL).

2. Hopkins Speech, Madison Square Garden, June 22, 1942, Box 12, Hopkins Papers, FDRL.

3. For the most detailed account of his mission to Moscow, see the drafts of "The Stalin-Hitler Grudge Fight," by Harry L. Hopkins, Hopkins Papers, Part I, Box 56, Folder 18, Special Collections Research Center, Lauinger Library, Georgetown

University. These drafts later evolved into "The Inside Story of My Meeting with Stalin," *The American Magazine*, December 1941.

4. Hopkins to FDR, July 25, 1941, President's Secretary's File (PSF), Safe File, Box 3, FDRL.

5. Harry L. Hopkins, draft of "We Can Win in 1945," for *The American Magazine*, October 1943, Box 8, Hopkins Papers, FDRL.

6. Joseph E. Davies to Hopkins, October 27, 1940, Joseph E. Davies Papers, Box 38, Folder 7, Manuscript Division, Library of Congress.

7. Attache Report by Ivan Yeaton, April 24, 1941, Box 190, Military Intelligence Reports, USSR, Hopkins Papers, FDRL.

8. Hopkins to Roosevelt, July 23, 1941, PSF Safe Files, Box 3, FDRL.

9. Roosevelt to Stalin, July 26, 1941, in Welles to Hopkins, July 27, 1941, Hopkins in Moscow File, Hopkins Papers, Box 306, FDRL.

10. Hopkins to Roosevelt, July 25, 1941, PSF Safe Files, Box 3, FDRL; Hopkins to Roosevelt, July 27, 1941, President's Personal Files (PPF) 4096, FDRL.

11. First Draft of "The Stalin-Hitler Grudge Fight."

12. Hopkins to Roosevelt, July 23, 1941, PSF Safe Files, Box 3, FDRL.

13. Roosevelt to Hopkins, July 26, 1941, PSF Safe Files, Box 3, FDRL.

14. First Draft of "The Stalin-Hitler Grudge Fight."

15. Hopkins to Roosevelt, July 27, 1941, PPF 4096, FDRL.

16. Hopkins, "Churchill-Roosevelt First Rough Draft."

17. Roosevelt to Stalin, in Welles to Hopkins, July 27, 1941, Hopkins in Moscow File, Hopkins Papers, Box 306, FDRL.

18. Churchill to Stalin, July 28, 1941, CHAR 20/41/63, Churchill Papers, Churchill College, Cambridge, United Kingdom.

19. First Draft of "The Stalin-Hitler Grudge Fight."

20. Interview with John Winant, September 13, 1946, File 1907, Sherwood Papers, Harvard.

21. First Draft of "The Stalin-Hitler Grudge Fight."

22. "Flight to Archangel, July–August 1941," Hopkins Papers, Part I, Box 60, Folder 9, Georgetown University; Interview with John Alison, Aviation Project, Columbia Center for Oral History, Butler Library, Columbia University, 15–16.

23. First Draft of "The Stalin-Hitler Grudge Fight."

24. First Draft of "The Stalin-Hitler Grudge Fight."

25. Harry Hopkins, "Churchill-Roosevelt First Rough Draft."

26. Military Attache Comments on Current Events, by Ivan Yeaton, April 24, 1941, Box 190, Military Intelligence Reports, USSR, Hopkins Papers, FDRL.

27. Laurence Steinhardt to Robert Sherwood, February 9, 1948, File 767, Sherwood Papers, Harvard; Interview with Charles Bohlen, January 14, 1947, File 1873, Sherwood Papers, Harvard.

28. Attache Report, Ivan Yeaton, June 30, 1941, Box 190, Military Intelligence Reports, USSR, Hopkins Papers, FDRL.

29. Laurence Steinhardt to Robert Sherwood, October 30, 1946, File 767, Sherwood Papers, Harvard.

30. Interview with Joseph E. Davies, March 6, 1947, File 1880, Sherwood Papers, Harvard. For more detail on the controversies over the military attachés, see Mary E. Glantz, *FDR and the Soviet Union: The President's Battles over Foreign Policy* (Lawrence: University of Kansas Press, 2005), 2–3, 30–35.

31. Faymonville to Hopkins, October 11, 1941, Box 194, Hopkins Papers, FDRL.

32. Harry Hopkins, "Churchill-Roosevelt First Rough Draft."

33. Laurence Steinhardt to Sherwood, October 30, 1946, File 767, Sherwood Papers, Harvard.

34. Second Meeting at the Kremlin between Harry L. Hopkins and Mr. Stalin, July 31, 1941, Hopkins in Moscow File, Hopkins Papers, Box 306, FDRL.

35. First Draft of "The Stalin-Hitler Grudge Fight."

36. For Hopkins's memoranda of conversation about the meetings with Stalin see, for example, Conference at the Kremlin between Harry L. Hopkins and Mr. Stalin, July 30, 1941, Hopkins in Moscow File, Hopkins Papers, Box 306, FDRL; as well as First Draft of "The Stalin-Hitler Grudge Fight"; and also Laurence A. Steinhardt to Robert E. Sherwood, October 30, 1946, File 767, Sherwood Papers, Harvard. With regard to documents where there are differences between the published versions in the series *Foreign Relations of the United States* and the original, the original has been used.

37. First Draft of "The Stalin-Hitler Grudge Fight."

38. First Draft of "The Stalin-Hitler Grudge Fight."

39. Conference at the Kremlin between Hopkins and Stalin, July 30, 1941, Hopkins in Moscow File, Hopkins Papers, Box 306, FDRL. These meeting minutes are more accessibly available, but in a slightly redacted version, at *Foreign Relations of the United States*, 802–5.

40. Second Meeting at the Kremlin between Hopkins and Stalin, July 31, 1941, Hopkins in Moscow File, Hopkins Papers, Box 306, FDRL.

41. Conference at the Kremlin between Hopkins and Stalin, July 30, 1941, Hopkins in Moscow File, Hopkins Papers, Box 306, FDRL.

42. First Draft of "The Stalin-Hitler Grudge Fight."

43. Memorandum by Harry Hopkins, no date, Hopkins Papers, Box 302, FDRL.

44. First Draft of "The Stalin-Hitler Grudge Fight."

45. Harry L. Hopkins, "For the President's Eyes Only," July 31, 1941, Hopkins in Moscow File, Hopkins Papers, Box 306, FDRL.

46. First Draft of "The Stalin-Hitler Grudge Fight."

47. Conference at the Kremlin between Hopkins and Molotov, July 31, 1941, Hopkins in Moscow File, Hopkins Papers, Box 306, FDRL.

48. Laurence Steinhardt to Sherwood, October 30, 1946, File 767, Sherwood Papers, Harvard.

49. "Hopkins in Russia Offers Supplies," *New York Times*, July 31. 1941.

50. Hopkins to Herbert Morrison, August 9, 1941, Hopkins Papers, Part I, Box 15, Folder 28, Georgetown University.

51. Harry Hopkins to the President, the Secretary, and Undersecretary, August 1, 1941, *FRUS*, Vol. I, The Soviet Union, 814–15.

52. Hopkins to Brenden Bracken, August 8, 1941, Hopkins Papers, Part I, Box 2, Folder 36, Georgetown University.

53. Interview with Charles Bohlen, January 14, 1947, File 1873, Sherwood Papers, Harvard.

54. First Draft of "The Stalin-Hitler Grudge Fight."

55. Interview with Averell Harriman, Columbia Center for Oral History, 248–49.

56. Hopkins to Winant, October 25, 1943, Hopkins Papers, Box 218, FDRL.

57. Hopkins to Hastings Ismay, August 7, 1941, Hopkins Papers, Part I, Box 10, Folder 14, Georgetown University.

58. Harry Hopkins, "Churchill-Roosevelt First Rough Draft."

59. First Draft of "The Stalin-Hitler Grudge Fight."

60. Averell Harriman, Columbia Center for Oral History, 248–49.

61. Interview with Charles Bohlen, January 14, 1947, File 1873, Sherwood Papers, Harvard.

62. Harry Hopkins, "Churchill-Roosevelt First Rough Draft."

63. Harry Hopkins, "Churchill-Roosevelt First Rough Draft."

64. Memorandum to Harry Hopkins, "Aid to Russia," by Wayne Coy, August 18, 1941, Wayne Coy Papers, Box 8, FDRL; Conversation between Sidney Hyman and Dan Arnstein, June 26, 1947, Sherwood Papers, File 2416, Harvard.

65. Interview with Averell Harriman, Columbia Center for Oral History, 249.

66. Harry Hopkins, "Churchill-Roosevelt First Rough Draft."

67. Hopkins to Churchill, September 29, 1941, Hopkins Papers, Box 136, FDRL.

68. First Draft of "The Stalin-Hitler Grudge Fight."

69. First Draft of "The Stalin-Hitler Grudge Fight."

70. Sumner Welles to Hopkins, July 7, 1941, *FRUS*, The Far East, 1941, 670–71.

## Chapter 5

1. Marshall to Hopkins, December 18, 1942, George Marshall Papers, George C. Marshall Foundation, Virginia Military Institute, Lexington, Virginia.

2. "Pearl Harbor: Fireside Scene," *Time*, February 25, 1946. In 1946, the sole survivor of this scene on December 6, 1941, Commander Lester R. Schulz, told the story to the Congressional Pearl Harbor Investigative Committee in February 1946.

3. Memorandum by Harry Hopkins, December 7, 1941, Hopkins Papers, Part III, Folder 19, Box 6, Special Collections Research Center, Lauinger Library, Georgetown University.

4. Churchill to Hopkins, December 7, 1941, CHAR 20/46/42, Winston S. Churchill Papers, Churchill College, Cambridge, United Kingdom.

5. Interview with Edward R. Murrow, September 16, 1946, File 1902, Robert E. Sherwood Papers, Manuscript Collections, Houghton Library, Harvard.

6. "U.S. At War: Assistant President," *Time*, April 10, 1944.

7. "Presidential Agent," *Time*, January 22, 1945.

8. Hopkins to Missy LeHand, September 11, 1942, Hopkins Papers, Part I, Box 12, Folder 27, Georgetown University.

9. Interview with Vannevar Bush, October 31, 1946, File 1876, Sherwood Papers, Harvard.

10. Marshall to Hopkins, December 18, 1942, Marshall Papers.

11. Interview with General Eisenhower, January 14, 1947, File 1884, Sherwood Papers, Harvard.

12. Harry Hopkins Memorandum for the President, "First Priority of Military Strategy," December 19, 1941, PSF Safe Files, Box 3, FDRL; Marshall Memorandum for Harry Hopkins, January 15, 1942, Marshall Papers.

13. Interview with Henry Stimson, October 23, 1946, File 1906-b, Sherwood Papers, Harvard; Interview with General Dwight D. Eisenhower, January 14, 1947, File 1884, Sherwood Papers, Harvard.

14. Harry Hopkins Memorandum for the President, "First Priority of Military Strategy," December 19, 1941, PSF Safe Files, Box 3, FDRL; "Priority of Objectives," by Harry Hopkins, February 16, 1942, PSF, Safe Files, Box 3, FDRL.

15. Harry Hopkins Memorandum for the President, December 17, 1941, Hopkins Papers, Decisions on Grand Strategy, Box 313, FDRL.

16. Interview with George Marshall, July 23, 1947, File 1899, Sherwood Papers, Harvard.

17. Harry Hopkins Memorandum for the President, "First Priority of Military Strategy," December 19, 1941, PSF Safe Files, Box 3, FDRL; Marshall Memorandum for Hopkins, January 15, 1942, Marshall Papers.

18. Interview with Bernard Baruch, January 27–31, 1947, File 1872, Sherwood Papers, Harvard.

19. Interview with Vannevar Bush, October 31, 1946, File 1876, Sherwood Papers, Harvard.

20. Frank L. Kluckhohn, "Washington Success Story," *New York Times Magazine*, July 26, 1942.

21. Roosevelt to Chiang Kai-shek, July 4, 1942, *FRUS, China*, 1942, 95.

22. Frances Perkins, "People Mattered to Harry Hopkins," *Survey Mid-monthly*, February 1946, 38–39.

23. Beaverbrook to Hopkins, November 29, 1944, Hopkins Papers, Part I, Box 1, Folder 33, Georgetown University.

24. Hopkins to Churchill, July 28, 1942, CHAR 20/78/71, Churchill Papers.

25. "White House Romance," *Time*, July 13, 1942.

26. George Marshall to Louise Macy, July 3, 1942, Marshall Papers.

27. Hopkins to Lord Beaverbrook, September 26, 1942, Hopkins Papers, Part I, Box 1, folder 33, Georgetown University.

28. Roosevelt to Churchill, July 8, 1942, Hopkins Papers, Box 136, Folder 1, FDRL.

29. Hopkins Notes on Conversation between the President, Molotov, Hopkins, and Hull, May 29, 1942, *FRUS*, Vol. III, The Soviet Union, 1942, 571–72.

30. Hopkins Notes on White House Dinner with the President and Molotov, May 29, 1942, *FRUS*, 573–74.

31. Memorandum of Conversation among the President, Molotov, King, Marshall, Hopkins, May 30, 1942, *FRUS*, 575.

32. Hopkins Memorandum on Molotov visit, May 31, 1942, Hopkins Papers, Box 194, FDRL.

33. Hopkins Memorandum of Conversation with FDR, King, Marshall, May 31, 1942, Molotov Mission File, Box 194, Hopkins Papers, FDRL.

34. Interview with Averell Harriman, Columbia Center for Oral History, Butler Library, Columbia University, 251.

35. Hopkins to Winant, June 12, 1942, Hopkins Papers, Box 311, Molotov Visit file, 1942, FDRL.

36. Hopkins Speech, Madison Square Garden, June 22, 1942, Box 12, Hopkins Papers.

37. Hopkins to Churchill, April 2, 1942, Hopkins Papers, Box 136, folder 1, FDRL; Roosevelt to Hopkins, for Churchill, April 17, 1942, CHAR 20/73/118, Churchill Papers.

38. Hopkins to Churchill, April 3, 1942, CHAR 20/73/42, Churchill Papers.

39. War Cabinet Minutes 47 (42), April 13, 1942, CAB 65/26/8, British National Archives, Kew Gardens, United Kingdom.

40. Hopkins to Roosevelt, July 25, 1942, FO 954/18B/6959, British National Archives.

41. Interview with Admiral King, May 24–25, 1946, and March 12 and 18, 1947, File 1894, Sherwood Papers, Harvard; Interview with General Marshall, July 23, 1947, Sherwood Papers, File 1899, Harvard.

42. Minutes of Combined Staff Conference, July 20, 1942, Hopkins Papers, Box 308, FDRL; Marshall to Hopkins, December 18, 1942, Marshall Papers.

43. Minutes of Combined Staff Conference, July 22, 1942, Hopkins Papers, Box 308, FDRL.

44. Roosevelt to Hopkins, Marshall, King, July 24, 1942, Hopkins Papers, Box 308, FDRL.

45. Interview with General Eisenhower, January 14, 1947, File 1884, Sherwood Papers, Harvard.

46. Hopkins to Churchill, February 3, 1943, CHAR 20/142A/76, Churchill Papers; Churchill to Hopkins, February 13, 1943, CHAR 20/106/72-73, Churchill Papers.

47. Interview with Admiral Ernest J. King, Part I, May 24–25, 1946, File 1894, Sherwood Papers, Harvard.

48. Churchill to Hopkins, September 23, 1943, Box 332, Appointment of Eisenhower File, FDRL; Hopkins Memorandum for the President, October 4, 1943, Appointment of Eisenhower File, Box 332, Hopkins Papers, FDRL.

49. Interview with Admiral Ernest J. King, Part I, May 24–25, 1946, File 1894, Sherwood Papers, Harvard.

50. Churchill to Hopkins, October 14, 1943, Hopkins Papers, Box 332, Appointment of Eisenhower File, FDRL.

51. Marshall Memorandum for General Eisenhower re: Harry Hopkins, February 14, 1942, Marshall Papers; Eisenhower to Hopkins, May 4, 1942, Hopkins Papers, Box 334, FDRL.

52. Interview with General Eisenhower, January 14, 1947, File 1884, Sherwood Papers, Harvard.

53. General George C. Marshall to Robert Sherwood, February 25, 1947, File 548, Sherwood Papers, Harvard.

54. Interview with General Eisenhower, January 14, 1947, File 1884, Sherwood Papers, Harvard.

55. Churchill to Hopkins, September 25, 1941, Hopkins Papers, Box 136, FDRL.

56. Combined Chiefs of Staff Minutes, *FRUS*, The Casablanca Conference, 708–9; Roosevelt-Churchill Luncheon, January 23, 1943, *FRUS*, The Casablanca Conference, 704–5.

57. Draft of Harry L. Hopkins, "We Can Win in 1945," for *The American Magazine*, October 1943, Box 8, Hopkins Papers, FDRL.

58. "What Victory Will Bring Us," by Harry Hopkins, November 4, 1943, Hopkins Papers, Part I, Box 57, Folder 4, Georgetown University.

59. Hopkins to Churchill, September 23, 1942, CHAR 20/80/73, Churchill Papers; Hopkins Memorandum of Conversations with FDR and Eden, March 15, 1943, Hopkins Papers, Eden in Washington File, Box 329, FDRL.

60. Memorandum for Hopkins from Combined Chiefs of Staff, "Importance of Soviet Relationship and Suggestions for Improving Them," December 1, 1942, Hopkins Papers, Box 217, Russia File, FDRL.

61. Oscar Cox to Hopkins, April 26, 1943, Growing Crises in Poland File, Hopkins Papers, Box 337, FDRL.

62. Hopkins to Winant, October 25, 1943, Hopkins Papers, Box 218, FDRL.

63. Interview with Joseph E. Davies, March 6, 1947, File 1880, Sherwood Papers, Harvard.

64. Harriman to Roosevelt, July 5, 1943 in Harriman to Hopkins, July 5, 1943, Hopkins Papers, Box 157, FDRL.

65. Eden to Churchill, March 26, 1943, CHAR 20/108/104, Churchill Papers.

66. Interview with Joseph E. Davies, March 6, 1947, File 1880, Sherwood Papers, Harvard.

67. See President Roosevelt to Marshall Stalin, May 5, 1943, in Susan Butler, ed., *My Dear Mr. Stalin: The Complete Correspondence of Franklin D. Roosevelt and Joseph V. Stalin* (New Haven: Yale University Press, 2006), 129–30.

68. Roosevelt to Charles Bohlen, November 30, 1943, Papers of Charles E. Bohlen, Box 34, Manuscript Collection, Library of Congress.

69. Hopkins to FDR, December 1, 1943, Hopkins Papers, Part 1, Box 19, Folder 3, Georgetown University.

70. Averell Harriman, Columbia Oral History Collection, 248–49.

71. Hopkins Notes, December 1, 1943, *FRUS*, Conferences at Cairo and Teheran, 593; Hopkins-Eden-Molotov Luncheon Meeting, November 30, 1943, *FRUS*, Conferences at Cairo and Teheran, 568–75.

72. Tripartite Luncheon Meeting, December 1, 1943, *FRUS*, 587; Hopkins Notes on Turkey at the Teheran Conference, December 1, 1943, *FRUS*, 593.

73. Luncheon Minutes by Charles Bohlen, December 1, 1943, *FRUS*, Conferences at Cairo and Teheran, 585–87.

74. Robert Sherwood, *Roosevelt and Hopkins: An Intimate History* (New York: Enigma Books, reprint 2008), 619.

75. Charles Bohlen, *Witness to History* (New York: W.W. Norton, 1973), 244.

## Chapter 6

1. Hopkins to Winant, June 12, 1942, Hopkins Papers, Box 311, Molotov Visit File, 1942, FDRL.

2. Harry L. Hopkins, Speech at Madison Square Garden, June 22, 1942, Box 12, Hopkins Papers, FDRL.

3. "What Victory Will Bring Us," by Harry Hopkins, November 4, 1943, Hopkins Papers, Part I, Box 57, Folder 4, Special Collections Research Center, Lauinger Library, Georgetown University.

4. Hopkins to Winant, June 12, 1942, Hopkins Papers, Box 311, Molotov Visit File, 1942, FDRL.

5. Memorandum for Hopkins from Combined Chiefs of Staff, "Importance of Soviet Relationship and Suggestions for Improving Them," December 1, 1942, Hopkins Papers, Box 217, Russia File, FDRL.

6. Conference at the Kremlin between Hopkins and V. M. Molotov, July 31, 1941, Hopkins in Moscow File, Hopkins Papers, Box 306, FDRL.

7. Dictation by Harry Hopkins, July 20, 1945, Hopkins Papers, Part I, Box 57, Folder 12, Georgetown University.

8. "What Victory Will Bring Us."

9. Interview with Admiral King, May 24–25, 1946, and March 12 and 18, 1947, File 1894, Sherwood Papers, Harvard; Interview with General Marshall, July 23, 1947, Sherwood Papers, File 1899, Harvard.

10. Dictation by Harry Hopkins, July 20, 1945, Hopkins Papers, Part I, Box 57, Folder 12, Georgetown University.

11. Hopkins to FDR, April 9, 1942, *FRUS*, 629–30.

12. See Warren Kimball editor's commentary for Churchill to Hopkins, May 31, 1942, in *Churchill and Roosevelt: The Complete Correspondence*, vol. 1, Warren Kimball, ed. (Princeton: Princeton University Press, 1984), 501; Hopkins to Churchill, June 1, 1942, CHAR 20/76/9, Churchill Papers.

13. Churchill to Roosevelt, April 12, 1942, in Kimball, ed., *Churchill and Roosevelt*, vol. I, 447–48.

14. Roosevelt to Churchill, in Roosevelt to Hopkins, April 11, 1942, in Kimball, ed., *Churchill and Roosevelt*, vol. I, 446–47.

15. Churchill to Hopkins, May 31, 1942, Hopkins Papers, Box 136, Folder 1, FDRL; Churchill to Hopkins, May 28, 1942, CHAR 20/75/99, Churchill Papers.

16. Dictation by Harry Hopkins, July 20, 1945, Hopkins Papers, Part I, Box 57, Folder 12, Georgetown University.

17. Dictation by Harry Hopkins, July 20, 1945, Hopkins Papers, Part I, Box 57, Folder 12, Georgetown University.

18. Dictation by Harry Hopkins, July 20, 1945, Hopkins Papers, Part I, Box 57, Folder 12, Georgetown University.

19. Conversation between Sidney Hyman and Dan Arnstein, Hopkins's special representative to Burma, June 26, 1947, Sherwood Papers, File 2416, Harvard.

20. Hopkins to Roosevelt, December 5, 1942, Hopkins Papers, Box 331, Chinese Affairs File, FDRL.

21. Conversation between Sidney Hyman and Dan Arnstein, June 26, 1947, Sherwood Papers, File 2416, Harvard.

22. Hopkins Speech, Madison Square Garden, June 22, 1942, Box 12, Hopkins Papers; "New Deal Emerging in Far East," *Washington Post*, June 28, 1942.

23. "Memorandum for the President: Matters of Immediate Military Concern," by Harry Hopkins, March 14, 1942, PSF 138, FDRL.

24. Memorandum by Harry L. Hopkins, "Arrival of Madame Chiang Kai-Shek in the United States," November 30, 1942, Hopkins Papers, Box 331, China Affairs File, FDRL.

25. "What Victory Will Bring Us."

26. Memorandum of Conversation between Harry Hopkins and Madame Chiang Kai-Shek, February 27, 1943, Hopkins Papers, Box 331, Chinese Affairs File, FDRL.

27. Hopkins Memorandum for the President, January 30, 1942, Chinese Requirements File, Box 314, Hopkins Papers, FDRL.

28. Hopkins to T. V. Soong, November 28, 1942, Map Room Files, Box 13, FDRL.

29. Memorandum by Hopkins, "Arrival of Madame Chiang Kai-Shek in the United States," November 30, 1942, China Affairs File, Hopkins Papers, Box 331, FDRL.

30. Memorandum of Conversation between Harry Hopkins and Madame Chiang Kai-Shek, February 27, 1943, Hopkins Papers, Box 331, Chinese Affairs File, FDRL.

31. Roosevelt to Hopkins, for Churchill, April 17, 1942, CHAR 20/73/118, Churchill Papers; Interview with George Marshall, July 23, 1947, File 1899, Sherwood Papers, Harvard.

32. Alsop to Hopkins, December 10, 1942, Hopkins Papers, Box 331, China Affairs File, FDRL; Davies to Hopkins, December 31, 1943 "Chiang Kai-Shek and China," Box 334, Hopkins Papers, FDRL.

33. Chennault to Hopkins, February 8, 1944, PSF 138, FDRL; Gen. Chennault to Hopkins, January 26, 1944, "Serious Trouble in China" File, Hopkins Papers, Box 334, FDRL.

34. Hopkins to Lauchlin Currie, June 9, 1943, Hopkins Papers, Box 331, Chinese Affairs File, FDRL; Hopkins to Marshall, May 19, 1943, Marshall Papers.

35. See Hopkins-Chiang Conversation, November 26, 1943, Evening, Roosevelt's Villa, *FRUS, The Conferences at Cairo and Tehran*, 367.

36. Memorandum of Conversation between Hopkins and Madame Chiang Kai-Shek, February 27, 1943, Hopkins Papers, Box 331, Chinese Affairs File, FDRL.

37. Interview with George Marshall, July 23, 1947, File 1899, Sherwood Papers, Harvard.

38. Memorandum of Conversation in the President's Study, by Harry Hopkins, July 15, 1943, Hopkins Papers, Box 331, Chinese Affairs File, FDRL.

39. According to Stilwell's diaries, he had an immediate dislike of Hopkins upon meeting him back in February 1942, disdaining Hopkins's cordiality toward him as softness and loathing his very appearance. See Entry for February 9, 1942, *The Stilwell Papers*, Theodore H. White, ed. (New York: W. Sloan Associates, 1948), 36.

40. Hopkins Memorandum on Madame Chiang Kai-Shek, September 11, 1944, "Serious Trouble in China" File, Hopkins Papers, Box 334, FDRL.

41. Hopkins Memorandum for the President, September 8, 1944, "Serious Trouble in China" File, Hopkins Papers, Box 334, FDRL; "The Generalissimo's Dilemmas," by John Davies, December 9, 1944, Hopkins Papers, Box 334, FDRL.

42. "China and the Kremlin," by John Davies, January 4, 1945, Hopkins Papers, Box 334, FDRL.

43. Dictation by Harry Hopkins, July 20, 1945, Hopkins Papers, Part I, Box 57, Folder 12, Georgetown University.

44. Dictation by Harry Hopkins, July 20, 1945, Hopkins Papers, Part I, Box 57, Folder 12, Georgetown University.

45. Raoul Aglion, *Roosevelt and de Gaulle: Allies in Conflict: A Personal Memoir of Allies in Conflict* (New York: Free Press, 1988), 129.

46. Dictation by Harry Hopkins, July 20, 1945, Hopkins Papers, Part I, Box 57, Folder 12, Georgetown University.

47. Dictation by Harry Hopkins, July 20, 1945, Hopkins Papers, Part I, Box 57, Folder 12, Georgetown University.

48. Minutes by Bohlen, December 1, 1943, *FRUS, Conferences at Cairo and Teheran*, 585–87.

49. Hopkins Notes on Casablanca, Entry for January 22, 1943, Casablanca File II, Box 330, FDRL.

50. "Notes by the President's Special Assistant," by Harry Hopkins, January 24, 1943, *FRUS, Casablanca*, 839.

51. Hopkins-Macmillan Conversation, January 24, 1943, *FRUS*, 723.

52. Harry L. Hopkins, "Notes by the President's Special Assistant," Casablanca, January 24, 1943, *FRUS, Casablanca*, 840.

53. Memorandum by Harry L. Hopkins, "Casablanca," January 22, 1943, Hopkins Papers, Box 330, FDRL.

54. Memorandum by Harry L. Hopkins, "Casablanca," January 22, 1943, Hopkins Papers, Box 330, FDRL; Hopkins Papers, Box 257, FDRL. Hopkins to Winant, November 11, 1942: Good on Free French: Hopkins to Winant, October 25, 1943.

55. Harry L. Hopkins, "Notes by the President's Special Assistant," January 24, 1943, *FRUS, Casablanca*, 840.

56. Hopkins-Eden-Molotov Luncheon Meeting, November 30, 1943, *FRUS, Cairo and Teheran*, 568–75.

57. Dictation by Harry Hopkins, July 20, 1945, Hopkins Papers, Part I, Box 57, Folder 12, Georgetown University.

58. Harry Hopkins, Observations on Yalta, October 19, 1945, Hopkins Papers, Part I, Manuscripts, Box 57, folder 14 (Yalta), Georgetown University; Memorandum of Conversation between Hopkins and Bidault, January 29, 1945, Hopkins Papers, Box 337, Hopkins in Paris, FDRL; Aglion, *Roosevelt and de Gaulle*, 198; Charles Bohlen, *Witness to History* (New York: W.W. Norton, 1973), 170.

59. Witness Comment by Etienne Burin des Roziers, in Kim Munholland, "The United States and Free France," in Robert O. Paxton and Nicholas Wahl, eds., *De Gaulle and the United States: A Centennial Reappraisal* (Oxford: Berg Publishers, 1994), 100–1.

60. Robert Sherwood, *Roosevelt and Hopkins: An Intimate History* (New York: Enigma Books, reprint 2008), 659.

61. Witness Comment by Etienne Burin des Roziers.

62. Hopkins to Roosevelt, February 5, 1945, *FRUS, The Yalta Conference*, III, 634; Hopkins to Roosevelt, February 7, 1945, *FRUS, The Yalta Conference*, III, 729.

63. Dictation by Harry Hopkins, July 20, 1945, Hopkins Papers, Part I, Box 57, Folder 12, Georgetown University.

64. "What Victory Will Bring Us"; Draft of Harry L. Hopkins, "We Can Win in 1945."

# Chapter 7

1. Robert E. Sherwood, *Roosevelt and Hopkins: An Intimate History* (New York: Enigma Books, 2008), 674.

2. Hopkins to Pamela Churchill, May 17, 1943, Hopkins Papers, Part I, Box 4, Folder 3, Special Collections Research Center, Lauinger Library, Georgetown University.

3. Harry Hopkins to Robert Hopkins, February 2, 1944, Hopkins Papers, Part III, Box 5, Folder 9, Georgetown University.

4. Harry Hopkins to Stephen Hopkins, February 2, 1944, Hopkins Papers, Part II, Box 3, Folder 6, Georgetown University.

5. Sherwood, *Roosevelt and Hopkins*.

6. Harry Hopkins to Robert Hopkins, February 14, 1944, Hopkins Papers, Part III, Box 5, Folder 9, Georgetown University.

7. Hopkins to Churchill, February 3, 1943, CHAR 20/142A/76, Churchill Papers.

8. Churchill to Hopkins, February 13, 1944, CHAR 20/142A/22, Churchill Papers.

9. Interview with Robert Kerr, October 12, 1947, File 1893, Sherwood Papers, Harvard; Roosevelt to Ethel Hopkins, February 21, 1944, PSF 138, FDRL.

10. Harry Hopkins to Robert Hopkins, February 29, 1944, Hopkins Papers, Part III, Box 5, Folder 9, Georgetown University.

11. Hopkins to Harriman, March 25, 1944, Hopkins Papers, Part I, Box 8, Folder 37, Georgetown University.

12. Frances Perkins to Hopkins, March 29, 1944, Hopkins Papers, Part I, Box 14, Folder 33, Georgetown University.

13. George Marshall to Harry Hopkins, March 29, 1944, Hopkins Papers, Box 6, FDRL.

14. Hopkins to Churchill, August 28, 1944, Box 13, Map Room Files, FDRL.

15. Interview with Charles Bohlen, January 14, 1947, File 1873, Sherwood Papers, Harvard; Charles Bohlen to Robert Sherwood, July 8, 1948, File 94, Sherwood Papers, Harvard.

16. Hopkins to Churchill, August 7, 1944, Box 13, Map Room Files, FDRL.

17. "U.S. at War: Assistant President," *Time*, April 10, 1944.

18. George Marshall to Harry Hopkins, April 7, 1944, Personal Health File, 1942–1944, Hopkins Papers, Box 6, FDRL.

19. Frances Perkins to Hopkins, June 17, 1944, Hopkins Papers, Part I, Box 17, Folder 33, Georgetown University.

20. Interview with Joseph E. Davies, March 6, 1947, File 1880, Sherwood Papers, Harvard.

21. Charles Bohlen, "Memorandum to Harry Hopkins," October 3, 1944, Hopkins Papers, Churchill in Moscow, Box 335, FDRL.

22. Bohlen Minutes, Tripartite Dinner Meeting, November 28, 1943, *FRUS, Conferences at Cairo and Teheran*, 512.

23. Hopkins-Eden-Molotov Luncheon Meeting, November 30, 1943, *FRUS, Conferences at Cairo and Teheran*, 568–75.

24. Interview with Charles E. Bohlen, January 14, 1947, File 1873, Sherwood Papers, Harvard.

25. Charles Bohlen, *Witness to History, 1929–1969* (New York: W.W. Norton, 1973), 162–63.

26. Charles Bohlen to Robert Sherwood, July 8, 1948, File 94, Sherwood Papers, Harvard.

27. Roosevelt to Harriman, October 4, 1944, Hopkins Papers, Churchill in Moscow File, Box 335, FDRL.

28. Hopkins draft of Roosevelt to Stalin, October 4, 1944, Hopkins Papers, Churchill in Moscow File, Box 335, FDRL. See also, Susan Butler, ed., *My Dear Mr. Stalin: The Complete Correspondence of Franklin D. Roosevelt and Joseph V. Stalin* (New Haven: Yale University Press, 2006), 260–61.

29. Interview with Charles E. Bohlen, January 14, 1947, File 1873, Sherwood Papers, Harvard.

30. Stalin to Roosevelt, in President to Harriman, October 9, 1944, Churchill-Stalin Conference, October 9–16, 1944, Special Files, Map Room, Box 32, FDRL.

31. Harriman to the President, October 9, 1944, Churchill-Stalin Conference, October 9–16, 1944, Special Files, Map Room, Box 32, FDRL; Interview with Charles E. Bohlen, January 14, 1947, File 1873, Sherwood Papers, Harvard.

32. Interview with Charles Bohlen, January 14, 1947, File 1873, Sherwood Papers, Harvard.

33. Harriman Cable 1342, to Roosevelt, October 10, 1944, Churchill-Stalin Conference File, October 9–16, 1944, Special Files, Map Room, Box 32, FDRL.

34. Roosevelt to Harriman, October 11, 1944, Churchill-Stalin Conference file, October 9–16, 1944, Special Files, Map Room, Box 32, FDRL.

35. Harriman to the President, October 11, 1944, Map Room Files, Box 32, FDRL.

36. Churchill to Hopkins, October 12, 1944, CHAR 20/173/32-33, Churchill Papers; Interview with Charles Bohlen, January 14, 1947, File 1873, Sherwood Papers, Harvard.

37. Churchill to Hopkins, October 12, 1944, CHAR 20/173/32-33, Churchill Papers.

38. Churchill to Hopkins, October 13, 1944, CHAR 20/173/36, Churchill Papers.

39. As Beaverbrook wrote to Hopkins regarding Moscow: "In any case, I received one injunction after another, 'This is not to be told.' And God knows, it should not be, although I would like very much to be recounting them to you in this letter." Beaverbrook to Hopkins, October 23, 1944, Hopkins Papers, Part III, Box 6, Folder 8, Georgetown University.

40. Interview with Bob Hannegan, May 25, 1946, File 1888, Sherwood Papers, Harvard.

41. Ickes Diaries, November 7, 1943, 8335, Library of Congress.

42. Florence Kerr, Columbia Center for Oral History, Butler Library, Columbia University, 106.

43. Ickes Diaries, August 6, 1944, 9151–9152, Library of Congress; Interview with Bob Hannegan, May 25, 1946, File 1888, Sherwood Papers, Harvard.

44. Ickes Diaries, January 1, 1944, 8504–8505, Ickes, Papers, Library of Congress.

45. Hopkins to the President, August 5, 1944, Hopkins Papers, Box 214, Franklin D. Roosevelt file, FDRL.

46. Beaverbrook to Hopkins, May 16, 1944, Hopkins Papers, Part I, Box 1, Folder 33, Georgetown University.

47. Churchill Telegram to Hopkins, November 7, 1944, CHAR 20/174/93, Churchill Papers.

48. Hopkins Cable to Churchill, November 7, 1944, CHAR 20/174/99, Churchill Papers.

49. Hopkins to Churchill, November 7, 1944, Hopkins Papers, Part I, Box 4, Folder 5, Georgetown University.

50. Harry Hopkins to Robert Hopkins, November 23, 1944, Hopkins Papers, Part III, Box 5, Folder 9, Georgetown University.

51. Hopkins to Henry Wallace, November 14, 1944, Hopkins Papers, Part I, Box 22, Folder 36, Georgetown University.

52. Hopkins to Harry S Truman, November 10, 1944, Hopkins Papers, Part I, Box 22, Georgetown University.

53. Ickes Diaries, December 2, 1944, 9365–9366, 9385, Library of Congress; Arthur Krock, Columbia Center for Oral History, Butler Library, Columbia University, 93–94.

54. Interview with Charles Bohlen, January 14, 1947, File 1873, Sherwood Papers, Harvard.

55. Edward Stettinius, *Roosevelt and the Russians: The Yalta Conference* (Garden City: Doubleday, 1949), 52–53.

56. Interview with Joseph E. Davies, March 6, 1947, File 1880, Sherwood Papers, Harvard.

57. Memorandum of 5th Conversation at the Kremlin, Subject: Poland, May 31, 1945, Box 338, Hopkins in Moscow File, Hopkins Papers, FDRL.

58. Winant to Hopkins, December 10, 1944, Growing Crises in Greece, Box 337, Hopkins Papers, FDRL.

59. Churchill to Hopkins, December 10, 1944, Map Room Files, Box 13, FDRL; Churchill to Hopkins, December 11, 1944, Growing Crises in Greece, Box 337, Hopkins Papers, FDRL.

60. Churchill to Hopkins, December 10, 1944, Growing Crises in Greece, Box 337, Hopkins Papers, FDRL.

61. Harry Hopkins, Memorandum on Greece, December 14, 1944, File 2414, Sherwood Papers, Harvard.

62. Hopkins to Churchill, December 16, 1944, Growing Crises in Greece, Box 337, Hopkins Papers, FDRL.

63. Churchill to Hopkins, December 17, 1944, CHAR 20/177/88, Churchill Papers.

64. Hopkins to Churchill, December 23, 1944, CHAR 20/178/23, Churchill Papers.

65. Hopkins to Winant, January 8, 1945, Box 257, Hopkins Papers, FDRL.

66. Memorandum for Mr. Hopkins, by Charles Bohlen, September 11, 1944, Growing Crises in Poland File, Box 337, Hopkins Papers, FDRL; Harriman to Hopkins, September 10, 1944, Box 13, Map Room Files, FDRL; Hopkins to Roosevelt, September 11, 1944, Growing Crises in Poland File, Box 337, Hopkins Papers, FDRL.

67. Harry Hopkins, Observations on Yalta, October 19, 1945, Hopkins Papers, Part I, Manuscripts, Box 57, Folder 14 (Yalta), Georgetown University.

68. Stalin to Roosevelt, October 19, 1944, Map Room Files, Box 32, FDRL.

69. Harry Hopkins, Observations on Yalta, October 19, 1945, Hopkins Papers, Part I, Manuscripts, Box 57, folder 14 (Yalta), Georgetown University.

70. "Return," *Time*, October 9, 1944; "Presidential Agent," *Time*, January 22, 1945.

71. Interview with Charles E. Bohlen, January 14, 1947, File 1873, Sherwood Papers, Harvard; Memorandum, January 15, 1945, Background for Yalta File, Box 337, Hopkins Papers, FDRL.

72. Roosevelt to Churchill, January 12, 1945, in Kimball, ed. 507–8.

73. Harry Hopkins, Observations on Yalta, October 19, 1945, Hopkins Papers, Part I, Manuscripts, Box 57, Folder 14 (Yalta), Georgetown University.

74. Hopkins to Roosevelt, January 24, 1945, Map Room Files, Box 13, FDRL.

75. Stettinius, *Roosevelt and the Russians: The Yalta*.

76. "Yalta Conference: Notes," Anna Roosevelt Halsted Papers, Box 84, FDRL.

77. Lord Moran, *Churchill: The Struggle for Survival* (Washington: Basic Books), 274–75.

78. "Yalta Conference: Notes," Anna Roosevelt Halsted Papers, Box 84, FDRL.

79. "Conversation with Stalin at Yalta," Robert Hopkins Papers, Box 4, Georgetown University.

80. Hopkins to Roosevelt, February 7, 1945, *FRUS*, Yalta, III, 729.

81. Roosevelt to Stalin, February 6, 1945, in Susan Butler ed., *My Dear Mr. Stalin*, 291–92.

82. Harry Hopkins, Observations on Yalta, October 19, 1945, Hopkins Papers, Part I, Manuscripts, Box 57, Folder 14 (Yalta), Georgetown University.

83. Secretary of State Stettinius to the President, March 13, 1945, PSF 29, FDRL.

84. Sherwood, *Roosevelt and Hopkins: An Intimate History*, 674; Harry Hopkins, Observations on Yalta, October 19, 1945, Hopkins Papers, Part I, Manuscripts, Box 57, Folder 14 (Yalta), Georgetown University; Dictation by Harry Hopkins, July 20, 1945, Hopkins Papers, Part I, Box 57, Folder 12, Georgetown University.

85. Hopkins to Roosevelt, February 5, 1945, *FRUS, Conferences at Malta and Yalta*, 633.

86. Hopkins to the President, February 10, 1945, *FRUS, Conferences at Malta and Yalta*, 920.

87. Charles Bohlen to Robert Sherwood, July 8, 1948, File 94, Sherwood Papers, Harvard.

88. Harry Hopkins to Louise Hopkins, February 15, 1945, Charles Bohlen Papers, Box 34, Library of Congress Manuscript Division; David Roll, *The Hopkins Touch* (London: Oxford University Press, 2013), 377–78.

89. Interview with George Marshall, July 23, 1947, File 1899, Sherwood Papers, Harvard.

90. Sherwood, *Roosevelt and Hopkins: An Intimate History*.

## Chapter 8

1. Interview with George Marshall, July 23, 1947, File 1899, Sherwood Papers, Harvard.

2. Charles Bohlen, *Witness to History, 1929–1969* (New York: W.W. Norton, 1973), 209.

3. Hopkins to Churchill, April 12, 1945, Map Room Files, Box 13, FDRL; Hopkins to Churchill, April 13, 1945, Map Room Files, Box 13, FDRL.

4. Churchill to Hopkins, April 13, 1945, CHAR 20/199/108, Winston S. Churchill Papers, Churchill College, Cambridge, United Kingdom.

5. Hopkins to Clementine Churchill, April 17, 1945, Hopkins Papers, Part I, Box 8, Folder 25, Special Collections Research Center, Lauinger Library, Georgetown University.

6. Brendan Bracken to Hopkins, April 19, 1945, Hopkins Papers, Part I, Box 11, Folder 36, Special Collections Research Center, Lauinger Library, Georgetown University.

7. Hopkins to Marshall Stalin, April 13, 1945, Map Room Files, Box 13, FDRL.

8. Hopkins to Chiang Kai Shek, April 13, 1945, Map Room Files, Box 13, FDRL.

9. Robert Sherwood, *Roosevelt and Hopkins: An Intimate History* (New York: Enigma Books, reprint 2008), 682.

10. Sherwood, *Roosevelt and Hopkins*.

11. Frank Costigliola, *Roosevelt's Lost Alliances: How Personal Politics Helped Start the Cold War* (Princeton: Princeton University Press, 2011), 317–18.

12. Interview with Bob Hannegan, May 25, 1946, File 1888, Sherwood Papers, Harvard.

13. Molotov, Stettinius, Eden to Hopkins, May 4, 1945, Hopkins Papers, Part I, Box 15, Folder 16, Georgetown University.

14. Churchill to Hopkins, May 9, 1945, CHAR 20/218/51, Winston S. Churchill Papers, Churchill College, Cambridge, United Kingdom.

15. George C. Marshall to Hopkins, May 13, 1945, Hopkins Papers, Part III, Box 14, Folder 33, Georgetown University.

16. Hopkins V-E Day Address, National Broadcasting Company (NBC), May 8, 1945, Hopkins Papers, Part I, Box 62, Folder 14, Georgetown University.

17. Hopkins to Prime Minister William Lyon Mackenzie King, April 13, 1945, Map Room File 13, FDRL.

18. Interview with Charles Bohlen, January 14, 1947, File 1873, Sherwood Papers, Harvard; Oscar Cox to Hopkins, "US-USSR Relations," May 14, 1945, Box 337, Post-Yalta Deterioration File, Hopkins Papers, FDRL.

19. "What Victory Will Bring Us," by Harry Hopkins, November 4, 1943, Hopkins Papers, Part I, Box 57, Folder 4, Georgetown University.

20. Memorandum of Conversation between Grew and Stettinius, May 21, 1945, *FRUS*, 22–23.

21. Averell Harriman, Columbia Center for Oral History, Butler Library, Columbia University, 268.

22. Bohlen, *Witness to History*.

23. Hopkins to President Truman, May 27, 1945, Box 338, Hopkins in Moscow File, Hopkins Papers, FDRL.

24. Memorandum by Harry Hopkins, October 19, 1945, Hopkins Papers, Part III, Box 6, Folder 31, Georgetown University.

25. See Costigliola, 318–19, 350. For evidence that Hopkins was still committed to pursing good relations with the USSR, see his comments on U.S.-Soviet relations in the unpublished "Dictation by Harry Hopkins," July 20, 1945, Hopkins Papers, Part I, Box 57, Folder 12, Georgetown University.

26. Marshall to Hopkins, May 13, 1945, Hopkins Papers, Part III, Box 14, Folder 33, Georgetown University.

27. Interview with George Marshall, July 23, 1947, File 1899, Sherwood Papers, Harvard.

28. Ickes Diaries, May 24, 1945, 9745, Ickes Papers, Library of Congress.

29. Harry Hopkins, "Notes on Negotiations during Moscow Visit," June 13, 1945, Hopkins Papers, Part III, Box 6, Folder 31, Georgetown University.

30. Truman to Marshal Stalin, May 19, 1945, *FRUS, The Conference of Berlin*, 21.

31. Memorandum by Harry Hopkins, October 19, 1945, Hopkins Papers, Part III, Box 6, Folder 31, Georgetown University.

32. Hopkins meeting can be found at Memorandum of First Conversation at the Kremlin, May 26, 1945, *FRUS*, the Hopkins Mission to Moscow, 23, but the original

documents are preferable owing to a series of key ommissions in the *FRUS* version. Memorandum of 1st Conversation at the Kremlin, May 26, 1945, Box 338, Hopkins in Moscow File, Hopkins Papers, FDRL.

33. Dictation by Harry Hopkins, July 20, 1945, Hopkins Papers, Part I, Box 57, Folder 12, Georgetown University.

34. Memorandum of 1st Conversation at the Kremlin, May 26, 1945, Box 338, Hopkins in Moscow File, Hopkins Papers, FDRL.

35. Memorandum of 1st Conversation at the Kremlin, May 26, 1945, Box 338, Hopkins in Moscow File, Hopkins Papers, FDRL.

36. Hopkins to Truman, May 26, 1945, Box 338, Hopkins Papers, FDRL.

37. Memorandum of 2nd Conversation at the Kremlin, May 27, 1945, Box 338, Hopkins Papers, FDRL.

38. Hopkins to Truman, May 28, 1945, Box 338, Hopkins Papers, FDRL.

39. Hopkins Dictation, July 20, 1945, Hopkins Papers, Part I, Box 57, Folder 12, Georgetown University.

40. Memorandum of 3rd Conversation at the Kremlin, May 28, 1945, Box 338, Hopkins Papers, FDRL.

41. Hopkins to Truman, May 29, 1945, Box 338, Hopkins Papers, FDRL.

42. Hopkins to Truman, May 30, 1945, Box 338, Hopkins Papers, FDRL.

43. Dictation by Harry Hopkins, July 20, 1945, Hopkins Papers, Part I, Box 57, Folder 12, Georgetown University.

44. Memorandum of 4th Conversation at the Kremlin, May 30, 1945, Box 338, Hopkins Papers, FDRL.

45. Memorandum of 5th Conversation at the Kremlin, May 31, 1945, Box 338, Hopkins Papers, FDRL.

46. Hopkins to Truman, May 31, 1945, Box 338, Hopkins Papers, FDRL.

47. Hopkins to Truman, June 1, 1945, Box 338, Hopkins Papers, FDRL.

48. Memorandum of Conversation during Dinner at the Kremlin, June 1, 1945, Box 338, Hopkins Papers, FDRL.

49. Memorandum of Conversation during Dinner at the Kremlin, June 1, 1945, Box 338, Hopkins Papers, FDRL.

50. Truman to Churchill, June 1, 1945, *FRUS*, 1945, vol. V, 314.

51. Churchill to Truman, June 2, 1945, *FRUS*, 1945, vol. V, 317.

52. Churchill to Hopkins, June 2, 1945 in Archibald Clark Kerr to Harry Hopkins, June 2, 1945, Box 338, Hopkins Papers, FDRL.

53. Hopkins to Churchill, June 3, 1945, CHAR 20/220/66, Churchill Papers.

54. President Truman to Harry Hopkins, June 5, 1945, Box 338, Hopkins Papers, FDRL.

55. Memorandum of 6th Conversation at the Kremlin, June 6, 1945, Box 338, Hopkins Papers, FDRL.

56. Stalin to Churchill, May 30, 1945, CHAR 20/220/32, Churchill Papers; Hopkins to Truman, June 6, 1945, Box 338, Hopkins Papers, FDRL; President Truman to Prime Minister Churchill, June 3, 1945, Box 338, Hopkins Papers, FDRL.

57. Truman to Hopkins, June 5, 1945, Box 338, Hopkins Papers, FDRL.

58. Interview with General Eisenhower, January 14, 1947, File 1884, Sherwood Papers, Harvard.

59. Harry Hopkins, "Notes on Negotiations during Moscow Visit," June 13, 1945 Hopkins Papers, Part III, Box 6, Folder 31, Georgetown University.

60. Truman to Hopkins, Note Affixed to "Proposal for the Establishment of a Council of Foreign Ministers," June 25, 1945, Potsdam Conference File, Hopkins Papers, Box 338, FDRL.

61. Interview with Charles Bohlen, January 14, 1947, File 1873, Sherwood Papers, Harvard.

62. Harry S Truman to Hopkins, July 3, 1945, Hopkins Papers, Part III, Box 6, Folder 18, Georgetown University.

63. Hopkins to Truman, July 2, 1945, Hopkins Papers, Box 214, Franklin D. Roosevelt File, FDRL.

64. Hopkins to Beaverbrook, July 6, 1945, Hopkins Papers, Part I, Box 1, Folder 33, Georgetown University.

65. Hopkins to Marshall, September 10, 1945, Hopkins Papers, Part I, Box 14, Folder 33, Georgetown University.

66. Marshall to Hopkins, July 4, 1945, Hopkins Papers, Part I, Box 14, Folder 33, Georgetown University.

67. Beaverbrook to Hopkins, June 29, 1945, Hopkins Papers, Part I, Box 1, Folder 33, Lauinger Library, Georgetown University.

68. Arthur Krock, "Hopkins' War Role," *New York Times*, July 4, 1945.

## Conclusion

1. "Good and Faithful Servant," *Time*, February 11, 1946.

2. Hopkins to Eleanor Roosevelt, June 26, 1945, Hopkins Papers, Box 19, Folder 1, Special Collections Research Center, Lauinger Library, Georgetown University; Hopkins to General Marshall, June 27, 1945, Box 338, Hopkins Papers, FDRL.

3. Hopkins to Harriman, July 4, 1945, Hopkins Papers, Part I, Box 8, Folder 37, Georgetown.

4. George McJimsey, *Harry Hopkins: Ally of the Poor and Defender of Democracy* (Cambridge: Harvard University Press, 1987), 345, 362.

5. Hopkins to Lord Beaverbrook, July 6, 1945, Hopkins Papers, Part I, Box 1, Folder 33, Georgetown University.

6. Dictation by Harry Hopkins, July 20, 1945, Hopkins Papers, Part I, Box 57, Folder 12, Georgetown.

7. Frances Perkins, "The People Mattered," *Survey Midmonthly*, February 1946, 38–39.

8. Lewis Hopkins to Sherwood, November 5, 1947, File 389, Sherwood Papers, Harvard.

9. "What Victory Will Bring Us," by Harry Hopkins, November 4, 1943, Hopkins Papers, Part I, Box 57, Folder 4, Georgetown.

10. Hopkins to Brendan Bracken, December 18, 1941, Hopkins Papers, Part I, Box 2, Folder 36, Georgetown.

11. Harry Hopkins to Robert Hopkins, January 22, 1946, Georgetown.

12. Hopkins to Churchill, January 22, 1946, Hopkins Papers, Part I, Box 4, Folder 5, Georgetown.

13. "Good and Faithful Servant."

14. Perkins, "The People Mattered."

15. "Harry L. Hopkins," *Washington Post*, January 30, 1946.

16. "Good and Faithful Servant."

17. Arthur Krock, Columbia Center for Oral History, Butler Library, Columbia University, 63.

18. "John Steinbeck's Memorial to Harry Hopkins," Read by Burgess Meredith, May 22, 1946, Hopkins Papers, Part IV, Box 1, Folder 45, Georgetown.

19. Ethel Hopkins to Robert Sherwood, September 23, 1947, File 386, Sherwood Papers, Harvard.

20. Winston Churchill to Robert Sherwood, August 17, 1946, File 168, Sherwood Papers, Harvard.

21. Hopkins to Winant, October 25, 1943, Hopkins Papers, Box 218, FDRL.

22. Hopkins-Eden-Molotov Luncheon Meeting, November 30, 1943, *FRUS, Conferences at Cairo and Teheran*, 568–75.

23. Interview with Anthony Eden, August 27, 1947, File 1883, Sherwood Papers, Harvard; Anthony Eden to Robert Sherwood, November 7, 1947, File 251, Sherwood Papers, Harvard.

24. Harriman, Columbia Center for Oral History, Butler Library, Columbia University, 246–50.

25. Dictation by Harry Hopkins, July 20, 1945, Hopkins Papers, Part I, Box 57, Folder 12, Georgetown.

26. Hopkins to Harry S Truman, November 10, 1944, Hopkins Papers, Part I, Box 22, Georgetown.

27. Dictation by Harry Hopkins, July 20, 1945, Hopkins Papers, Part I, Box 57, Folder 12, Georgetown.

28. John Lewis Gaddis, *George F. Kennan: An American Life* (New York: Penguin Press, 2011), 202.

29. Charles Bohlen, *Witness to History, 1929–1969* (New York: W.W. Norton, 1973), 243–44.

30. Harry L. Hopkins, Speech at Madison Square Garden, June 22, 1942, Box 12, Hopkins Papers, FDRL.

31. Averell Harriman, Columbia Center for Oral History, Butler Library, Columbia University, 273–74.

32. Dictation by Harry Hopkins, July 20, 1945, Hopkins Papers, Part I, Box 57, Folder 12, Georgetown.

# Index

Alaska, 89, 90
Allied Control Commission for
    Germany, 106
Allies. *See* Grand Alliance
Alsop, Joseph, 99
Americans: relief views of, 13, 27; on
    Soviet Union, 72–73, 130–31, 135,
    147; workers, 142; on WWII, 54
Appleby, Paul, 18, 27, 40
Asia, 6, 78, 79, 93–98, 102, 119, 122,
    123, 148. *See also* China
Athens, Greece, 117–18
Atlantic Charter, 55
Atlantic Conference, 21, 47, 54–56, 72
*Augusta*, USS, 54–55
austerity, 28, 35–37
Axis powers, 12, 4, 8, 48–49, 60, 73,
    79, 95, 103, 144. *See also* Germany;
    Italy; Japan

Balkans, 84, 91, 94, 103, 111, 113, 114,
    116, 148
Baltic, 87, 95, 148
Baruch, Bernard, 16
Beaverbrook (lord), 79, 138, 139, 141

Belgium, 38
Bering Straits, 89, 90
Berlin, Germany, 106, 108, 121–22,
    130, 132, 135 *138*, 141
Berlin Conference, 128, 135, 136, 137,
    138, 148
Biddle, Anthony, 9
Big Three, 6–7, 87, 91, 110, 111, 118,
    119, 128, 130, 135. *See also* Berlin
    Conference; Grand Alliance;
    Teheran Conference; Yalta
    Conference; Yalta formula
Blackstone Hotel, 49, 50–51
Bohlen, Charles, 9, 71, 109, 111–12,
    118, 122,125, 128, *138*, 148
boondoggling, 28, 30
Bracken, Brendan, 57–58, 70, 126, 142
Britain. *See* Great Britain
British: China interest of, 94, 96–97;
    Greek actions of, 116, 117, 133, 136;
    imperial objectives of, 94–97; Italian
    actions of, 116–17, 118; Pacific
    interest of, 94; Second Front and,
    83–85; spheres of influence, 97, 113
British War Cabinet, 54

Bruenn, Howard, 121
Bulgaria, 113–14
Burma Road, 97, 99–100
Burns, James H., 2
Business Advisory Council, 39
business confidence, 35–36
Byrnes, Jimmy, 115, 121, 13738, 148–50

Cairo, Egypt, 86, 99
cancer, 32, 33–34, 42, 108
Caribbean, 52
Casablanca Conference, 59, 103–4, 105
Catledge, Turner, 47
Chennault, Clair, 99–100
Chequers, 58, 63
Chiang Kai-shek, 2, 6, 80, 93, 96–101, 103, 126, 134–35
Chicago, Illinois, 19, 49–51, 50
Chiefs of Staff. See military chiefs
China, 2, 3–4, 6, 60, 78, 80, 93–103, 134–35; British as interested in, 94, 96–97; Churchill, Winston, influencing, 99; Hopkins, Harry, supporting, 78, 93–94; Japan and, 97–98, 99; problems of, 101–2; as regional power, 93; Stalin on, 134–35; in UN, 101; U.S. and, 97–100, 102. See also empires; Grand Alliance
Chinese, 1,6, 93–103
Christodora House, 18–19
Churchill, Clementine, 126
Churchill, Pamela, 107
Churchill, Winston, 6–7, 20, 79, 108, 148; on alcohol, 59, 120; at Casablanca Conference, 103; eccentric operations of, 84, 91, 94; goals of, 60; Hopkins, Harry, communicating with, 117–18, 125, 136–37, 142; Hopkins, Harry, meeting with, 52–53, 54, 55–56, 57–60, 83–85, 137; Hopkins, Harry, on, 56, 128; Hopkins,

Harry's, objectives influencing, 60; Hopkins, Harry's, relationship with, 56–60, 84, 118; on Hopkins, Harry, 1–2, 45, 58, 127, 144; imperial objectives of, 94–97, 148–49; as intermediary, 88, 89, 90; at Moscow Conference, 109, 110–14; Perkins on, 55; press and, 59–60; reelection worrying, 115, 122, 129, 135; Roosevelt, Franklin Delano, and, 5, 55, 58, 59, 111–13, 120–21, 125; Second Front and, 83–85, 87, 94; Soviet Union and, 63, 72, 73; Stalin and, 64, 72, 87, 109, 110–14, 146; Truman and, 129, 136, 137. See also Moscow Conference; Yalta Conference
Civil Works Administration (CWA), 4, 13, 27–28, 30, 40, 79, 106
Claridge's Hotel, 52
cloak and suit industry, 142
clothes, of Hopkins, Harry, 21, 42
Colbert, Claudette, 35
Cold War, 3, 147–48
Commerce Department, 38–39
communism, Hopkins, Harry, on, 66
Cone, Howard, 105
Congress, 36–37
Costigliola, Frank, 128–29
Coy, Wayne, 14
Crimea, 119–20
criticism: of Hopkins, Harry, 7–9, 16, 31–32, 37, 41–42; of New Deal, 28–29, 30; of Roosevelt, Franklin Delano, 131. See also Ickes, Harold
cross-channel invasion, weather influencing, 85. See also Overlord; Second Front
CWA. See Civil Works Administration

Davies, John Paton, 99, 101
Davies, Joseph E., 88, 129
Davis, Chester, 18

death: of Hopkins, Barbara, 32, 34–35; of Hopkins, Harry, 25, 142–44; of Roosevelt, Franklin Delano, 126–27, 129–30, 131
demand, spending stimulating, 36–37
Democratic Convention, 19, 49–51, 50, 114–15
Democratic Party, 38–41, 49–51, 50, 115, 121
Des Moines Economic Club, 41
Dewey, Thomas E., 115–16, 119
diplomacy, 150
direct relief, 29, 30
Distinguished Service Medal, 138–39
divorce, of Hopkins, Harry, 20
Duncan, Barbara. *See* Hopkins, Barbara

Eastern Europe, 116, 131, 148
Eastern Front, 91, 93–94
Eden, Anthony, 87, 91, 111–14, 120, 127, 144–45, 155
Eisenhower, Dwight D., 5–6, 9, 58, 77–78, 85–86, 141
Elizabeth (queen), 42
empires, 6, 57, 60, 94–97, 148–49
Europe, 106, 111. *See also* Eastern Europe; World War I; World War II
European Recovery Program. *See* Marshall Plan

family: of Hopkins, Harry, 17–18, 20, 32, 45, 80–82, 121–22; of Roosevelt, Franklin Delano, 33, 34, 45
Far East. *See* Asia
Farley, Jim, 39–40, 49
fascism, 3–4, 6, 48, 57, 66. *See also* nazism
Faymonville, Philip R., 67
Federal Emergency Relief Administration (FERA), 27–28, 29
federal spending. *See* spending
FERA. *See* Federal Emergency Relief Administration

Finland, 133
Flanagan, Hallie, 18
*Foreign Relations of the United States* (FRUS) (State Department), 3
Forrestal, James, 4, 9, 16, 47, 48
Fort Dix, 46
Fourteenth Air Force, 100
France, 82–85, 103, 104, 105–6. *See also* Free French; de Gaulle, Charles
Frank, Jerome, 20–21
Frankfurter, Felix, 16
Free France. *See* France
Free French, 2–3, 6, 8, 102, 104
French North Africa, 84–85
FRUS. *See Foreign Relations of the United States*

Garner, John Nance, 39–40
de Gaulle, Charles, 2, 3, 8, 102–6
Geneva Convention, 82
George VI (king), 42
Germans, 5, 43, 61–62
Germany: defeat of, 84, 127; Japan influenced by, 73; Soviet Union invaded by, 61–63, 66–67; Stalin on, 69; as threat, 47
Giraud, Henri, 103
Goddard, Paulette, 81
government relief. *See* relief
Grand Alliance: dynamics of, 8–9; Hitler driving wedge into, 87–88; Hopkins, Harry, as key to, 1–4, 5–7, 56–57, 60, 78–79, 86–87, 93–106, 102–3, 104, 105, 105–6, 107–24, 143, 144, 149. *See also* Big Three
Grand Design, 6, 149–50
Great Britain, 5, 6–7, 52–53, 56, 58–59, 148. *See also* Grand Alliance
Great Depression, Americans on, 13, 27
Greece, 7, 111, 113–14, 116–118, 133, 136, 144
Grinnell, Iowa, 17, 18–19, 34, 41
Grinnell College, 18–19

Gromyko, Andrei, 119
Gross, Ethel, 20

Hague, Frank, 50
Hale, Dorothy Donovan, 35
Hale, Gardner, 35
Hamlin, Hannibal, 115
Harding, Warren G., 49
Harriman, W. Averell, 9, 47, 48, 57, 88, 91, 109, 112, 113–14, *124*, 128, 145–46, *146*, 150
health: of Hopkins, Harry, 32, 33–34, 42, 81–82, 108, 109, 120, 121, 138, 141, 142, 149; of Roosevelt, Franklin Delano, 109
Hearst press, 139
Hertz, John, *50*
Hitler, Adolf, 3, 4, 45, 52, 54, 61, 62–64, 66, 73, 76, 78, 79, 82, 83, 93–94, 117, 144, 150; Grand Alliance wedge driven by, 87–88; Hopkins, Harry, finding, 137; Japan fled to by, 132; Katyn massacre used by, 87–88; Soviets finding body of, 132; Stalin on, 68–69, 70, 132, 137
Hodson, Bill, 19
Honolulu, Hawaii, 75–76
Hoover, Herbert, 29, 38, 40
Hopkins, Adah, 20
Hopkins, Ann, 17–18
Hopkins, Barbara, 20, 32, 34–35
Hopkins, David Aldona, 18, *50*, 80, 107
Hopkins, Diana, 20, *33*, 34, 41, 42, 46, *48, 50*
Hopkins, Ethel, 19, 34, 144
Hopkins, Harry, *12, 14*, 20–21, 22, *23, 24, 33, 48, 50, 105, 123, 138*; accusations against, 7–8; appearance of, 21, 41–42; as assistant president, 5–6, 53–54, 76–92, 80, 89, 90, 109–10; characteristics of, 17–18, 20–22, 24–25, 49; controversy about, 7–8; goals measured against objectives

of, 3–4; humor of, 17; life of, 11–13, 34–35; papers of, 20; as recalled, 43; source material on, 3; statecraft duties of, 49; strategic sense of, 78–79; strengths possessed by, 16; as writer, 19. *See also* New Deal
Hopkins, Lewis, 17, 33, 34, 42, 142
Hopkins, Louise, 81–82, *138*
Hopkins, Robert, 42, 46, 49, 80, 107, 108, 121–22, 142
Hopkins, Stephen, 80, 107–9
Howe, Louis McHenry, 15
*How the Other Half Lives* (Riis), 11
Hull, Cordell, 9, 39–40, *48*, 75, 76, 77, 82, 91, 102, 112, 116
Hungary, 113, 114
Hurley, Patrick, 101

Iceland, 54
Ickes, Harold, 17, 30–32, 35, 129; on Churchill, Winston, 53; on farm life, 41; on presidential nomination, 40; rivalry of, 31–32, 46, 115; and Hopkins with women, 31–32
Imperial Japanese Army. *See* Japanese
India, 93, 95–96
International Red Cross, 8, 82
Iowa, 17, 18–19, 38, 41
Italy, 91, 116–17, 118

James, William, 4
Japan, 6–7; China providing attack on, 97–101; Churchill, Winston, on, 76; Germany influencing, 73; Hitler fleeing to, 132; Roosevelt, Franklin Delano, on, 75, 76; Soviet Union's war with, 122, 123, 134–35, 137; Stalin on, 134, 135, 150; as threat, 47; U.S. attacked by, 75–76
Japanese, 6, 97–98
jobs, public works creating, 29–30, 32
Johnson, Andrew, 115
Joint Chiefs of Staff. *See* military chiefs

Kahlo, Frida, 35
Katyn massacre, 87–88
Kelly, Ed, 49, 50
Kennan, George, 148
Kerr, Archibald Clark, 129
Kerr, Florence, 15, 18, 34, 41, 108
Kerr, Robert, 19, 34, 41, 108
King, Ernest J., 5, 6, 9, 57, 58, 60, 78, 83, 84, 85, 99, 103, 118, *124*
*King George*, HMS, 47, 54
Knox, Frank, 75–76, 77
Krock, Arthur, 1, 19–20, 37, 40–41, 47, 139, 143
Kuter, Major General L. S., *124*
Kwajalein, 108

Leahy, William, 9, 77–78, 85, 100, *105*, 118, *124*, 150
LeHand, Marguerite, *14*, 32, 34, 35, 42, 43, 77
Lehman, Herbert, 19
Lend-Lease, 4, 5; to Great Britain, 52–53, 56, 58–59; to Soviet Union, 59, 66, 67, 68, 70, 86–87; spending, 53
liberalism, 11
Lincoln, Abraham, 115
Lincoln Study, 43, 45–47
Lippmann, Walter, 38
Litvinov, Maxim, 83
Livadia Palace, *124*
logistics, 78–79
London, Great Britain, 8–9, 52–53, 54, 83–85, 95–96
London Poles, 87–88, 118, 132
Lowlands, 43
Luce, Henry, 143

Macy, Louise. *See* Hopkins, Louise
Madam Chiang Kai-shek. *See* Soong Mei-ling
Madison Square Garden, 83, 93
Maisky, Ivan, 64

Malay Straits, 76
Manchuria, 122, 134–35
Manhattan. *See* New York City, New York
Mao Zedong, 134
marriages, of Hopkins, Harry, 20, 35, 81–82
Marshall, George C., *124*; in conference, 76; Hopkins, Harry, and, 1, 5–6, 9, 14–15, 46, 60, 75, 77, 78–79, 81, 100, 109, 110, *123*, 125, 127, 129, 138–39, 141, 142–43; Overlord led by, 85, 86; Second Front and, 83–85; on WWII, 1
Marshall Plan, 106
mass graves, 87–88
Mayo Clinic, 33, 42, 108, 109, 125
McAdoo, William Gibbs, 81
McCormick press, 139
McIntyre, Ross, 33
Memorial Hospital, 142
Meredith, Burgess, 143–44
military chiefs, 60, 84–85
Molotov, Vyacheslav, 8, 67, 70, 82–83, *90*, 91, 94, 114, 127, 144
Montana, 18, 19
Morgenthau, Henry, 11, 13, 35–36, 48, 149
Morgenthau Plan, 109
Morocco, 59
Moscow, Soviet Union, 7, 8–9; Hopkins, Harry, and, 61–72, *65*, 66–67, 70, 88, 117, 128–37, 148; London Poles' relations with, 87–88, 118; Poland threatened by, 87–88; Roosevelt, Franklin Delano, approving trip to, 63–64; wives leaving, 62
Moscow Conference, 109, 110–14, 116, 117
Munitions Assignments Board, 76–79
Murrow, Edward R., 52, 76
Mussolini, Benito, 117

National Defense Research Committee (NDRC), 79
nazism, 2, 3–4, 66, 69, 71, 88, 130, 141
NDRC. *See* National Defense Research Committee
Nehru, Jawaharlal, 95–96
New Deal, 77; Churchill, Winston, as curious about, 54; criticism of, 28–29; Hopkins, Harry's, abandonment of, 47, 48; record of, 28; Roosevelt, Franklin Delano, on, 28; spending, 27–28, 29, 32; transformational impact of, 28–29; WWII influenced by, 28
New Dealers, 39–40, 127. *See also* Ickes, Harold
New York City, New York, 18–19, 142
New York State Temporary Emergency Relief Administration (TERA), 19
New York Tuberculosis and Health Association, 19, 20
North Africa, 84–85

obituary, 143
Operation Overlord. *See* Overlord
Operation Sledgehammer, 82
Operation Torch, 84–85
organized labor, 40–41
Overlord, 85–86, 91, 110

Pacific, 84, 94, 132
Panic of 1893, 18
Pearl Harbor, Hawaii, 75–76
Perkins, Frances, 11, 16, 19, 20, *22*, 31, 48–49, 51–52, 55, 57, 80, 109, 110, 142, 143
Pius XI (pope), 21
Poland: 7, 87–88, 118, 128–37, 144; Churchill, Winston, on, 111, 113, 114; Greece compared with, 117, 133, 136; Hopkins, Harry, on, 132; Moscow threatening, 87–88; Stalin on, 131, 132–34, 136, 137; at Yalta Conference, 122, 132–33

Polish government-in-exile. *See* London Poles
Polish leaders, 136
political machines, 36, 40–41, 51
postwar conflict, 127
postwar foreign policies of Soviet Union, 146–47
Potsdam Conference. *See* Berlin Conference
poverty, 19
presidential nomination, 37–42, 43, 49, 50–51
press, 21, 45, 46–47, 59–60, 139
prison camps, 8, 82
public works, 29–30, 32
Public Works Administration (PWA), 31, 32
PWA. *See* Public Works Administration

realpolitik, 78–79
recession, 35–37
Red Army, 2, 3, 5, 7, 61–72, 78, 82, 83, 87–88, 91, 93, 101, 117, 121–22, 133–37
reelection, 114–16, 122, 129, 135
relief: direct, 29, 30; necessity of, 28, 30; as right, 13; unemployment influenced by, 13, 29, 36–37. *See also* New Deal
resignation, 42, 51, 127
Riis, Jacob, 11
Rochester, Minnesota, 33, 42
Romania, 113, 114
Roosevelt, Anna, 4, 15, 120–21
Roosevelt, Betsey, 31, 32, *33*, 34
Roosevelt, Eleanor, *14*, 31, 33, 34, 40, 45–46, 48, 51, 81, 141
Roosevelt, Franklin Delano, 3, 6–7, 13, *14*, *33*, 48, 82, *105*, *124*, 127–28; Churchill, Winston, and, 5, 55, 58, 59, 111–13, 120–21; crisis faced by, 43; criticism of, 131; death of, 126–27, 129–30, 131; Democratic

Party influenced by, 39–41, 49–51, 50; diplomatic style of, 150; family of, 33, 34, 45; goals of, 6–7; Greece and, 117–18; as guardian, 34; health of, 109; Hopkins, Harry, and, 14–16, 19–20, 31–32, 33–34, 35, 42, 45–47, 79, 80, 112, 120, 123, 143; on Japan, 75, 76; Moscow trip approved by, 63–64; on New Deal, 28; purge of, 39; reelection of, 114–16; Second Front and, 83–85; sons of, 80; Soviet Union speculated on by, 72; Stalin and, 64, 83, 88–92, 90, 112–13, 144, 145, 146; as stubborn, 15; on U.S.-Soviet relations, 145, 146. *See also* Yalta Conference

Roosevelt, Franklin Delano, Jr., 14, 33

Roosevelt, Jimmy, 31, 33, 34

Roosevelt, Sara, 32, 33

Roosevelt, Teddy, 28, 39–40

*Roosevelt and Hopkins* (Sherwood), 3, 17

*Roosevelt's Lost Alliances* (Costigliola), 128–29

Rosenman, Sam, 38–39, 46

Round Up, 84–85

Roziers, Etienne Burin des, 104, 105

Russia. *See* Soviet Union

Sandberg, Carl, 19

San Francisco Conference, 127, 130, 137

Second Cairo Conference, 86

Second Front, 82–85, 87, 91, 94, 103

Second Quebec Conference, 109

Secretary of Commerce, 38–39, 40, 42, 51

Secretary of Welfare, 38

Secret Service, U.S., 103–4

Security Council, 101, 106

self-determination, 96, 133

self-government of India, 95–96

Senate, U.S., 36–37, 115

Sforza, Carlo, 116–17

Shakespeare, William, 108

Sherwood, Robert, 3–4, 17, 91–92, 123–24, 126, 144

Siberia, 89, 90

small countries, Red Army reoccupying, 88

Social Gospel, 11–12, 17, 48–49

Soong, T. V., 2, 98

Soong Mei-ling, 98–99

Soviets, 113, 132

Soviet Union, 38; Americans on, 72–73, 130–31, 135, 147; Churchill, Winston, and, 63, 72, 73; Germans in, 5; Germany invading, 61–63, 66–67; Hopkins, Harry, and, 3–4, 5, 7–8, 61–72, 65, 86–87, 93–94, 127; interests of, 131, 148; Japan's war with, 122, 123, 134–35; Lend-Lease to, 59, 66, 67, 68, 70, 86–87; Pacific War entered by, 132; postwar conflict with, 127; postwar foreign policies of, 146–47; prison camps of, 8, 82; Roosevelt, Franklin Delano, speculating on, 72; Stalin analyzing, 68, 69–70, 72; world role of, 93, 94. *See also* Grand Alliance; U.S.-Soviet relations

spending, 22, 27–28, 29, 32, 35–37, 53

spheres of influence, 97, 113

Stalin, Joseph, 20, 45, 126; on China, 134–35; Churchill, Winston, and, 64, 72, 87, 109, 110–14, 146; Eastern Front focus of, 94; Eden making commitments to, 87; on Germany, 69; goals of, 6–7; as grateful, 71–72; on Greece, 117, 133, 136; on Hitler, 68–69, 70, 132, 137; Hopkins, Harry, and, 61–72, 65, 91, 128–37; on Japan, 134, 135; London Poles hated by, 132; negotiations with, 1–2, 7; objectives of, 148–49; on Poland, 131, 132–34, 136, 137; Roosevelt, Franklin Delano, and, 64, 83, 88–92,

90, 112–13, 144, 145, 146; Soviet
Union analyzed by, 68, 69–70, 72;
Truman communicating with, 129;
U.S. wringing concessions from, 150.
*See also* Moscow Conference; Yalta
Conference
Stark, Harold, 54–55, 75, 76
State Department, U. S., 3, 63–64, 82,
116, 149–50
Steinbeck, John, 25, 143–44
Steiner, Edward, 18
Steinhardt, Laurence, 67, 70, 88
Stettinius, Edward, 4, 9, 47, 48, 116,
120, 123, *124*, 127, 128, 149
Stilwell, Joseph, 99–101
Stimson, Henry, 6, 9, 76, 77
Sullivan, Mark, 41
superweapons, 79
Supreme Commander, 85–86

Teheran Conference, 90, 90–92, 118,
144
TERA. *See* New York State Temporary
Emergency Relief Administration
Thompson, Dorothy, 35
Tito, Joseph Broz, 134
Tolstoy, Leo, 18
Tolstoy conference. *See* Moscow
Conference
Torch, 84–85
Truman, Harry S., 7, 115, 116, 128;
Churchill, Winston, and, 129, 136,
137; Hopkins, Harry, and, 126–27,
129, 132, 137, 138, 141, 147; oath
of office taken by, 126–27; Stalin
communicated with by, 129; State
Department influenced by, 149–50;
U.S.-Soviet relations influenced by,
148, 149
Truman Committee, 126–27
Turkey, 91

unemployment, 13, 29, 36–37. *See also*
jobs
Union of Polish Patriots, 88
United Nations (UN), 7, 96, 101, 106,
116, 119, 122
United States (U.S.): Asia objectives
of, 94, 95; China's relationship with,
102; China supported by, 97–100;
interests of, 148; Japan attacking,
75–76; Moscow Conference
jeopardizing objectives of, 116;
self-determination supported by,
96; Stalin's concessions to, 150. *See
also* Grand Alliance; U.S.-Soviet
relations
U.S.-Soviet relations, 124; challenges
to, 147; complicating of, 87–92, 89,
90; deterioration of, 128–29, 144,
145; Hopkins, Harry, on, 71, 86–87,
88, 144, 146–47, 148, 150; Moscow
visit on, 128–37; Roosevelt, Franklin
Delano, on, 145, 146; Truman and,
129, 148, 149
USSR. *See* Soviet Union

vice presidency, 50, 51

Wallace, Henry, 39–40, 51, 95, 114–15,
114–16, 143
War Cabinet, 53–54
War Department, 38
Warm Springs, Georgia, 36, 125
War Production Board, 76
weather, cross-channel invasion
influenced by, 85
Wedemeyer, Albert C., 101
Wehrmacht. *See* Germans
Welfare Department, 38
Welles, Sumner, 55, 63, 73, 95, 102
White House, Lincoln Study of, 43,
45–47

Williams, Aubrey, *24*, 25
Williams, Frank Wood, 20
Willkie, Wendell, 114–15
Wilson, Charles McMoran, 121
Winant, John, 64, 83, 93
workers, 142
Works Progress Administration (WPA),
   27–28, 30–31, 32, 35, 37, 38–39, 106
World War I (WWI), 19
World War II (WWII): Americans
   on, 54; as different, 79; diplomacy
   of, 150; New Deal influencing, 28;

as UN war, 96; victory in, 1, 47,
   127
WPA. *See* Works Progress
   Administration

Yalta Conference, 90, 104, 105–6, 107,
   118–24, *123*, *124*, 129–35, 144
Yalta formula, 6–7, 131, 149–50
Yeaton, Ivan, 66–67
Yugoslavia, 66, 113, 134

Zhukov, Georgy, 141

~

# About the Author

**Christopher D. O'Sullivan** is the author of several other books about world affairs, including *FDR and the End of Empire: The Origins of American Power in the Middle East* (2012); *Colin Powell: A Political Biography* (2010); *Sumner Welles: Postwar Planning and the Quest for a New World Order* (2008); and *The United Nations* (2005). He teaches history at the University of San Francisco.